Kirkham's Grammar

Kirkham's Grammar

The Book That Shaped Lincoln's Prose

Samuel Kirkham

Octavo Press
An Imprint of Templegate Publishers
Springfield, Illinois

Published by Octavo Press
An Imprint of Templegate Publishers

The special contents of this edition
Copyright © 1999 by Templegate Publishers

Templegate Publishers
302 East Adams Street
Post Office Box 5152
Springfield, Illinois 62705
217-522-3353
www.templegate.com

ISBN 0-87243-243-2
Library of Congress Catalog Card Number: 99-71179

Manufactured in the United States of America

ENGLISH GRAMMAR,

IN

FAMILIAR LECTURES;

ACCOMPANIED BY

A COMPENDIUM

EMBRACING

A NEW SYSTEMATIC ORDER OF PARSING

A NEW SYSTEM OF PUNCTUATION,

EXERCISES IN FALSE SYNTAX,

AND

A SYSTEM OF PHILOSOPHICAL GRAMMAR,

IN NOTES:

TO WHICH ARE ADDED,

AN APPENDIX AND A KEY TO THE EXERCISES

DESIGNED

FOR THE USE OF SCHOOLS AND PRIVATE LEARNERS.

BY SAMUEL KIRKHAM.

STEREOTYPE EDITION.

NEW YORK:

ROBERT B. COLLINS,

254 PEARL STREET.

AN ESSAY ON ELOCUTION,

DESIGNED FOR THE USE OF SCHOOLS AND PRIVATE LEARNERS

BY SAMUEL KIRKHAM.

This work is mainly designed as a Reading-Book for Schools. In the first part of it, the *principles* of reading are developed and explained in a scientific and *practical* manner, and so familiarly illustrated in their application to practical examples as to enable even the juvenile mind very readily to comprehend their nature and character, their design and use, and thus to acquire that high degree of excellence, both, in reading and speaking, which all desire, but to which few attain.

The last part of the work, contains *Selections* from the greatest master-pieces of rhetorical and poetical composition, both ancient and modern. Many of these selections are taken from the most elegant and classical American authors—writers whose noble productions have already shed an unfading lustre, and stamped immortality, upon the literature of our country.—In the select part of the work, *rhetorical marks* are also employed to point out the application of the principles laid down in the first part.—The very favorable reception of the work by the public, and its astonishingly rapid introduction into schools, since its first publication in 1833, excites in the author the most sanguine hopes in regard to its future success.

NOTICES.

After a careful perusal of this work, we are decidedly of opinion, that it is the only *successful* attempt of the kind. The rules are copious, and the author's explanations and illustrations *are happily adapted to the comprehension of learners*. No school should be without this book, and it ought to find a place in the library of every gentleman who values the attainment of a just and forcible elocution.—*Pittsburgh Mer. April,* 1834.

Mr. Kirkham has given rules for inflections and emphasis, and has followed them by illustrative examples, and these by remarks upon the inflection which he has adopted, and the reasons for his preference of one inflection to another—a most admirable plan for such a work. Copious examples occur in which all the various inflections and the shades of emphasis are distinguished with great accuracy and clearness. The catechetical appendages of each chapter, give the work new value in a school, and the selections made for the exercise of scholars, evince good taste and judgment.
U. S. Gazette, Philadelphia, Sept. 17, 1834.

The Essay now before us, needs not depend on any former work of its author for a borrowed reputation ; it has intrinsic merits of its own. It lays down principles clearly and concisely. It presents the reader with many new and judicious selections, both in prose and poetry ; and altogether evinces great industry, combined with taste and ingenuity.—*Courier of Upper Canada, York, Oct.* 12, 1833.

Of the talent and judgment of Mr. Kirkham, we have already had occasion to speak in terms of honest praise. His work on Elocution raises him still higher in our estimation.—The book would be of great utility in schools—such a one as has long been wanted ; and we are glad to see it forthcoming.—*Baltimore Visitor, July,* 1833.

Every facility for teaching Elocution, which I have so often needed, but never before found, is exactly furnished in this work :—principles are clearly and concisely laid down, and *are very happily adapted to the comprehension of the learner.* Thoroughly convinced of its utility, I shall lose no time in introducing it into my school.
Hartford, Conn. Aug. 20, 1834.   NATHANIEL WEBB.

RECOMMENDATIONS.

It is well known that the recommendations which generally accompany new books have very little weight with the public. This is as it should be, for that work which rests more on its written testimonials, than on its intrinsic merits for support, asserts no claims to permanent patronage. But recommendations which analyze the merits of a work, and which, by exhibiting its prominent features in a striking light, are calculated to carry conviction to the reader that the system recommended is meritorious, the author is proud to have it in his power to present in this volume. The following are *some* of the numerous testimonials which he has received, and for which he tenders his grateful acknowledgments to those literary gentlemen to whose liberality and politeness he is indebted for them. More than *six hundred* others presented to the author, and many of which are equally flattering with these, he has not room to insert.

———

The following notice of this work is extracted from the "Western Review," This journal is ably conducted by the Rev. Timothy Flint, author of "Francis Berrian," "History and Geography of the Miss. Valley," and many other popular and valuable works.

We had not, at that time, seen Mr. Kirkham's "Grammar in familiar Lectures," but have since given it a cursory perusal. If we comprehend the author's design, it is not so much to introduce new principles, as to render more easy and intelligible those which have been long established, and to furnish additional facilities to an accurate and thorough knowledge of our language. In this we think he has been successful.

It is to be expected that a modest, unassuming writer, on presenting himself before the public tribunal as an author, will, as far as is consistent with his plan, avail himself of the authority of such as have written well on the subject before him. Mr. Kirkham has accordingly followed Mr. Murray in the old beaten track of English writers on grammar, in the general principles of his science; endeavoring, at the same time, to avoid whatever appeared to be erroneous or absurd in the writings of that author, and adopting an entirely new arrangement. The most useful matter contained in the treatise of Mr. Murray, is embraced in this; but in the definitions and rules, it is simplified, and rendered much more intelligible. Though our author follows Mr. Murray, in the general principles of his work, he has, in numerous instances, differed from him, pursuing a course that appears to be his own, and introducing some valuable improvements.

Among these may be mentioned some additional rules and explanatory notes in syntax, the arrangement of the parts of speech, the mode of explaining them, manner of parsing, manner of explaining some of the pronouns, and the use of a synopsis which presents the essentials of the science at one view, and is well calculated to afford assistance to learners.

In his arrangement of the parts of speech, Mr. Kirkham seems to have endeavored to follow *the order of nature;* and we are not able to see how he could have done better. The noun and verb, as being the most important parts of speech, are first explained, and afterwards those which are considered in a secondary and subordinate character. By following this order, he has avoided the absurdity so common among authors, of defining the minor parts before their principals, of which they were designed to be the appendages, and has rationally prepared the way for conducting the learner by easy advances to a correct view of the science.

In his illustrations of the various subjects contained in his work, our author appears to have aimed, not at a flowery style, nor at the appearance of being learned, but at being understood. The clearness and perspicuity of his remarks, and their application to familiar objects, are well calculated to arrest the attention, and aid the understanding of the pupil, and thereby to lessen the labor of the instructer. The principles of the science *are simplified, and rendered so perfectly easy of comprehension,* we should think no ordinary mind, having such help, could find them difficult. It is in this particular that the work appears to possess its chief merit, and on this account it cannot fail of being preferred to many others.

It gives us pleasure to remark, in reference to the success of the amiable and modest author whose work is before us, that we quote from the fifth edition.

Cincinnati, Aug. 24, 1827.

The following is from the pen of a gentleman of the Bar, formerly a distinguished[1] Classical teacher. [Extract from the "National Crisis."]

As a friend to literature, and especially to genuine merit, it is with peculiar pleasure I allude to a notice in a late paper of this city, in which Mr. S. Kirkham proposes to deliver a course of Lectures on English Grammar. To such as feel interested in acquiring a general and practical knowledge of this useful science, an opportunity is now

presented which ought not to be neglected. Having myself witnessed,`in several in-
stances, within the last ten months, the practical results of Mr. Kirkham's plan, I am
enabled to give a decisive opinion of its merits. The extensive knowledge acquired in
one course by his class in Pittsburgh, and the great proficiency evinced by his classes
elsewhere, are a demonstration of the utility and superiority of his method of teaching, and a higher encomium on him than I am able to bestow.

The principles on which Mr. Kirkham's "New system of Grammar" is predicated,
are judiciously compiled, and happily and briefly expressed; but the great merit of
his work consists in the lucid illustrations accompanying the principles, and the simple
and gradual manner in which it conducts the learner along from step to step through
the successive stages of the science. The explanations blended with the theory, are
addressed to the understanding of the pupil in a manner so familiar, that they cannot
fail to excite in him a deep interest; and whatever system is calculated to bring into
requisition the mental powers, must, I conceive, be productive of good results. In my
humble opinion, the system of teaching introduced into this work, will enable a diligent pupil to acquire, without any other aid, a practical knowledge of grammar, *in less
than one-fourth* part of the time usually devoted.

My views of Mr. Kirkham's system are thus publicly given, with the greater pleasure, on account of the literary empiricisms which have been so extensively practised
in many parts of the western country.

Cincinnati, April 26, 1826.

From Mr. Blood, Principal of the Chambersburgh Academy, Pa.

Mr. Kirkham,—It is now almost twenty years since I became a teacher of youth,
and, during this period, I have not only consulted all, but have used many of the different systems of English grammar that have fallen in my way; and, sir, I do assure you,
without the least wish to flatter, that yours far exceeds any I have yet seen.

Your arrangement and systematic order of parsing are most excellent; and experience has convinced me, (having used it, and it only, for the last twelve or thirteen
months,(that a scholar will learn more of the nature and principles of our language in
one quarter, from your system, than in a *whole year* from any other I had previously
used. I do, therefore, most cheerfully and earnestly recommend it to the public at
large, and especially to those who, anxious to acquire a knowledge of our language,
are destitute of the advantages of an instructer.

Yours, very respectfully,   SAMUEL BLOOD.
Chambersburgh Academy, Feb. 12, 1825.

From Mr. N. R. Smith, editor of a valuable literary journal, styled "The Hesperus."

Mr. Kirkham,

Sir, I have examined your Lectures on English Grammar with that degree of minute-
ness which enables me to yield my unqualified approbation of the work as a grammatical system. The engaging manner in which you have explained the elements of grammar, and accommodated them to the capacities of youth, is an ample illustration of the
utility of your plan. In addition to this, the critical attention you have paid to an
analytical development of grammatical principles, while it is calculated to encourage
the perseverance of young students in the march of improvement, is sufficient, also, to
employ the researches of the literary connoisseur. I trust that your valuable compila-
tion will be speedily introduced into schools and academies.

With respect, yours,   N. R. SMITH, A. M.
Pittsburgh, March 22, 1825.

From Mr. Jungmann, Principal of the Frederick Lutheran Academy :—Extract.

Having carefully examined Mr. S. Kirkham's new system of "English Grammar in
familiar Lectures," I am satisfied that the pre-eminent advantages it possesses over our
common systems, will soon convince the public, that it is not one of those feeble
efforts of quackery which have so often obtruded upon our notice. Its decided *superiority over all other systems*, consists in adapting the subject-matter to the capacity of
the young learner, and the happy mode adopted of communicating it to his mind in a
manner so clear and simple, that he can easily comprehend the nature and the application of every principle that comes before him.

In short, all the intricacies of the science are *elucidated so clearly*, I am confident that
even a private learner, of common docility, can, by perusing this system attentively
acquire a better practical knowledge of this important branch of literature in *three
months*, than is ordinarily obtained in *one year*.

Frederick, Md. Sept. 17, 1824.   JOHN E. JUNGMANN.

RECOMMENDATIONS.

Extract: from De Witt Clinton, late Gov. of New-York.

I consider the Compendium of English Grammar, by Samuel Kirkham, a work deserving encouragement, and well calculated to facilitate the acquisition of this useful science.

DE WITT CLINTON.

Albany, Sept. 25, 1824.

S. Kirkham, Esq.—I have examined your Grammar with attention, and with a particular view to benefit the Institution under my charge. I am fully satisfied, that it is the *best form* in which Murray's principles have been given to the public. The lectures are ample, and given in so familiar and easy language, as to be readily understood, even by a *tyro* in grammar.

I feel it due to you to say, that I commenced the examination of your work, under *a strong prejudice against it*, in consequence of the numerous "improved systems" with which the public has been inundated, of late, most of which are by no means improvements on Murray, but the productions of individuals whom a "*little grammar* has rendered grammatically insane." My convictions, therefore, are the result of *investigation*. I wish you, Sir, success in your publication.

Respectfully,   EBER WHEATON,
Pr. of Mechanics' Society School.

With the opinion of Mr. Wheaton respecting Mr. Kirkham's English Grammar, we heartily concur.

NATHAN STARK, Pr. Acad.
(Rev.) JOHN JOHNSTON,

Newburgh, Aug. 4, 1829.   (Rev.) WM. S. HEYER.

From the Rev. C. P. McIlvaine, and others.

So far as I have examined the plan of grammatical instruction by Samuel Kirkham, I am well satisfied that *it meets the wants* of elementary schools in this branch, and deserves to be patronised.

CHARLES P. McILVAINE.

Brooklyn, L. I. July 9, 1829.

We fully concur in the above.

ANDREW HAGEMAN,
E. M. JOHNSON.

EXTRACT.

From the partial examination which I have given Mr. S. Kirkham's English Grammar, I do not hesitate to recommend it to the public as the *best of the class I have ever seen*, and as filling up an important and almost impassable chasm in works on grammatical science.

D. L. CARROLL.

Brooklyn, L. I. June 29, 1829.

We fully concur in the foregoing recommendation.

B. B. HALLOCK,
E. KINGSLEY,
T. S. MAYBON.

From A. W. Dodge, Esq.

New-York, July 15, 1829.

The experience of every one at all acquainted with the business of instruction, must ave taught him that the study of grammar, important as it is to every class of learners, is almost invariably a dry and uninteresting study to young beginners, and for the very obvious reason, that the systems in general use in the schools, are *far beyond* the comprehension of youth, and ill adapted to their years. Hence it is, that their lessons in this department of learning, are considered as *tasks*, and if committed at all, committed to *the memory, without enlightening their understandings*; so that many a pupil who has *been through* the English grammar, is totally unacquainted with the nature even of the simplest parts of speech.

The work of Mr. Kirkham on grammar, is well calculated to remedy these evils, and supply a deficiency which has been so long and so seriously felt in the imperfect education of youth in the elementary knowledge of their own language. By a simple, familiar, and lucid method of treating the subject, he has rendered what was before irksome and unprofitable, pleasing and instructive. In one word, the grammar of Mr. Kirkham furnishes a *clew* by which the youthful mind is guided through the intricate labyrinth of verbs, nouns and pronouns; and the path which has been heretofore so difficult and uninviting, as to dampen the ardor of youth, and waste their energies in fruitless attempts to surmount its obstacles, is cleared of these obstructions by this *pioneer* to the youthful mind, and planted, at every turn, with friendly *guide-boards* **to** *direct them in the right road.* The slightest perusal of the work alluded to, will convince even the most skeptical of the truth of these remarks, and satisfy every one who is not wedded by prejudice to old rules and forms, that it will meet the wants of the community.

ALLEN W. DODGE.

RECOMMENDATIONS.

Philadelphia, Aug. 10, 1829

Having, for several years, been engaged in lecturing on the science of grammar and, during this period, having *thoroughly tested* the merits of Mr. S. Kirkham's system of "English Grammar in Familiar Lectures" by using it as a text-book for my classes, I take pleasure in giving this testimonial of my cordial approbation of the work. Mr. Kirkham has attempted to improve upon this branch of science, chiefly by unfolding and explaining the principles of grammar in a manner so clear and simple, as *to adapt them completely to the understanding* of the young learner, and by adopting a new arrangement, which enables the pupil to commit the principles by a simultaneous application of them to practical examples. The public may rest assured, that he has been successful in his attempt *in a pre-eminent degree*. I make this assertion under a full conviction that it will be corroborated by every candid judge of the science who becomes acquainted with the practical advantages of this manual.

The explicit brevity and accuracy of the rules and definitions, the novel, the striking, the lucid, and critical illustrations accompanying them, the peculiar and advantageous arrangement of the various parts of the subject, the facilities proffered by the "systematic mode of parsing" adopted, the convenient and judicious introduction and adaptation of the exercises introduced, and the deep researches and critical investigations displayed in the "Philosophical Notes," render this system of grammar *so decidedly superior to all others extant*, that, to receive general patronage, it needs but to be known. ·

My knowledge of this system from experience in teaching it, and witnessing its effects in the hands of private learners, warrants me in saying, that a learner will, by studying this book *four months without a teacher*, obtain a more clear conception of the nature and proper construction of words and phrases, than is ordinarily obtained in common schools and academies, *in five times four months*.

It is highly gratifying to know, that wherever this system has been circulated, it is very rapidly supplanting those works of dulness which have so long paralyzed the energies of the youth of our country.

I think the specimens of verbal criticism, additional corrections in orthography and orthoepy, the leading principles of rhetoric, and the improvements in the illustrations generally, which Mr. K. is about introducing into his ELEVENTH EDITION, will render it quite *an improvement on the former editions of this work*.   H. WINCHESTER.

From the Rev. S. Center, Principal of a Classical Academy.

I have examined the last edition of Kirkham's Grammar with peculiar satisfaction. The improvements which appear in it, do, in my estimation, give it a decided preference to any other system now in use. To point out the peculiar qualities which secure to it claims of which no other system can boast, would be, if required, perfectly easy. At present it is sufficient to remark, that it imbodies all that is essentially excellent and useful in other systems; while it is entirely free from that tediousness of method and prolixity of definition which so much perplex and embarrass the learner.

The peculiar excellence of Mr. Kirkham's grammar is, *the simplicity of its method*, and *the plainness of its illustrations*. Being conducted by familiar lectures, the teacher and pupil are necessarily brought into agreeable contact by each lesson. Both are improved by the same task, without the slightest suspicion, on the part of the pupil, that there is anything hard, difficult, or obscure in the subject: a conviction, this, which must inevitably precede all efforts, or no proficiency will be made. In a word, the treatise I am recommending, is a *practical* one; and for that reason, if there were no others to be urged, it ought to be introduced into all our schools and academies. From actual experiment I can attest to the practicability of the plan which the author has adopted. Of this fact any one may be convinced who will take the pains to make the experiment.   SAMUEL CENTER.

Albany, July 10, 1829.

From a communication addressed to S. Kirkham, by the Rev. J. Stockton, author of the "Western Calculator" and "Western Spelling-Book."

Dear Sir.—I am much pleased with both the *plan* and *execution* of your "English Grammar in Familiar Lectures." In giving a *systematic mode of parsing*, calculated alike to exercise the *understanding* and *memory* of the pupil, and also free the teacher from the *drudgery* of continued interrogation, you have made your grammar what every elementary school book ought to be—*plain, systematic*, and *easy* to be understood.

This, with the copious definitions in every part of the work, and other improvements so judiciously introduced, gives it a *decisive superiority* over the imperfect grammar of Murray, now so generally used.   JOSEPH STOCKTON, A. M.

Allegheny-Town (near Pittsburgh,) March 18, 1825.

The author is free to acknowledge, that since this treatise first ventured on the wave of public opinion, the gales of patronage which have wafted it along, have been far more favorable than he had reason to anticipate. Had any one, on its first appearance, predicted, that the demand for it would call forth *twenty-two thousand* copies during the past year, the author would have considered the prediction extravagant and chimerical. In gratitude, therefore, to that public which has smiled so propitiously on his humble efforts to advance the cause of learning, he has endeavored, by unremitting attention to the improvement of his work, to render it as useful and as unexceptionable as his time and talents would permit.

It is believed that the *tenth* and *eleventh* editions have been greatly improved ; but the author is apprehensive that his work is not yet as accurate and as much simplified as it may be. If, however, the disadvantages of lingering under a broken constitution, and of being able to devote to this subject only a small portion of his time, snatched from the active pursuits of a business life, (*active* as far as his imperfect health permits him to be,) are any apology for its defects, he hopes that the candid will set down the apology to his credit. This personal allusion is hazarded with the additional hope, that it will ward off some of the arrows of criticism which may be aimed at him, and render less pointed and poisonous those that may fall upon him. Not that he would beg a truce with the gentlemen critics and reviewers. Any compromise with them would betray a want of self-confidence and moral courage which he would, by no means, be willing to avow. It would, moreover, be prejudicial to his interest ; for he is determined, if his life be preserved, to avail himself of the advantages of any judicious and candid criticisms on his production, that may appear, and, two or three years hence, *revise* his work, and present to the public another and a better edition.

The improvements in the *tenth* edition, consisted mainly in the addition of many important principles ; in rendering the illustrations more critical, extensive, accurate, and lucid ; in connecting more closely with the genius and philosophy of our language, the general principles adopted ; and in adding a brief view of philosophical grammar interspersed in notes. The introduction into the ELEVENTH EDITION, of many verbal criticisms, of additional corrections in orthography and orthoepy, of the leading principles of rhetoric, and of general additions and improvements in various parts of the work, render *this edition*, it is believed, *far preferable* to any of the former editions of the work.

Perhaps some will regard the philosophical notes as a useless exhibition of pedantry. If so, the author's only apology is, that some investigations of this nature seemed to be called for by a portion of the community whose minds, of late, appear to be under the influence of a kind of *philosophical mania ;* and to such these notes are respectfully submitted for just what *they* may deem their real value. The author's own opinion on this point, is, that they proffer no *material* advantages to common learners ; but that they may profitably engage the attention of the curious, and perhaps impart a degree of interest to the literary connoisseur

New-York, August 22, 1829.

CONTENTS.

PREFACE.

There appears to be something assuming in the act of writing, and thrusting into public notice, a new work on a subject which has already employed many able pens; for who would presume to do this, unless he believed his production to be, in some respects, superior to every one of the kind which had preceded it? Hence, in presenting to the public this system of English Grammar, the author is aware that an apology will be looked for, and that the arguments on which that apology is grounded, must inevitably undergo a rigid scrutiny. Apprehensive, however, that no explanatory effort, on his part, would shield him from the imputation of arrogance by such as are blinded by self-interest, or by those who are wedded to the doctrines and opinions of his predecessors, with *them* he will not attempt a compromise, being, in a great measure, indifferent either to their praise or their censure. But with the candid, he is willing to negotiate an amicable treaty, knowing that they are always ready to enter into it on honorable terms. In this negotiation he asks nothing more than merely to rest the merits of his work on its practical utility, believing that, if it prove uncommonly successful in facilitating the progress of youth in the march of mental improvement, *that* will be its best apology.

When we bring into consideration the numerous productions of those learned philologists who have labored so long, and, as many suppose, so successfully, in establishing the principles of our language; and, more especially, when we view the labors of some of our modern compilers, who have displayed so much ingenuity and acuteness in attempting to arrange those principles in such a manner as to form a correct and an easy medium of mental conference; it does, indeed, appear a little like presumption for a young man to enter upon a subject which has so frequently engaged the attention and talents of men distinguished for their erudition. The author ventures forward, however, under the conviction, that most of his predecessors are very deficient, at least, in *manner*, if not in *matter;* and this conviction, he believes, will be corroborated by a majority of the best judges in community. It is admitted, that many valuable improvements have been made by some of our late writers, who have endeavored to simplify and render this subject intelligible to the young learner, but they have all overlooked what the author considers a very important object, namely, *a systematic order of parsing;* and nearly all have neglected to *develop and explain* the principles in such a manner as to enable the learner, without great difficulty, to comprehend their nature and use.

By some this system will, no doubt, be discarded on account of its *simplicity;* while to others its simplicity will prove its principal recommendation. Its design is an humble one. It proffers no great advantages to the recondite grammarian; it professes not to instruct the literary connoisseur; it presents no attractive graces of style to charm, no daring flights to astonish, no deep researches to gratify him; but in the humblest simplicity of diction, it attempts to accelerate the march of the juvenile mind in its advances in the path of science, by dispersing those clouds that so often bewilder it, and removing those obstacles that generally retard its progress. In this way it endeavors to render interesting and delightful a study which has hitherto been considered tedious, dry, and irksome. Its leading object is to adopt a correct and an easy method, in which pleasure is blended with the labors of the learner, and which is calculated to excite in him a spirit of inquiry, that shall call forth into vigorous and useful exercise, every latent energy of his mind; and thus enable him soon to become thoroughly acquainted with the nature of the principles, and with their practical utility and application.

Content to be useful, instead of being brilliant, the writer of these pages has endeavored to shun the path of those whose aim appears to have been to dazzle, rather than to instruct. As he has aimed not so much at origi-nality as utility, he has adopted the thoughts of his predecessors whosu labors have become public stock, whenever he could not, in his opinior, furnish better and brighter of his own. Aware that there is, in the pub-lic mind, a strong predilection for the doctrines contained in Mr. Murray's grammar, he has thought proper, not merely from motives of policy, but from choice, to select his *principles* chiefly from that work; and, more-over, to adopt, as far as consistent with his own views, the language of that eminent philologist. In no instance has he varied from him, unless he conceived that, in so doing, some practical advantage would be gained. He hopes, therefore, to escape the censure so frequently and so justly awarded to those unfortunate innovators who have not scrupled to alter, mutilate, and torture the text of that able writer, merely to gratify an itching propensity to figure in the world as authors, and gain an ephemeral popularity by arrogating to themselves the credit due to another.

The author is not disposed, however, to disclaim all pretensions to origi-nality; for, although his principles are chiefly selected, (and who would presume to make new ones?) the manner of arranging, illustrating, and applying them, is principally his own. Let no one, therefore, if he hap-pen to find in other works, ideas and illustrations similar to *some* contain ed in the following lectures, too hastily accuse him of plagiarism. It is well known that similar investigations and pursuits often elicit correspond-ing ideas in different minds: and hence it is not uncommon for the same thought to be strictly *original* with many writers. The author is not here attempting to manufacture a garment to shield him from rebuke, should he unjustly claim the property of another; but he wishes it to be under-stood, that a long course of teaching and investigation, has often produced in his mind ideas and arguments on the subject of grammar, exactly or nearly corresponding with those which he afterwards found, had, under similar circumstances, been produced in the minds of others. He hopes, therefore, to be pardoned by the critic, even though he should not be willing to reject a good idea *of his own*, merely because some one else has, at some time or other, been blessed with the same thought.

As the plan of this treatise is far more comprehensive than those of or-dinary grammars, the writer could not, without making his work unrea-sonably voluminous, treat some topics as extensively as was desirable. Its design is to embrace, not only all the most important principles of the science, but also exercises in parsing, false syntax, and punctuation, suffi-ciently extensive for all ordinary, practical purposes, and a key to the ex ercises, and, moreover, a series of illustrations so full and intelligible, as *completely to adapt the principles to the capacities of common learners* Whether this design has been successfully or unsuccessfully executed, is left for the public to decide. The general adoption of the work into schools, wherever it has become known, and the ready sale of *forty thou-sand* copies, (though *without hitherto affording the author any pecuniary profit*,) are favorable omens.

In the selection and arrangement of principles for his work, the author has endeavored to pursue a course between the extremes, of taking blindly on trust whatever has been sanctioned by prejudice and the authority of venerable names, and of that arrogant, innovating spirit, which sets at de-fiance all authority, and attempts to overthrow all former systems, and con-vince the world that all true knowledge and science are wrapped up in a crude system of vagaries of its own invention. Notwithstanding the author is aware that public prejudice is powerful, and that he who ventures much by way of innovation, will be liable to defeat his own purpose by falling into neglect; yet he has taken the liberty to think for himself, to investigate the subject critically and dispassionately, and to adopt such principles only as he deemed the least objectionable, and best calculated to effect the object he had in view. But what his system claims as improvements on others, consists not so much in bettering the principles themselves, as *in the method adopted of communicating a knowledge of them to the mind of the learner.* That the work is defective, the author is fully sensible: and he is free to acknowledge, that its defects arise, in part, from his own want of judgment and skill. But there is another and a more serious cause of them, namely, the anomalies and imperfections with which the language abounds. This latter circumstance is also the cause of the existence of so widely different opinions on many important points; and, moreover, the reason that the grammatical principles of our language can never be indisputably settled. But principles ought not to be rejected because they admit of exceptions.—He who is thoroughly acquainted with the genius and structure of our language, can duly appreciate the truth of these remarks

₊ Should parents object to the Compendium, fearing it will soon be destroyed by their children, they are informed that the pupil will not have occasion to use it one-tenth part as much as he will the book which it accompanies: and besides, if it be destroyed, he will find all the definitions and rules which it contains, recapitulated in the series of Lectures.

HINTS TO TEACHERS AND PRIVATE LEARNERS.

As this work proposes a new mode of parsing, and pursues an arrangement essentially different from that generally adopted, it may not be deemed improper for the author to give some directions to those who may be disposed to use it. Perhaps they who take only a slight view of the order of parsing, will not consider it *new*, but blend it with those long since adopted. Some writers have, indeed, attempted plans somewhat similar; but in no instance have they reduced them to what the author considers a *regular systematic order.*

The methods which they have generally suggested, require the teacher to *interrogate* the pupil as he proceeds; or else he is permitted to parse without giving any explanations at all. Others hint that the learner ought to apply definitions in a general way, but they lay down no systematic arrangement of questions as his guide. The *systematic* order laid down in this work, if pursued by the pupil, compels him to apply every definition and every rule that appertains to each word he parses, without having a question put to him by the teacher; and, in so doing, he explains every word fully as he goes along. This course enables the learner to proceed independently; and proves, at the same time, a great relief to the instructer. The convenience and advantage of this method, are far greater than can be easily conceived by one who is unacquainted with it. The author is, therefore, anxious to have the absurd practice, wherever it has been established, of causing learners to commit and recite definitions and rules without any simultaneous application of them to practical examples, immediately abolished. This system obviates the necessity of pursuing such a stupid course of drudgery; for the young beginner who pursues it, will have, in a few weeks, all the most important definitions and rules perfectly committed, simply by applying them in parsing.

If this plan be once adopted, it is confidently believed that every teacher who is desirous to consult, either his own convenience, or the advantage of his pupils, will readily pursue it in preference to any former method. This belief is founded on the advantages which the author himself has experienced from it in the course of several years, devoted to the instruction of youth and adults. By pursuing this system, he can, with less labor, advance a pupil farther in a practical knowledge of this abstruse science, in *two months*, than he could in *one year* when he taught in the "old way." It is presumed that no instructer, who once gives this system a fair trial, will doubt the truth of this assertion.

Perhaps some will, on a first view of the work, disapprove of the transposition of many parts; but whoever examines it attentively, will find that, although the author has not followed the common "artificial and unnatural arrangement adopted by most of his predecessors," yet he has endeavored to pursue a more judicious one, namely, "the order of the understanding."

The learner should commence, *not by committing and rehearsing*, but by reading attentively the first *two* lectures several times over. He ought then to parse, according to the *systematic order*, the examples given for that purpose; in doing which, as previously stated, he has an opportunity of committing all the definitions and rules belonging to the parts of speech included in the examples.

The COMPENDIUM, as it presents to the eye of the learner a condensed but comprehensive view of the whole science, may be properly considered an "Ocular Analysis of the English language." By referring to it, the young student is enabled to apply all his definitions and rules from the very commencement of his parsing. To some, this mode of procedure may seem rather tedious; but it must appear obvious to every person of discernment, that a pupil will learn more by parsing *five* words critically, and explaining them fully, than he would by parsing *fifty* words superficially, and without understanding their various properties. The teacher who pursues this plan, is not under the necessity of hearing his pupils recite a single lesson of *definitions* committed to memory, for he has a fair opportunity of discovering their knowledge of these as they evince it in parsing. All other directions necessary for the learner in school, as well as for the *private learner*, will be given in the succeeding pages of the work. Should these feeble efforts prove a saving of much time and expense to those young persons who may be disposed to pursue this science with avidity, by enabling them easily to acquire a critical knowledge of a branch of education so important and desirable, the author's fondest anticipations will be fully realized ; but should his work fall into the hands of any who are expecting, by the acquisition, to become grammarians, and yet, have not sufficient ambition and perseverance to make themselves acquainted with its contents, it is hoped that the blame for their nonimprovement, will not be thrown upon *him*.

To those enterprising and intelligent gentlemen who may be disposed to lecture on this plan, the author takes the liberty to offer a few hints by way of encouragement.

Any judicious instructer of grammar, if he take the trouble to make himself familiar with the contents of the following pages, will find it an easy matter to pursue this system. One remark only to the lecturer, is sufficient. Instead of causing his pupils to acquire a knowledge of the nature and use of the principles by intense application, let him communicate it verbally ; that is, let him first take up one part of speech, and, in an oral lecture, unfold and explain all its properties, not only by adopting the illustrations given in the book, but also by giving others that may occur to his mind as he proceeds. After a part of speech has been thus elucidated, the class should be interrogated on it, and then taught to parse it, and correct errors in composition under the rules that apply to it. In the same manner he may proceed with the other parts of speech, observing, however, to recapitulate occasionally, until the learners become thoroughly acquainted with whatever principles may have been presented. If this plan be faithfully pursued, rapid progress, on the part of the learner, will be the inevitable result ; and that teacher who pursues it, cannot fail of acquiring distinction, and an enviable popularity in his profession.   S. KIRKHAM.

FAMILIAR LECTURES

ON

ENGLISH GRAMMAR.

LECTURE I.

DIVISIONS OF GRAMMAR.—ORTHOGRAPHY.

TO THE YOUNG LEARNER.

You are about to enter upon one of the most useful, and, when rightly pursued, one of the most interesting studies in the whole circle of science. If, however, you, like many a misguided youth, are under the impression that the study of grammar is dry and irksome, and a matter of little consequence, I trust I shall succeed in removing from your mind, all such false notions and ungrounded prejudices; for I will endeavor to convince you, before I close these lectures, that this is not only a pleasing study, but one of real and substantial utility; a study that directly tends to adorn and dignify human nature, and meliorate the condition of man. Grammar is a leading branch of that learning which alone is capable of unfolding and maturing the mental powers, and of elevating man to his proper rank in the scale of intellectual existence;—of that learning which lifts the soul from earth, and enables it to hold converse with a thousand worlds. In pursuing any and every other path of science, you will discover the truth of these remarks, and feel its force; for you will find, that, as grammar opens the door to every department of learning, a knowledge of it is indispensable: and should you not aspire at distinction in the republic of letters, this knowledge cannot fail of being serviceable to you, even if you are destined to pass through the humblest walks of life. I think it is clear, that, in one point of view, grammatical knowledge possesses a decisive advantage over every other branch of learning. Penmanship, arithmetic, geography, astronomy, botany, chemistry, and so on, are highly useful in their respective places; but not one of them is so universally applicable to practical purposes, as this. In every situation, under all circumstances, on all occasions;—when you speak,

2

read, write, or think, a knowledge of grammar is of essential utility.

Doubtless you have heard some persons assert, that they could detect and correct any error in language by the ear, and speak and write accurately without a knowledge of grammar. Now your own observation will soon convince you, that this assertion is incorrect. A man of refined taste, may, by perusing good autors, and conversing with the learned, acquire that knowledge of language which will enable him to avoid those glaring errors that offend the ear; but there are other errors equally gross, which have not a harsh sound, and, consequently, which cannot be detected without a knowledge of the rules that are violated. Believe me, therefore, when I say, that without the knowledge and application of grammar rules, it is impossible for any one to think, speak, read, or write with accuracy. From a want of such knowledge, many often express their ideas in a manner so improper and obscure as to render it impossible for any one to *understand* them: their language frequently amounts, not only to *bad* sense, but *non*-sense. In other instances several different meanings may be affixed to the words they employ; and what is still worse, is, that not unfrequently their sentences are so constructed, as to convey a meaning quite the reverse of that which they intended. Nothing of a secular nature can be more worthy of your attention, then, than the acquisition of grammatical knowledge.

The path which leads to grammatical excellence, is not all the way smooth and flowery, but in it you will find some thorns interspersed, and some obstacles to be surmounted; or, in simple language, you will find, in the pursuit of this science, many intricacies which it is rather difficult for the juvenile mind completely to unravel. I shall, therefore, as I proceed, address you in plain language, and endeavor to illustrate every principle in a manner so clear and simple, that you will be able, *if you exercise your mind,* to understand its nature, and apply it to practice as you go along; for I would rather give you one useful idea, than fifty high-sounding words, the meaning of which you would probably be unable to comprehend.

Should you ever have any doubts concerning the meaning of a word, or the sense of a sentence, you must not be discouraged, but persevere, either by studying my explanations, or by asking some person competent to inform you, till you obtain a clear conception of it, and till all doubts are removed. By carefully examining, and frequently reviewing, the following lectures, you will soon be able to discern the grammatical construction of our language, and fix in your mind the principles by which it is governed. Nothing delights youth so much, as a clear and distinct knowledge of any branch of science which they are pursuing; and, on the other hand, I know they are apt to be discouraged with any branch of learning which requires much time and attention to be understood. It is the evidence of a weak mind, however, to be discouraged by the obstacles with which the young learner must expect to meet; and the best means that you can adopt, in order to enable you to overcome the difficulties that arise in the incipient stage of your studies, is to cultivate the habit of *thinking methodically and soundly* on all subjects of importance which may engage your attention. Nothing will be more effectual in enabling you to think, as well as to speak and write, correctly, than the study of English grammar, according to the method of pursuing it as prescribed in the following pages. This system is designed, and, I trust, well calculated, to expand and strengthen the intellectual faculties, in as much as it involves a process by which the mind is addressed, and a knowledge of grammar communicated in an interesting and familiar manner.

You are aware, my young friend, that you live in an age of light and knowledge;—an age in which science and the arts are marching onward with gigantic strides. You live, too, in a land of liberty;—a land on which the smiles of Heaven beam with uncommon refulgence. The trump of the warrior and the clangor of arms no longer echo on our mountains, or in our valleys; "the garments dyed in blood have passed away;" the mighty struggle for independence is over; and you live to enjoy the rich boon of freedom and prosperity which was purchased with the blood of our fathers. These considerations forbid that you should ever be so unmindful of your duty to your country, to your Creator, to yourself, and to succeeding generations, as to be content to grovel in ignorance. Remember that "knowledge is power;" that an enlightened and a virtuous people can never be enslaved; and that, on the intelligence of our youth, rest the future liberty, the prosperity, the happiness, the grandeur, and the glory of our beloved country. Go on then, with a laudable ambition, and an unyielding perseverance, in the path which leads to honor and renown. Press forward. Go, and gather laurels on the hill of science; linger among her unfading beauties;. "drink deep" of her crystal fountain; and then join in "the march of fame." Become learned and virtuous, and you will be great. Love God and serve him, and you will be happy.

LANGUAGE.

LANGUAGE, in its most extensive sense, implies those signs by which men and brutes communicate to each other their thoughts, affections, and desires.

Language may be divided, 1. into natural and artificial; 2. into spoken and written.

NATURAL LANGUAGE consists in the use of those natural signs which different animals employ in communicating their feelings one to another. The meaning of these signs all perfectly understand by the principles of their nature. This language is common both to man and brute. The elements of natural language in man, may be reduced to three kinds; modulations of the voice, gestures, and features. By means of these, two savages who have no common, artificial language, can communicate their thoughts in a manner quite intelligible : they can ask and refuse, affirm and deny, threaten and supplicate ; they can traffick, enter into contracts, and plight their faith. The language of brutes consists in the use of those *inarticulate* sounds by which they express their thoughts and affections. Thus, the chirping of a bird, the bleating of a lamb, the neighing of a horse, and the growling, whining, and barking of a dog, are the language of those animals, respectively.

ARTIFICIAL LANGUAGE consists in the use of words, by means of which mankind are enabled to communicate their thoughts to one another.—In order to assist you in comprehending what is meant by the term *word*, I will endeavor to illustrate the meaning of the term.

Idea. The *notices* which we gain by sensation and perception, and which are treasured up in the mind to be the materials of thinking and knowledge, are denominated ideas. For example, when you place your hand upon a piece of ice, a sensation is excited which we call *coldness.* That faculty which notices this sensation or change produced in the mind, is called *percep-tion ;* and the abstract notice itself, or notion you form of this sensation, is denominated an *idea.* This being premised, we will now proceed to the consideration of words.

Words are *articulate* sounds, used by common consent, not as natural, but as artificial, signs of our ideas. Words have no meaning in themselves. They are merely the artificial representatives f those ideas affixed to them by compact or agreement among hose who use them. In English, for instance, to a particular kind of metal we assign the name *gold ;* not because there is, in that sound, any peculiar aptness which suggests the idea we wish to convey, but the application of that sound to the idea signified, is an act altogether arbitrary. Were there any natural connexion between the sound and the thing signified, the word *gold* would convey the same idea to the people of other countries as it does to ourselves. But such is not the fact. Other nations make use of different sounds to signify the same thing. Thus, *aurum* denotes the same idea in Latin, and *or* in French. Hence it follows, that it is by custom only we learn to annex particular ideas to particular sounds.

Spoken Language or speech is made up of articulate sounds uttered by the human voice.

The voice is formed by air which, after it passes through the glottis, (a small aperture in the upper part of the wind-pipe,) is modulated by the action of the throat, palate, teeth, tongue, lips, and nostrils.

Written Language. The elements of written language consist of letters or characters, which, by common consent and general usage, are combined into words, and thus made the ocular representatives of the articulate sounds uttered by the voice.

GRAMMAR.

GRAMMAR is the science of language.

Grammar may be divided into two species, universal and particular.

Universal Grammar explains the principles which are common to all languages.

Particular Grammar applies those general principles to a particular language, modifying them according to its genius, and the established practice of the best speakers and writers by whom it is used. Hence,

The established practice of the best speakers and writers of any language, is the standard of grammatical accuracy in the use of that language.

By the phrase, *established practice*, is implied reputable, national, and present usage. A usage becomes *good* and *legal*, when it has been long and generally adopted.

The best speakers and writers, or such as may be considere good authority in the use of language, are those who are deservedly in high estimation; speakers, distinguished for their elo-

2*

cution and other literary attainments, and writers, eminent for correct taste, solid matter, and refined manner.

In the grammar of a *perfect* language, no rules should be admitted, but such as are founded on fixed principles, arising out of the genius of that lan guage and the nature of things; but our language being *im*-perfect, it becomes necessary, in a *practical* treatise, like this, to adopt some rules to direct us in the use of speech as regulated by *custom.* If we had a permanent and surer standard than capricious custom to regulate us in the transmission of thought, great inconvenience would be avoided. They, however, who introduce usages which depart from the analogy and philosophy of a language, are conspicuous among the number of those who form that language, and have power to control it.

Language is conventional, and not only invented, but, in its progressive advancement, *varied* for purposes of practical convenience. Hence it assumes any and every form which those who make use of it choose to give it. We are, therefore, as *rational* and *practical* grammarians, compelled to submit to the necessity of the case; to take the language as it *is*, and not as it *should be*, and bow to custom.

PHILOSOPHICAL GRAMMAR investigates and develops the principles of language, as founded in the nature of things and the original laws of thought. It also discusses the grounds of the classification of words, and explains those procedures which practical grammar lays down for our observance.

PRACTICAL GRAMMAR adopts the most convenient classification of the words of a language, lays down a system of definitions and rules, founded on scientific principles and good usage, illustrates their nature and design, and enforces their application.

PRINCIPLE. A principle in grammar is a peculiar construction of the language, sanctioned by good usage.

DEFINITION. A definition in grammar is a principle of language expressed in a definite form.

RULE. A rule describes the peculiar construction or circumstantial relation of words, which custom has established for our observance.

ENGLISH GRAMMAR.

ENGLISH GRAMMAR is the art of speaking and writing the English language with propriety.

GRAMMAR teaches us *how to use words in a proper manner.* The most important use of that faculty called speech, is, to convey our thoughts to others. If, therefore, we have a store of words, and even know what they signify, they will be of no real use to us unless we can also apply them to practice, and make them answer the purposes for which they were invented. *Grammar*, well understood, enables us to express our thoughts fully and clearly ; and, consequently, in a manner which will defy the ingenuity of man to give our words any other meaning thar that which we ourselves intend them to express. To be able to speak and write our vernacular tongue with accuracy and elegunce, is, certainly, a consideration of the highest moment.

Grammar is divided into four parts ;

1. ORTHOGRAPHY,	3. SYNTAX,
2. ETYMOLOGY,	4. PROSODY.

ORTHOGRAPHY teaches the nature and powers of letters, and the just method of spelling words.

ORTHOGRAPHY means *word-making*, or *spelling*. It teaches us the different kinds and sounds of letters, how to combine them into syllables, and syllables into words.

As this is one of the first steps in the path of literature, I presume you already understand the nature and use of letters, and the just method of spelling words. If you do, it is unnecessary for you to dwell long on this part of grammar, which, though very important, is rather dry and uninteresting, for it has nothing to do with parsing and analyzing language. And, therefore, if you can *spell correctly*, you may omit Orthography, and commence with Etymology and Syntax.

Orthography treats, 1st, of *Letters*, 2ndly, of *Syllables*, and 3dly, of *Words*.

I. LETTERS. A letter is the first principle, or least part, of a word.

The English Alphabet contains twenty-six letters. They are divided into vowels and consonants.

A vowel is a letter that can be perfectly sounded by itself. The vowels are *a*, *e*, *i*, *o*, *u*, and sometimes *w* and *y*. *W* and *y* are consonants when they begin a word or syllable ; but in every other situation hey are vowels.

A consonant is a letter that cannot be perfectly sounded without the help of a vowel ; as, *b*, *d*, *f*, *l*. All letters except the vowels are consonants.

Consonants are divided into mutes and semi-vowels. The mutes cannot be sounded *at all* without the aid of a vowel. They are *b, p, t, d, k,* and *c* and *g* hard.

The semi-vowels have an imperfect sound of themselves. They are *f, l, m, n, r, v, s, z, x,* and *c* and *g* soft.

Four of the semi-vowels, namely, *l, m, n, r,* are called *liquids,* because they readily unite with other consonants, and flow, as it were, into their sounds.

A diphthong is the union of *two* vowels, pronounced by a single impulse of the voice; as *oi* in voice, *ou* in sound.

A triphthong is the union of *three* vowels pronounced in like manner; as, *eau* in beau, *iew* in view.

A *proper* diphthong has *both* the vowels sounded; as, *ou* in ounce. An *improper* diphthong has only *one* of the vowels sounded; as, *oa* in boat.

II. SYLLABLES. A Syllable is a distinct sound, uttered by a single impulse of the voice; as, *a, an, ant.*

A word of one syllable, is termed a Monosyllable; a word of two syllables, a Dissyllable; a word of three syllables, a Trisyllable; a word of four or more syllables, a Polysyllable.

III. WORDS. Words are articulate sounds, used by common consent, as signs of our ideas.

Words are of two sorts, primitive and derivative.

A *primitive* word is that which cannot be reduced to a simpler word in the language; as, *man, good.*

A *derivative* word is that which may be reduced to a simpler word; as, *manful, goodness.*

There is little or no difference between derivative and compound words. The terminations or added syllables, such as *ed, es, ess, est, an, ant, en, ence, ent, dom, hood, ly, ous, ful, ness,* and the like, were, originally, distinct and separate words, which, by long use, have been contracted, and made to coalesce with other words.

OF THE SOUNDS OF THE LETTERS.

A.—*A* has four sounds; the long; as in *name, basin;* the broad; as in *ball, wall;* the short; as in *fagot, glass;* and the flat, Italian sound; as in *bar, farther.*

The improper diphthong, *aa,* has the short sound of *a* in *Balaam, Canaan, Isaac;* and the long sound of *a* in *Baal, Gaal, Aaron.*

The Latin diphthong, *æ,* has the long sound of *e* in *ænigma, Cæsar,* and some other words. But many authors reject this useless excrescence of antiquity, and write, *enigma, Cesar.*

The diphthong, *ai,* has the long sound of *a;* as in *pail, sail;* except in *plaid, said, again, raillery, fountain, Britain,* and some others.

Au is sounded like broad *a* in *taught,* like flat *a* in *aunt,* like long *o* in *hautboy,* and like short *o* in *laurel.*

Aw has always the sound of broad *a;* as in *bawl, crawl.*

Ay has the long sound of *a;* as in *pay, delay.*

B.—*B* has only one sound; as in *baker, number, chub.*

B is silent when it follows *m* in the same syllable; as in *lamb,* &c. except in *accumb, rhomb,* and *succumb.* It is also silent before *t* in the same syllable; as in *doubt, debtor, subtle,* &c.

C.—*C* sounds like *k* before *a, o, u, r, l, t,* and at the end of syllables; as in *cart, cottage, curious, craft, tract, cloth; victim, flaccid.* It has the sound of *s* before *e, i,* and *y;* as in *centre, cigar, mercy. C* has the sound of *sh* when followed by a diphthong, and is preceded by the accent, either primary or secondary; as in *social, pronunciation,* &c.; and of *z* in *discern, sacrifice, sice, suffice.* It is mute in *arbuscle, czar, czarina, endict, victuals, muscle.*

Ch is commonly sounded like *tsh;* as in *church, chin;* but in words derived from the ancient languages, it has the sound of *k;* as in *chemist, chorus;* and likewise in foreign names; as in *Achish, Enoch.* In words from the French, *ch* sounds like *sh;* as in *chaise, chevalier;* and also like *sh* when preceded by *l* or *n;* as in *milch, bench, clinch,* &c.

Ch in *arch,* before a vowel, sounds like *k;* as in *arch-angel,* except in *arched, archery, archer, archenemy;* but before a consonant, it sounds like *tsh;* as in *archbishop. Ch* is silent in *schedule, schism, yacht, drachm.*

D.—*D* has one uniform sound; as in *death, bandage.* It sounds like *dj* or *j* when followed by long *u* preceded by the accent; as in *educate, verdure.* It also sounds like *j* in *grandeur, soldier.*

The termination, *ed,* in adjectives and participial adjectives, retains its distinct sound; as, a *wick-ed* man, a *learn-ed* man, *bless-ed* are the meek; but in verbs the *e* is generally dropped; as, *passed, walked, flashed, aimed, rolled,* &c. which are pronounced, *past, walkt, flasht, aimd, rold.*

E.—*E* has a long sound; as in *scheme, severe;* a short sound; as in *men, tent;* and sometimes the sound of flat *a;* as in *sergeant;* and of short *i;* as in *yes, pretty, England,* and generally in the unaccented terminations, *es, et, en.*

F.—*F* has one unvaried sound; as in *fancy, muffin;* except in *of,* which, when uncompounded, is pronounced *ov.* A wive's portion, a calve's head, are improper. They should be, *wife's* portion, *calf's* head.

G.—*G* has two sounds. It is hard before *a, o, u, l,* and *r,* and at the end of a word; as in *gay, go, gun, glory; bag, snug.* It is soft before *e, i,* and *y;* as in *genius, ginger, Egypt.* Exceptions; *get, gewgaw, gimlet,* and some others. G is silent before *n;* as in *gnash.*

H.—*H* has an articulate sound; as in *hat, horse, hull.* It is silent after *r;* as in *rhetoric, rhubarb.*

I. —*I* has a long sound; as in *fine;* and a short one; as in *fin*. Before *r* it is often sounded like *u* short; as in *first, third;* and in other words, like short *e;* as in *birth, virtue*. In some words it has the sound of long *e;* as in *machine, profile*.

J.—*J* has the sound of soft *g;* except in *hallelujah*, in which it is pronounced like *y*.

K.—*K* has the sound of *c* hard, and is used before *e, i,* and *y*, where *c* would be soft; as *kept, skirt, murky*. It is silent before *n;* as in *knife, knell, knocker*.

L.—*L* has always a soft liquid sound; as in *love, billow*. It is often silent; as in *half, talk, almond*.

M.—*M* has always the same sound; as in *murmur, monumental;* except in *comptroller*, which is pronounced *controller*.

N.—*N* has two sounds; the one pure; as in *man, net, noble;* the other a compound sound; as in *ankle, banquet, distinct,* &c., pronounced *angkl, bangkwet*. *N* final is silent when preceded by *m;* as in *hymn, autumn*.

O.—*O* has a long sound; as in *note, over;* and a short one; as in *not, got*. It has the sound of *u* short; as in *son, attorney, doth, does;* and generally in the terminations, *op, ot, or, on, om, ol, od,* &c.

P.—*P* has but one uniform sound; as in *pin, slipper;* except in *cupboard clapboard*, where it has the sound of *b*. It is mute in *psalm, Ptolemy, tempt, empty, corps, raspberry, and receipt*.

Ph has the sound of *f* in *philosophy, Philip;* and of *v* in *nephew, Stephen*.

Q.—*Q* is sounded like *k*, and is always followed by *u* pronounced like *w;* as in *quadrant, queen, conquest*.

R.—*R* has a rough sound; as in *Rome, river, rage;* and a smooth one; as in *bard, card, regard*. In the unaccented termination *re*, the *r* is sounded after the *e;* as in *fibre, centre*.

- S.—*S* has a flat sound like *z;* as in *besom, nasal;* and, at the beginning of words, a sharp, hissing sound; as in *saint, sister, sample*. It has the sound of *sh* when preceded by the accent and another *s* or a liquid, and followed by a diphthong or long *u;* as in *expulsion, censure*. *S* sounds like *zh* when preceded by the accent and a vowel, and followed by a diphthong or long *u ·* as in *brasier, usual*. It is mute in *isle, corps, demesne, viscount*.

T.—*T* is sounded in *take, temper*. *T* before *u*, when the accent precedes, and generally before *eou*, sounds like *tsh;* as, *nature, virtue, righteous*, are pronounced *natshure, virtshue. richeus*. *Ti* before a vowel, preceded by the accent, has the sound of *sh;* as in *salvation, negotiation;* except in such words as *tierce, tiara,* &c. and unless an *s* goes before; as, *question;* and excepting also derivatives from words ending in *ty;* as in *mighty, mightier*.

Th, at the beginning, *middle*, and end of words, is sharp; as in *thick, panther, breath*. Exceptions; *then, booth, worthy,* &c.

U.—*U* has three sounds; a long; as in *mule, cubic;* a short; as in *dull, custard;* and an obtuse sound; as in *full, bushel*. It is pronounced like short *e* in *bury;* and like short *i* in *busy, business*.

V.—*V* has uniformly the sound of flat *f;* as in *vanity, love*.

W.—*W*, when a consonant, has its sound, which is heard in *wo, beware*.

W is silent before *r;* as in *wry, wrap, wrinkle;* and also in *answer, sword,* &c. Before *h* it is pronounced as if written after the *h;* as in *why, when, what;—hwy, hwen, hwat*. When heard as a vowel, it takes the sound of *u;* as in *draw, crew, now*.

X.—*X* has a sharp sound, like *ks*, when it ends a syllable with the accent on it; as, *exit, exercise;* or when it precedes an accented syllable which begins with any consonant except *h;* as, *excuse, extent;* but when the following accented syllable begins with a vowel or *h*, it has, generally, a flat sound, like *gz;* as in *exert, exhort.* *X* has the sound of *Z* at the beginning of proper names of Greek original; as in *Xanthus, Xenophon, Xerxes.*

Y.—Y, when a consonant, has its proper sound; as in *youth, York, yes, new-year.* When *y* is employed as a vowel, it has exactly the sound that *i* would have in the same situation; as in *rhyme, system, party, pyramid*

Z.—Z has the sound of flat *s;* as in *freeze, brazen.*

RULES FOR SPELLING.

SPELLING is the art of expressing a word by its proper letters.

The following rules are deemed important in practice, although they assist us in spelling only a small portion of the words of our language. This useful art is to be chiefly acquired by studying the spelling-book and dictionary, and by strict attention in reading.

RULE I. Monosyllables ending in *f, l,* or *s,* double the final or ending consonant when it is preceded by a *single* vowel; as, *staff, mill, pass.* Exceptions; *of, if, is, as, has, was, yes, his, this, us,* and *thus.*

False Orthography for the learner to correct.—Be thou like the gale that moves the gras, to those who ask thy aid.—The aged hero comes forth on his staf; his gray hair glitters in the beam.—Shal mortal man be more just than God?—Few know the value of health til they lose it.—Our manners should be neither gros, nor excessively refined.

    And that is not the lark, whose notes do beat
    The vaulty heaven so high above our heads:
    I have more care to stay, than wil to go.

RULE II. Monosyllables ending in any consonant but *f, l,* or *s,* never double the final consonant when it is preceded by a *single* vowel; as, *man, hat.* Exceptions; *add, ebb, butt, egg, odd, err, inn, bunn, purr,* and *buzz.*

False Orthography.—None ever went sadd from Fingal.—He rejoiced over his sonn.—Clonar lies bleeding on the bedd of death.—Many a trapp is set to insnare the feet of youth.

    The weary sunn has made a golden sett,
    And, by the bright track of his golden carr,
    Gives token of a goodly day to-morrow.

RULE III. Words ending in *y,* form the plural of nouns, the persons of verbs, participial nouns, past participles, comparatives, and superlatives, by changing *y* into *i,* when the *y* is preceded by a *consonant;* as, *spy, spies; I carry, thou carriest, he carries; carrier, carried; happy, happier, happiest.*

The present participle in *ing,* retains the *y* that *i* may not be doubled; as, *carry, carrying.*

But when *y* is preceded by a *vowel*, in such instances as the above, it is not changed into *i ;* as, *boy, boys ; I cloy, he cloys ;* except in the words *lay, pay,* and *say ;* from which are formed *laid, paid,* and *said ;* and their compounds, *unpaid, unsaid,* &c.

False Orthography.—Our fancys should be governed by reason.—Thou wearyest thyself in vain.—He denyed himself all sinful pleasures.
Win straiing souls with modesty and love;
Cast none away.
The truly good man is not dismaied by poverty.
Ere fresh morning streak the east, we must be risen to reform yonder allies green.

RULE IV. When words ending in *y,* assume an additional syllable beginning with a consonant, the *y,* if it is preceded by a consonant, is commonly changed to *i ;* as, *happy, happily, happiness.*

But when *y* is preceded by a vowel, in such instances, it is very rarely changed to *i ;* as, *coy, coyless ; boy, boyish ; boyhood ; joy, joyless, joyful.*

False Orthography.—His mind is uninfluenced by fancyful humors.—The vessel was heavyly laden.—When we act against conscience, we become the destroiers of our own peace.
Christiana, mayden of heroic mien!
Star of the north! of northern stars the queen!

RULE V. Monosyllables, and words accented on the last syllable, ending with a single consonant that is preceded by a single vowel, double that consonant when they assume another syllable that begins with a vowel ; as, *wit, witty ; thin, thinnish ; to abet, an abetter.*

But if a diphthong precedes, or the accent is *not* on the last syllable, the consonant remains single ; as, *to toil, toiling ; to offer, an offering ; maid, maiden.*

False Orthography.—The business of to-day, should not be defered till to-morrow.—That law is annuled.—When we have outstriped our errors we have won the race.—By defering our repentance, we accumulate our sorrows.—The Christian Lawgiver has prohibitted many things which the heathen philosophers allowed.
At summer eve, when heaven's aerial bow
Spans with bright arch the glitterring hills below.—
Thus mourned the hapless man ; a thunderring sound
Rolled round the shudderring walls and shook the ground.

RULE VI. Words ending in double *l,* in taking *ness, less, ly,* or *ful,* after them, generally omit one *l ;* as, *fulness, skilless, fully, skilful.*

But words ending in any double letter but *l,* and taking *ness, less, ly,* or *ful,* after them, preserve the letter double ; as, *harmlessness, carelessness, carelessly, stiffly, successful.*

False Orthography.—A chillness generally precedes a fever.—He is wed to dulness.

The silent stranger stood amazed to see
Contempt of wealth and willful poverty.

Restlesness of mind impairs our peace.—The road to the blisful regions, is as open to the peasant as to the king.—The arrows of calumny fall harmlessly at the feet of virtue.

RULE VII. *Ness, less, ly,* or *ful,* added to words ending in silent *e,* does not cut it off; as, *paleness, guileless, closely, peaceful :* except in a few words ; as, *duly, truly, awful.*

False Orthography.—Sedatness is becoming.
All these with ceasless praise his works behold.
Stars rush : and final ruin fiercly drives
Her ploughshare o'er creation !
————————————Nature made a pause,
An aweful pause ! prophetic of her end !

RULE VIII. When words ending in silent *e,* assume the termination, *ment,* the *e* should not be cut off; as, *abatement, chastisement.*

Ment, like other terminations, changes *y* into *i* when the *y* is preceded by a consonant ; as, *accompany, accompaniment ; merry, merriment.*

False Orthography.—A judicious arrangment of studies facilitates improvment.—Encouragment is greatest when we least need it.
To shun allurments is not hard,
To minds resolv'd, forwarn'd, and well prepar'd.

RULE IX. When words ending in silent *e,* assume the termination, *able* or *ible,* the *e* should generally be cut off; as, *blame, blamable ; cure, curable ; sense, sensible.* But if *c* or *g* soft comes before *e* in the original word, the *e* is preserved in words compounded with *able ;* as, *peace, peaceable ; change, changeable.*

False Orthography.—Knowledge is desireable.—Misconduct is inexcuseable.—Our natural defects are not chargable upon us.—We are made to bo servicable to others as well as to ourselves.

RULE X. When *ing* or *ish* is added to words ending in silent *e,* the *e* is almost always omitted ; as, *place, placing ; lodge, lodging ; slave, slavish ; prude, prudish.*

False Orthography.—Labor and expense are lost upon a droneish spirit.—An obligeing and humble disposition, is totally unconnected with a servile and cringeing humor.
Conscience anticipateing time,
Already rues th' unacted crime.

One self-approveing hour, whole years outweighs
Of stupid starers, and of loud huzzas.

RULE XI. Compound words are generally spelled in the same

manner as the simple words of which they are compounded; as, *glasshouse, skylight, thereby, hereafter.*   Many words ending in double *l,* are exceptions to this rule ; as, *already, welfare, wilful, fulfil ;* and also the words, *wherever, christmas, lammas, &c.*

False Orthography.—The Jew's pasover was instituted in A M. 2513.— They salute one another by touching their forheads.—That which is some times expedient, is not allways so.

Then, in the scale of reas'ning life 'tis plain,
There must be, somwhere, such a rank as man.
Till hymen brought his lov-delighted hour,
There dwelt no joy in Eden's rosy bower.
The head reclined, the loosened hair,
The limbs relaxed, the mournful air:—
See, he looks up ; a wofull smile
Lightens his wo-worn cheek awhile.

You may now answer the following
QUESTIONS.

What is language ?—How is language divided ?—What is natural language ?—What are the elements of natural language in man ?—Wherein consists the language of brutes ?—What is artificial language ?—What is an idea ?—What are words ?—What is grammar ?—What does Universal grammar explain ?—Wherein does Particular grammar differ from universal ?—What is the standard of grammatical accuracy ?—What is Philosophical grammar?—What is Practical grammar?—What is a principle of grammar ?—A definition ?—A rule ?—What is English grammar ?— Into how many parts is grammar divided ?—What does Orthography teach ?

ETYMOLOGY AND SYNTAX.

—

LECTURE II.

OF NOUNS AND VERBS.

ETYMOLOGY treats of the different sorts of words, their various modifications, and their derivation.

SYNTAX treats of the agreement and government of words, and of their proper arrangement in a sentence.

The word ETYMOLOGY signifies the *origin* or *pedigree of words.*
Syn, a prefix from the Greek, signifies *together.*   *Syn-tax,* means *placing together ;* or, as applied in grammar, *sentence making.*

The rules of syntax, which direct to the proper choice of words, and their judicious arrangement in a sentence, and thereby enable us to correct and avoid errors in speech, are chiefly based on principles unfolded and explained by Etymology. Etymological knowledge, then, is a prerequisite to the study of Syntax ; but, in parsing, under the head of Etymology, you are required to apply the rules of Syntax. It becomes necessary, therefore, in a practical work of this sort, to treat these two parts of grammar in connexion.

Conducted on scientific principles, Etymology would comprehend the exposition of the origin and meaning of words, and, in short, their whole ·history, including their application to things in accordance with the laws of nature and of thought, and the caprice of those who apply them ; but to follow up the current of language to its various sources, and analyze the springs from which it flows, would involve a process altogether too·arduous and extensive for an elementary work. It would lead to the study of all those languages from which ours is immediately derived, and even compel us to trace many words through those languages to others more ancient, and so on, until the chain of research would become, if not endless, at least, too extensive to be traced out by one man. I shall, therefore, confine myself to the following, limited views of this part of grammar.

1. Etymology treats of the *classification* of words.

2. Etymology explains the *accidents* or *properties* peculiar to each class or sort of words, and their present *modifications*. By modifications, I mean the changes produced on their *endings*, in consequence of their assuming different relations in respect to one another. These changes, such as fruit, fruit*s*, fruit'*s*; he, h*is*, h*im*; write, write*st*, write*th*, write*s*, wr*ote*, wr*itten*, writ*ing*, writ*er*; a, a*n*; ample, ampl*y*, and the like, will be explained in their appropriate places.

3. Etymology treats of the *derivation* of words; that·is, it teaches you *how one word comes from*, or *grows out of* another. For example, from the word speak, come the words speak*est*, speak*eth*, speak*s*, speak*ing*, sp*oke*, sp*oken*, speak*er*, speak*er's*, speak*ers*. These, you perceive, are all one and the same word, and all, except the last three, express the same kind of action. They differ from each other only in the termination. These changes in termination are produced on the word in order to make it correspond with the various *persons* who speak, the *number* of persons, or the *time* of speaking; as, *I* speak, *thou* spea*est*, the *man* speak*eth*, or speak*s*, the *men* speak, *I* sp*oke*; The speak*er* speak*s* another speak*er's* spe*ech*.

The third part of Etymology, which is intimately connected with the second, will be more amply expanded in Lecture XlV. and in the Philosophical notes; but I shall not treat largely of that branch of derivation which consists in tracing words to foreign languages. This is the province of the lexicographer, rather than of the philologist. It is not the business of him who writes a practical, English grammar, to trace words to the Saxon, nor to the Celtic, the Greek, the Dutch, the Mexican, nor the Persian; nor is it his province to explain their meaning in Latin, French, or Hebrew, Italian, Mohegan, or Sanscrit; but it is his duty to explain their properties, their powers, their connexions, relations, dependancies, and. bearings, not at the period in which the Danes made an irruption into the island of Great Britain, nor in the year in which Lamech paid his addresses to Adah and Zillah, but *at the particular period in which he writes*. His words are already derived, formed, established, and furnished to his hand, and he is bound to take them and explain them as he finds them *in his day*, without any regard to their ancient construction and application.

CLASSIFICATION.

In arranging the parts of speech, I conceive it to be the legitimate object of the practical grammarian, to consult *practical convenience*. The true principle of classification seems to be, not a reference to essential differences in the *primitive* meaning of words, nor to their original combinations, but to the *manner in which they are at present employed*. In the early and rude state of society, mankind are quite limited in their knowledge, and having but few ideas to communicate, a small number of words answers their purpose in the transmission of thought. This leads them to express their ideas in short, detached sentences, requiring few or none of those *connectives*, or words of transition, which are afterwards introduced into language by refinement, and which contribute so largely to its perspicuity and elegance. The argument appears to be conclusive, then, that every language must necessarily have more parts of speech in its refined, than in its barbarous state.

The part of speech to which any word belongs, is ascertained, not by the *original* signification of that word, but by its present *manner* of meaning, or, rather, *the office which it performs in a sentence.*

The various ways in which a word is applied to the idea which it represents, are called its *manner of meaning*. Thus, The painter dips his *paint* brush in *paint*, to *paint* the carriage. Here, the word *paint*, is first employed to *describe* the brush which the painter uses; in this situation it is, therefore, an *adjective ;* secondly, to *name* the mixture employed; for which reason it is a *noun ;* and, lastly, to *express the action* performed; it therefore, becomes a *verb ;* and yet, the meaning of the word is the same in all these applications. This meaning, however, is applied in different ways; and thus the same word becomes different parts of speech. Richard took *water* from the *water* pot, to *water* the plants.

ETYMOLOGY.

Etymology treats, first, of the *classification* of words.

THE ENGLISH LANGUAGE is derived chiefly from the Saxon, Danish, Celtic, and Gothic; but in the progressive stages of its refinement, it has been greatly enriched by accessions from the Greek, Latin, French, Spanish, Italian, and German languages.

The number of words in our language, after deducting proper names, and words formed by the inflections of our verbs, nouns, and adjectives, may be estimated at about *forty thousand*.

There are ten sorts of words, called parts of speech, namely, the NOUN or SUBSTANTIVE, VERB, ARTICLE, ADJECTIVE, PARTICIPLE, ADVERB, PREPOSITION, PRO-NOUN, CONJUNCTION, and INTERJECTION.

Thus you perceive, that all the words in the English language are included in these ten classes : and what you have to do in acquiring a knowledge of English Grammar, is merely to become acquainted with these ten parts of speech, and the rules of Syntax that apply to them. The *Noun* and *Verb* are the most important and leading parts of speech ; therefore they are first presented : all the rest (except the interjection) are either appendages or connectives of these two. As you proceed, you will find that it will require more time, and cost you more labor, to get a knowledge of the noun and verb, than it will to become familiar with all the minor parts of speech.

The principal use of words is, to *name* things, *compare* them. with each other, and *express their actions*.

Nouns, which are the names of entities or things, *adjectives* which denote the comparisons and relations of things by describing them, and expressing their qualities, and *verbs*, which express the actions and being of things, are the only classes of words necessarily recognised in a philosophical view of grammar. But in a treatise which consults, mainly, the *practical* advantages of the learner, it is believed, that no classification will be found more convenient or accurate than the foregoing, which divides words into ten sorts. To attempt to prove, in this place, that nothing would be gained by adopting either a less or a greater number f the parts of speech, would be anticipating the subject. I hall, therefore, give my reasons for adopting this arrangement in preference to any other, as the different sorts of words are respectively presented to you, for then you will be better prepared to appreciate my arguments.

OF NOUNS.

A NOUN is the name of any person, place, or thing; as, *man, Charleston, knowledge.*

Nouns are often improperly called *substantives.* A substantive is the name of a *substance* only; but a noun is the name either of a *substance* or a *quality.*

Noun, derived from the Latin word *nomen,* signifies *name.* The name of any thing* that exists, whether animate or inani-

---

* The word *thing*, from the Saxon verb *thingian*, to think, is almost unlimited in its meaning. It may be applied to every animal and creature in the universe. By the term creature, I mean that which has been created; as, a dog, water, dirt. This word is also frequently applied to actions; as, "To get drunk is a beastly *thing.*" In this phrase, it signifies neither animal nor creature; but it denotes merely an action; therefore this action is the thing.

NOTES ON PHILOSOPHICAL GRAMMAR.

Perhaps no subject has, in this age, elicited more patient research, and critical investigation of original, constituent principles, formations, and combinations, than the English language. The legitimate province of philology, however, as I humbly conceive, has, in some instances, been made to yield to that of philosophy, so far as to divert the attention from the combinations of our language which refinement has introduced, to radical elements and associations which no way concern the progress of literature, or the essential use for which language was intended. Were this retrogressive mode of in vestigating and applying principles, to obtain, among philologists, the ascend ency over that which accommodates the use of language to progressive re finement, it is easy to conceive the state of barbarism to which society would in a short time, be reduced. Moreover, if what some call the philosophy of language, were to supersede, altogether, the province of philology as it applies to the present, progressive and refined state of English literature, the great object contemplated by the learned, in all ages, namely, the approximation of language, in common with every thing else, to that point of perfection at which it is the object of correct philology to arrive, would be frustrated. The dubious and wildering track struck out by those innovators and visionaries who absurdly endeavor to teach modern English, by rejecting the

mate, or which we can see, hear, feel, taste, smell, or think of, is a noun. *Animal, bird, creature, paper, pen, apple, field, house, modesty, virtue, danger,* are all nouns. In order that you may easily distinguish this part of speech from others, I will give you a *sign,* which will be useful to you when you cannot tell it by the *sense.* Any word that will make sense with *the* before it, is a noun. Try the following words by this sign, and see if they are nouns: tree, mountain, soul, mind, conscience, understanding. *The* tree, *the* mountain, *the* soul, and so on. You perceive, that they will make sense with *the* prefixed; therefore you know they are *nouns.* There are, however, exceptions to this rule, for some nouns will not make sense with *the* prefixed. These you will be able to distinguish, if you exercise your mind, by their *making sense of themselves ;* as, *goodness, sobriety, hope, immortality.*

Nouns are used to denote the nonentity or absence of a thing, as well as its reality ; as, *nothing, naught, vacancy, non-existence, invisibility.*

Nouns are sometimes used as verbs, and verbs, as nouns, according to their *manner* of meaning ; and nouns are sometimes used as adjectives, and adjectives, as nouns. This matter will be explained in the concluding part of this lecture, where you will be better prepared to comprehend it.

---

authority and sanction of custom, and by conducting the learner back to the original combinations, and the detached, disjointed, and barbarous constructions of our progenitors, both prudence and reason, as well as a due regard for correct philology, impel me to shun. Those modest writers who, by bringing to their aid a little sophistry, much duplicity, and a wholesale traffic in the swelling phrases, " philosophy, reason, and common sense," attempt to overthrow the wisdom of former ages, and show that the result of all the labors of those distinguished philologists who had previously occupied the field of grammatical science, is nothing but error and folly, will doubtless meet the neglect and contempt justly merited by such consummate vanity and unblushing pedantry. Fortunately for those who employ our language as their vehicle of mental conference, custom will not yield to the speculative theories of the visionary. If it would, improvement in English literature would soon be at an end, and we should be tamely conducted back to the Vandalic age.

As the use of what is commonly called the philosophy of language, is evidently misapplied by those who make it the test of *grammatical certainty,* it may not be amiss to offer a few considerations with a view to expose the fallacy of so vague a criterion.

All reasoning and investigation which depend on the philosophy of language for an ultimate result, must be conducted *a posteriori.* Its office, according to the ordinary mode of treating the subject, is to trace language to its origin, not for the purpose of determining and fixing grammatical associations and dependances, such as the agreement, government, and mutual relations of words, but in order to analyze combinations with a view to develop the first principles of the language, and arrive at the primitive meaning of

Nouns are of two kinds, common and proper.

A *Common noun* is the name of a sort or species of things; as, *man, tree, river.*

A *Proper noun* is the name of an individual; as, *Charles, Ithaca, Ganges.*

A noun signifying many, is called a *collective noun*, or *noun of multitude*; as, the *people*, the *army.*

The distinction between a common and a proper noun, is very obvious. For example : *boy* is a common noun, because it is a name applied to *all* boys ; but *Charles* is a proper noun, because it is the name of an *individual* boy. Although many boys may have the same name, yet you know it is not a common noun, for the name Charles is *not* given to all boys. *Mississippi* is a proper noun, because it is the name of an individual river ; but *river* is a common noun, because it is the name of a *species* of things, and the name *river* is common to *all* rivers.

Nouns which denote the genus, species, or variety of beings or things, are always common ; as, *tree*, the genus ; *oak, ash, chestnut, poplar*, different species ; and red *oak*, white *oak*, black *oak*, varieties. The word earth, when it signifies a kind or quantity of dirt, is a common noun ; but when it denotes the planet we inhabit, it is a proper noun. The *words* person, place, river,

---

words. Now, it is presumed, that no one who has paid critical attention to the subject, will contend, that the original import of single words, has any relation to the syntactical dependances and connexions of words in general ;—to gain a knowledge of which, is the leading object of the student in grammar. And, furthermore, I challenge those who have indulged in such useless vagaries, to show by what process, with their own systems, they can communicate a practical knowledge of grammar. I venture to predict, that, if they make the attempt, they will find their systems more splendid in theory, than useful in practice.

Again, it cannot rationally be contended, that the radical meaning has any efficiency in controlling the signification which, by the power of association, custom has assigned to many words ;—a signification *essentially different* from the original import. Were this the case, and were the language now to be taught and understood in compliance with the original import of words, it would have to undergo a thorough change ; to be analyzed, divided, and subdivided, almost *ad infinitum*. Indeed, there is the same propriety in asserting, that the Gothic, Danish, and Anglo-Saxon elements in our language, ought to be pronounced separately, to enable us to understand our vernacular tongue, that there is in contending, that their primitive meaning has an as cendency over the influence of the principle of association in changing, and the power of custom in determining, the import of words. Many of our words are derived from the Greek, Roman, French, Spanish, Italian, and German languages ; and the only use we can make of their originals, is to render them subservient to the force of custom in cases in which general

mountain, lake, &c. are *common nouns*, because they are the names of whole *species*, or classes of things containing many sorts; but the *names* of persons, places, rivers, mountains, lakes, &c. are *proper nouns*, because they denote *individuals;* as, Augustus, Baltimore, Alps, Huron.

Physician, lawyer, merchant, and *shoemaker,* are common nouns, because these names are common to classes of men. *God* and *Lord,* when applied to Jehovah or Jesus Christ, are proper; but when employed to denote heathen or false *gods,* or temporal *lords,* they are common.

The Notes and remarks throughout the work, though of minor importance, demand your attentive and careful perusal.

NOTES.

1. When *proper* nouns have an article annexed to them, they are used after the manner of *common* nouns; as, " Bolivar is styled *the* Washington of South America."

2. *Common* nouns are sometimes used to signify *individuals,* when articles or pronouns are prefixed to them; as, " *The* boy is studious; *That* girl is discreet." In such instances, they are nearly equivalent to proper nouns.

3. *Common* nouns are sometimes subdivided into the following classes: *Nouns of Multitude;* as, The people, the parliament: *Verbal or participial nouns;* as, The beginning, reading, writing; and *Abstract nouns,* or the names of qualities abstracted from their substances; as, knowledge, virtue, goodness. Lest the student be led to blend the idea of abstract nouns with that of adjectives, both of which denote qualities, a farther illustration appears to be necessary, in order to mark the distinction between these two parts of speech. An abstract noun denotes a quality considered *apart* (that is, abstracted) *from* the substance or being to which it belongs; but an adjective denotes a quality *joined* (adjected) *to* the substance or being to which it belongs. Thus, *whiteness* and *white* both denote the same quality; but we

---

usage has not varied from the primitive signification. Moreover, let the advocates of a mere philosophical investigation of the language, extend their system as far as a radical analysis will warrant them, and, with Horne Tooke, not only consider adverbs, prepositions, conjunctions, and interjections, as abbreviations of nouns and verbs, but, on their own responsibility, apply them, in teaching the language, *in compliance with their radical import,* and what would such a course avail them against the power of custom, and the influence of association and refinement? Let them show me one grammarian, produced by such a course of instruction, and they will exhibit a " philosophical" miracle. They might as well undertake to teach architecture, by having recourse to its origin, as represented by booths and tents. In addition to this, when we consider the great number of obsolete words, from which many now in use are derived, the original meaning of which cannot be ascertained, and, also, the multitude whose signification has been changed by the principle of association, it is preposterous to think, that a mere philosophical mode of investigating and teaching the language, is the one by which its significancy can be enforced, its correctness determined, its use comprehended, and its improvement extended. Before what commonly passes for a philosophical manner of developing the language can successfully be made the medium through which it can be comprehended, in all its present combinations, relations, and dependances, it must undergo a thorough retrogres-

speak of whiteness as a distinct object of thought, while we use the word *white* always in reference to the noun to which it belongs; as, *white* paper, *white* nouse.

4. Some authors have proceeded to still more minute divisions and subdivisions of nouns; such, for example, as the following, which appear to be more complex than useful : *Natural nouns,* or names of things formed by nature ; as, man, beast, water, air : 2. *Artificial nouns,* or names of things formed by art ; as, book, vessel, house : 3. *Personal nouns,* or those which stand for human beings ; as, man, woman, Edwin : 4. *Neuter nouns,* or those which denote things inanimate ; as, book, field, mountain, Cincinnati. The following, however, is quite a rational division : *Material nouns* are the names of things formed of matter ; as, stone, book : *Immaterial nouns* are the names of things having no substance ; as, hope, immortality.

To nouns belong gender, person, number, and case.

GENDER.

GENDER is the distinction of sex. Nouns have three genders, the masculine, the feminine, and the neuter.

The *masculine gender* denotes males; as, a *man*, a *boy*.

The *feminine gender* denotes females; as, a *woman*, a *girl*.

The *neuter gender* denotes things without sex; as, a *hat*, a *stick*.

Neuter means *neither :* therefore neuter gender signifies neither gender ; that is, neither masculine nor feminine. Hence,

give change, in all those combinations, relations, and dependances, even to the last letter of the alphabet. And before we can consent to this radical modification and retrograde ratio of the English language, we must agree to revive the customs, the habits, and the precise language of our progenitors, the Goths and Vandals. Were all the advocates for the introduction of such philosophical grammars into common schools, at once to enter on their pilgrimage, and recede into the native obscurity and barbarity of the ancient Britons, Picts, and Vandals, it is believed, that the cause of learning and refinement would not suffer greatly by their loss, and that the good sense of the present age, would not allow many of our best teachers to be of the party.

The last consideration which I shall give a philosophical manner of investigating and enforcing the English language, is, that by this mode of analyzing and reducing it to practice, *it cannot, in this age, be comprehended* as the medium of thought. Were this method to prevail, our present literal language would become a dead letter. Of what avail is language, if it can not be understood ? And how can it be accommodated to the understanding, unless it receive the sanction of common consent? Even if we admit that such a manner of unfolding the principles of our language, is more rational and correct than the ordinary, practical method, I think it is clear that such a mode of investigation and development, does not meet the necessities and convenience of ordinary learners in school. To be consistent, that system which instructs by tracing a few of our words to their origin, must unfold the whole in the same manner. But the student in common schools and academies, cannot afford time to stem the tide of language up to its source,

neuter gender means *no gender.* Strictly speaking, then, as there are but two sexes, nouns have but *two* genders; but for the sake of practical convenience, we apply to them three genders, by calling that a gender which is *no* gender. The English and the pure Persian, appear to be the only languages which observe, in the distinction of sex, the natural division of nouns.—The genders of nouns are so easily known, that a farther explanation of them is unnecessary, except what is given in the following

NOTES.

1. The same noun is sometimes masculine *and* feminine, and sometimes masculine *or* feminine. The noun *parents* is of the masculine *and* feminine gender. The nouns *parent, associate, neighbor, servant, friend, child, bird, fish, &c.* if doubtful, are of the masculine *or* feminine gender.

2. Some nouns naturally neuter, are, when used figuratively, or *personified,* converted into the masculine or feminine gender. Those nouns are generally rendered masculine, which are conspicuous for the attributes of imparting or communicating, and which are by nature strong and efficacious; as, the *sun, time, death, sleep, winter, &c.* Those, again, are generally feminine, which are conspicuous for the attributes of containing or bringing forth, or which are very beautiful, mild, or amiable; as, the *earth, moon, church, boat, vessel, city, country, nature, ship, soul, fortune, virtue, hope, spring, peace, &c.* This principle for designating the sex of a personified object, which is quite rational, is generally adhered to in the English language; but, in some instances, the poet applies the sex according to his fancy.

The masculine and feminine genders are distinguished in three ways:

1. *By different words;* as,

Masculine	Feminine.	Masculine.	Feminine.
Bachelor	maid	Boy	girl
Boar	sow	Brother	sister

and there dive to the bottom of the fountain for knowledge. Such labor ought not to be required of him. His object is to become, not a philosophical antiquarian, but a practical grammarian. If I comprehend the design (if they have any) of our modern philosophical writers on this subject, it is to make grammarians by inculcating a few general principles, arising out of the genius of the language, and the nature of things, which the learner, by the exercise of his *reasoning powers,* must reduce to practice. His own judgment, *independent of grammar rules,* is to be his guide in speaking and writing correctly. Hence, many of them exclude from their systems, all exercises in what is called *false Syntax.* But these profound philological dictators appear to have overlooked the important consideration, that the great mass of mankind, and especially of boys and girls in common schools, *can never become philosophers;* and, consequently, can never comprehend and reduce to practice their metaphysical and obscure systems of grammar. I wish to see children treated as *reasoning* beings. But there should be a medium in all things. It is, therefore, absurd to instruct children as if they were already profound philosophers and logicians.

To demonstrate the utility, and enforce the necessity, of exercising the learner in correcting *false Syntax,* I need no other argument than the interesting and undeniable fact, that Mr. Murray's labors, in this department, have effected a complete revolution in the English language, in point of verbal accuracy. Who does not know, that the best writers of this day, are not guilty of *one* grammatical inaccuracy, where those authors who wrote before

Buck	doe	Lord	lady
Bull	cow	Man	woman
Cock	hen	Master	mistress
Dog	bitch	Milter	spawner
Drake	duck	Nephew	niece
Earl	countess	Ram	ewe
Father	mother	Singer	songstress or
Friar	nun		singer
Gander	goose	Sloven	slut
Hart	roe	Son	daughter
Horse	mare	Stag	hind
Husband	wife	Uncle	aunt
King	queen	Wizard	witch
Lad	lass	Sir	madam

2. *By a difference in termination;* as,

Abbot	abbess	Elector	electress
Actor	actress	Embassador	embassadress
Administrator	administratrix	Emperor	emperess
Adulterer	adulteress	Enchanter	enchantress
Ambassador	ambassadress	Executor	executrix
Arbiter	arbitress	Fornicator	fornicatress
Auditor	auditress	God	goddess
Author	authoress	Governor	governess
Baron	baroness	Heir	heiress
Benefactor	benefactress	Hero	heroine
Bridegroom	bride	Host	hostess
Canon	canoness	Hunter	huntress
Caterer	cateress	Inheritor	inheritress or
Chante.	chantress		inheritrix
Conductor	conductress	Instructer	instructress
Count	countess	Jew	Jewess
Czar	czarina	Lion	lioness
Deacon	deaconess	Marquis	marchioness
Detracter	detractress	Mayor	mayoress
Director	directress	Patron	patroness
Duke	dutchess	Peer	peeress

Mr. Murray flourished, are guilty of *five?* And what has produced this important change for the better? Ask the hundreds of thousands who have studied "Mr. Murray's exercises in FALSE SYNTAX." If, then, this view of the subject is correct, it follows, that the greater portion of our philosophical grammars, are far more worthy the attention of literary connoisseurs, than of the great mass of learners.

Knowing that a strong predilection for philosophical grammars, exists in the minds of some teachers of this science, I have thought proper, for the gratification of such, to intersperse through the pages of this work, under the head of "PHILOSOPHICAL NOTES," an entire system of grammatical principles as deduced from what appears to me to be the most rational and consistent philosophical investigations. They who prefer this theory to that exhibited in the body of the work, are, of course, at liberty to adopt it.

In general, a philosophical theory of grammar will be found to accord wit the practical theory embraced in the body of this work. Wherever such agreement exists, the system contained in these NOTES *will be deficient, and this deficiency may be supplied by adopting the principles contained in the other parts of the work.*

Poet	poetess	Sultan	sultaness **or**
Priest	priestess		sultana
Prince	princess	Tiger	tigress
Prior	prioress	Testator	testatrix
Prophet	prophetess	Traitor	traitress
Proprietor	proprietress	Tutor	tutoress
Protector	protectress	Tyrant	tyranness
Shepherd	shepherdess	Victor	victress
Songster	songstress	Viscount	viscountess
Sorcerer	sorceress	Votary	votaress·
Suiter	suitress	Widower	widow

3. *By prefixing another word ;* as,

A cock-sparrow	A hen-sparrow
A man-servant	A maid-servant
A he-goat	A she-goat
A he-bear	A she-bear
A male-child	A female-child
Male-descendants	Female-descendants

PERSON.

PERSON is a property of the noun and pronoun which varies the verb.

The *first person* denotes the speaker.

The *second person* denotes the person or thing spoken to ; as, " Listen, O *earth !* "

The *third person* denotes the person or thing spoken of ; as, " The *earth* thirsts."

Nouns have but *two* persons, the second and third. When a man speaks, the *pronoun* I or we is always used ; therefore nouns can never be in the *first* person. In examples like the following,

---

OF THE PHILOSOPHICAL CLASSIFICATION OF WORDS.

According to the method in which philosophical investigations of language have generally been conducted, all our words should be reduced to two classes ; for it can be easily shown, that from the noun and verb, all the other parts of speech have sprung. Nay, more. They may even be reduced to one. Verbs do not, in reality, *express* actions ; but they are intrinsically the mere *names* of actions. The idea of action or being communicated by them, as well as the *meaning* of words in general, is merely *inferential.* The principle of reasoning assumed by the celebrated Horne Tooke, if carried to its full extent, would result, it is believed, in proving that we have but one part of speech.

Adnouns or *adjectives* were originally nouns. *Sweet, red, white,* are the *names* of qualities, as well as *sweetness, redness, whiteness.* The former differ from the latter only in their *manner* of signification. To denote that the name of some quality or substance is to be used in connexion with some other name, or, that this quality is to be *attributed* to some other name, we sometimes affix to it the termination *en, ed,* or *y ;* which signifies *give, add,* or *join.* When we employ the words wood*en,* wooll*en,* wealth*y,* grass*y,* the terminations *en* and *y,* by their own intrinsic meaning, give notice that we

4

some philologists suppose the noun to be in the *first* person :—"This may certify, that I, *Jonas Taylor,* do hereby give and grant," &c. But it is evident, that the speaker or writer, in introducing his own name, speaks *of* himself; consequently the noun is of the *third person.*

If you wish to understand the persons of nouns, a little sober thought is requisite; and, by exercising it, all difficulties will be removed. If I say, my *son,* have you seen the young man? you perceive that the noun *son* is of the *second* person, because I address myself *to* him; that is, he is spoken *to ;* but the noun *man* is of the *third* person, because he is spoken *of.* Again, if I say, young *man,* have you seen my son? *man* is of the *second* person, and *son* is of the *third.*

"Hast thou left thy blue course in the heavens, golden-haired *sun* of the sky?"

"*Father,* may the Great Spirit so brighten the chain of friendship between us, that a child may find it, when the sun is asleep in his wig-wam behind the western waters."

"Lo, earth receives him from the bending skies! Sink down, ye *mountains,* and, ye *valleys,* rise!"

"Eternal *Hope,* thy glittering wings explore Earth's loneliest bounds, and ocean's wildest shore."

In these examples, the nouns, sun, father, mountains, valleys, and hope, are of the *second* person, and, as you will hereafter learn, in the nominative case independent. Course, heavens, sky, Spirit, chain, friendship, child, sun, wig-wam, waters, earth, skies, wings, earth, bounds, ocean, and shore, are all of the *third* person.

---

intend to *give, add,* or *join,* the names of some other substances in which are found the properties or qualities of *wood, wool, wealth,* or *grass.*

Pronouns are a class of nouns, used instead of others to prevent their disagreeable repetition. Participles are certain forms of the verb. Articles, interjections, adverbs, prepositions, and conjunctions, are contractions of abbreviations of nouns and verbs. *An (a, ane,* or *one)* comes from *ananad,* to add, to heap. *The* and *that,* from the Anglo-Saxon verb *thean,* to get, assume. *Lo* is the imperative of *look ; fy,* of *fian,* to hate; and *welcome* means, it is *well* that you are *come. In* comes from the Gothic noun *inna,* the interior of the body; and *about,* from *boda,* the first outward boundary. *Through* or *thorough* is the Teutonic noun *thuruh,* meaning passage, gate, door. *From* is the Anglo-Saxon noun *frum,* beginning, source, author. He came *from (beginning)* Batavia. *If* (formerly written *gif, give, gin*) is the imperative of the Anglo-Saxon verb *gifan,* to give. I will remain *if (give* or *grant that fact)* he will *(remain.) But* comes from the Saxon verb *beon-utan,* to be-out. I informed no one *but (be-out, leave-out)* my brother.

This brief view of the subject, is sufficient to elucidate the manner in which, according to Horne Tooke's principles, the ten parts of speech are reduced to one. But I am, by no means, disposed to concede, that this is the *true* principle of classification; nor that it is any more *philosophical* or *ra-*

NUMBER.

NUMBER is the distinction of objects, as one or more. Nouns are of two numbers, the singular and the plural.

The *singular* number implies but one; as, a *book*.

The *plural* number implies more than one; as, *books*

NOTES.

1 Some nouns are used only in the singular form; as, hemp, flax, barley, wheat, pitch, gold, sloth, pride, honesty, meekness, compassion, &c.; others only in the plural form; as, bellows, scissors, ashes, riches, snuffers, tongs, thanks, wages, embers, ides, pains, vespers, &c.

2. Some words are the same in both numbers; as, deer, sheep, swine; and, also, hiatus, apparatus, series, species.

3. The plural number of nouns is generally formed by adding *s* to the singular; as, dove, doves; face, faces; but sometimes we add *es* in the plural; as, box, boxes; church, churches; lash, lashes; cargo, cargoes.

4. Nouns ending in *f* or *fe*, are rendered plural by a change of that termination into *ves*; as, half, halves; wife, wives: except grief, relief, reproof, and several others, which form their plurals by the addition of *s*. Those ending in *ff*, have the regular plural; as, ruff, ruffs; except staff, staves.

5. Nouns ending in *y* in the singular, with no other vowel in the same syllable, change it into *ies* in the plural; as, beauty, beauties; fly, flies. But the *y* is not changed, where there is another vowel in the syllable; as, key, keys; delay, delays; attorney, attorneys; valley, valleys; chimney, chimneys.

6. *Mathematics, metaphysics, politics, optics, ethics, pneumatics, hydraulics, &c.* are construed either as singular or plural nouns.

7. The word *news* is always singular. The nouns *means, alms,* and *amends,* though plural in form, may be either singular or plural in signification. An

---

tional than one which allows a more practical division and arrangement of words. What has been generally received as "philosophical grammar," appears to possess no stronger claims to that imposing appellation than our common, practical grammars. Query. Is not Mr. Murray's octavo grammar more worthy the dignified title of a "Philosophical Grammar," than Horne Tooke's "Diversions of Purley," or William S. Cardell's treatises on language? What constitutes a *philosophical* treatise, on this, or on any other subject? *Wherein* is there a display of philosophy in a speculative, etymological performance, which attempts to develop and explain the elements and primitive meaning of words by tracing them to their origin, *superior* to the philosophy employed in the development and illustration of the principles by which we are governed in applying those words to their legitimate purpose, namely, that of forming a correct and convenient medium by means of which we can communicate our thoughts? Does philosophy consist in ransacking the mouldy records of antiquity, in order to *guess* at the ancient construction and signification of single words? or have such investigations, in reality, any thing to do with *grammar?*

Admitting that all the words of our language include, in their *origina* signification, the import of nouns or names, and yet, it does not follow, tha : they *now* possess no other powers, and, in their combinations and connexions in sentences, are employed for no other purpose, than *barely* to *name objects.* The *fact* of the case is, that words are variously combined and applied, to answer the distinct and diversified purposes of *naming* objects, *asserting*

tipodes, credenda, literati, and minutiæ, are always plural. *Bandit* is now used as the singular of Banditti.

8. The following nouns form their plurals not according to any general rule; thus, man, men; woman, women; child, children; ox, oxen; tooth, teeth; goose, geese; foot, feet; mouse, mice; louse, lice; brother, brothers or brethren; cow, cows or kine; penny, pence, or pennies when the coin is meant; die, dice *for play*, dies *for coining;* pea and fish, pease and fish when the species is meant, but *peas* and *fishes* when we refer to the number; s, six *peas,* ten *fishes.*

9. The following compounds form their plurals thus: handful, handfuls; cupful, cupfuls; spoonful, spoonfuls:—brother-in-law, brothers-in-law; court-martial, courts-martial.

The following words form their plurals according to the rules of the languages from which they are adopted.

Singular.	Plural.	Singular.	Plural.
Antithesis	antitheses	Genius -	genii*
Apex	apices	Genus	genera
Appendix	{ appendixes *or* appendices	Hypothesis	hypotheses
		Ignis fatuus	ignes fatui
Arcanum	arcana	Index	{ indices *or* indexes†
Automaton	automata		
Axis	axes	Lamina	laminæ
Basis	bases	Magus	magi
Beau	{ beaux *or* beaus	Memorandum	{ memoranda *or* memorandums
Calx	{ calces *or* calxes	Metamorphosis	metamorphoses
		Parenthesis	parentheses
Cherub	{ cherubim *or* cherubs	Phenomenon	phenomena
Crisis	crises	Radius	{ radii *or* radiuses
Criterion	criteria	Stamen	stamina
Datum	data	Seraph	{ seraphim *or* seraphs
Diæresis	diæreses		
Desideratum	desiderata	Stimulus	stimuli
Effluvium	effluvia	Stratum	strata
Ellipsis	ellipses	Thesis	theses
Emphasis	emphases	Vertex	vertices
Encomium	{ encomia *or* encomiums	Vortex	{ vortices *or* vortexes
Erratum	errata		

*. Genii, imaginary spirits: geniuses, persons of great mental abilities.

† Indexes, when pointers or tables of contents are meant: indices, when referring to algebraic quantities.

truths, *pointing out* and *limiting* objects, *attributing qualities* to objects, *connecting* objects, and so on; and on this *fact* is founded the *true philosophical principle of the classification of words.* Hence, an arrangement of words into classes according to this principle, followed by a development and illustration of the principles and rules that regulate us in the proper use and application of words in oral and written discourse, appears to approximate as near to a true definition of *philosophical grammar,* as any I am capable of giving.

Nouns, or the names of the objects of our perceptions, doubtless constituted the original class of words; (if I may be allowed to assume such a hypothesis as an *original* class of words;) but the ever-active principle of

CASE.

CASE, when applied to nouns and pronouns, means the different state, situation, or position they have in relation to other words. Nouns have three cases, the nominative, the possessive, and the objective.

I deem the essential qualities of *case*, in English, to consist, not in the *changes* or *inflections* produced on nouns and pronouns, but in the various offices which they perform in a sentence, by assuming different positions in regard to other words. In accordance with this definition, these cases can be easily explained on reasoning principles, founded in the nature of things.

Now, five grains of common sense will enable any one to comprehend what is meant by case. Its real character is extremely simple; but in the different grammars it assumes as many meanings as Proteus had shapes. The most that has been written on it, however, is mere verbiage. What, then, is meant by *case?* In speaking of a horse, for instance, we say he is in a good *case,* when he is fat, and in a bad *case,* when he is lean, and needs more oats; and in this sense we apply the term *case* to denote the *state* or *condition* of the horse. So, when we place a noun before a verb as actor or subject, we say it is in the *nominative case;* but when it follows a transitive verb or preposition, we say it has another *case;* that is, it assumes a new *position* or *situation* in the sentence: and this we call the *objective* case. Thus, the *boy* gathers fruit. Here the boy is represented as *acting*. He is, therefore, in the *nominative* case. But when I say, Jane struck the *boy,* I do not represent the boy as the *actor*, but as the *object* of the action. He is, therefore, in a new *case* or *condition*. And when I say, This is the *boy's* hat, I do not speak of the boy either as *acting* or as *acted upon;* but as possessing something: for which reason he is in the *possessive* case. Hence, it is clear, that nouns have three cases or positions.

As the nominative and objective cases of the noun are insepa-

---

association, soon transformed nouns into verbs, by making them, when employed in a particular manner, expressive of affirmation. This same principle also operated in appropriating names to the purpose of attributing qualities to other names of objects; and in this way was constituted the class of words called *adjectives* or *attributes*. By the same principle were formed all the other classes.

In the following exposition of English grammar on scientific principles, . shall divide words into *seven* classes; *Nouns* or *Names, Verbs, Adjectives, Adnouns,* or *Attributes, Adverbs, Prepositions, Pronouns,* and *Conjunctions* or *Connectives.*

For an explanation of the noun, refer to the body of the work.

rably connected with the verb, it is impossible for you to understand them until you shall have acquired some knowledge of this
part of speech. I will, therefore, now give you a partial description of the verb in connexion with the noun; which will enable
me to illustrate the cases of the noun so clearly, that you may
easily comprehend their nature.

In the formation of language, mankind, in order to hold converse
with each other, found it necessary, in the first place, to give *names*
to the various objects by which they were surrounded. Hence the
origin of the first part of speech, which we denominate the *noun*.
But merely to name the objects which they beheld or thought of,
was not sufficient for their purpose. They perceived that these
objects existed, moved, acted, or caused some action to be done.
In looking at a man, for instance, they perceived that he lived,
walked, ate, smiled, talked, ran, and so on. They perceived that
plants grow, flowers bloom, and rivers flow. Hence the necessity
of another part of speech, whose office it should be to express these
existences and actions. This second class of words we call

VERBS.

A VERB is a word which signifies to BE, to DO, or
to SUFFER; as, I *am; I rule; I am ruled.*

Verbs are of three kinds, active, passive, and
neuter. They are also divided into regular, irregular,
and defective.

The term *verb* is derived from the Latin word *verbum,* which
signifies a *word.* This part of speech is called a *verb* or *word,*
because it is deemed the most important word in every sentence:
and without a verb and nominative, either expressed or implied,
no sentence can exist. The noun is the original and leading
part of speech; the verb comes next in order, and is far more
complex than the noun. These two are the most useful in the
language, and form the basis of the science of grammar. The
other eight parts of speech are subordinate to these two, and, as
you will hereafter learn, of minor importance.

For all practical purposes, the foregoing definition and division
of the verb, though, perhaps, not philosophically correct, will be
found as *convenient* as any other. I adopt them, therefore, to be
consistent with the principle, that, in arranging the materials of
this treatise, I shall not alter or reject any established definition,
rule, or principle of grammar, unless, in my humble judgment,
some *practical advantage* to the learner is thereby gained. The
following, some consider a good definition.

A VERB is a word which *expresses affirmation.*

An *active verb* expresses action; and
The *nominative case* is the actor, or subject of the verb; as, *John writes.*

In this example, which is the *verb?* You know it is the word *writes*, because this word signifies to *do;* that is, it expresses *ac-*tion, therefore, according to the definition, it is an *active verb.* And you know, too, that the noun *John* is the *actor*, therefore John is in the *nominative case* to the verb writes. In the expressions, The man walks—The boy plays—Thunders roll—Warriors fight—you perceive that the words *walks, plays, roll*, and *fight*, are *active verbs;* and you cannot be at a loss to know, that the nouns *man, boy, thunders*, and *warriors*, are in the *nominative case.*

As no *action* can be produced without some agent or moving cause, it follows, that every active verb must have some *actor* or *agent.* This *actor, doer*, or *producer of the action*, is the nominative. *Nominative*, from the Latin *nomino*, literally signifies to *name;* but in the technical sense in which it is used in grammar, it means the noun or pronoun which is the *subject* of affirmation. This subject or nominative may be *active, passive*, or *neuter*, as hereafter exemplified.

A *neuter verb* expresses neither action nor passion, but *being*, or *a state of being;* as, *John sits.*

Now, in this example, *John* is not represented as *an actor*, but, as the *subject* of the verb *sits*, therefore John is in the *nominative case* to the verb. And you know that the word *sits* does not ex-

---

PHILOSOPHICAL NOTES.

Plausible arguments may be *advanced*, for rejecting *neuter* and passive verbs; but they have been found to be so convenient in practice, that the theory which recognises them, has stood the test of ages. If you tell the young learner, that, in the following expressions, The church *rests* on its foundation; The book *lies* on the desk; The boys *remain (are)* idle, the nouns *church, book*, and *boys*, are represented as acting, and, therefore, the verbs *rests, lies remain*, and *are*, are *active*, he will not believe you, because there is no action that is apparent to his senses. And should you proceed farther, and, by a labored and metaphysical investigation and development of the laws of motion, attempt to prove to him that "every portion of matter is influenced by different, active principles, tending to produce change," and, therefore, every thing in universal nature is *always* acting, it is not at all probable, that you could convince his *understanding*, in opposition to the clearer testimony of his senses. Of what avail to learners is a theory which they cannot comprehend?

Among the various theorists and speculative writers on philosophical grammar, the ingenious Horne Tooke stands pre-eminent; but, unfortunately, his principal speculations on the verb, have never met the public eye. William

press *apparent action*, but a *condition of being ;* that is, it represents John in a particular *state of existence ;* therefore *sits* is a
neuter verb. In speaking of the neuter gender of nouns, I informed you, that *neuter* means *neither;* from which it follows, that
neuter gender implies neither gender; that is, neither masculine
nor feminine. Hence, by an easy transition of thought, you
learn, that *neuter,* when applied to verbs, means neither of the
other two classes ; that is, a *neuter* verb is one which is neither
active nor passive. In these examples, The man stands—The
lady lives—The child sleeps—The world exists—the words *stands,
lives, sleeps,* and *exists,* are *neuter verbs ;* and the nouns, *man,
lady, child,* and *world,* are all in the *nominative case,* because each
is the *subject* of a verb. Thus you perceive, that when a noun
is in the nominative case to an *active* verb, it is the *actor ;* and
when it is nominative to a *neuter* verb, it is *not* an actor, but the
subject of the verb.

Some neuter verbs express *being in general ;* as, The man *is ;*
Kingdoms *exist.* Others express *being in some particular state ;*
as, The man *stands, sits, lies,* or *hangs.*

I will now give you two *signs,* which will enable you to distinguish the verb from other parts of speech, when you cannot
tell it by its signification. Any word that will make sense with
to before it, is a verb. Thus, to run, to write, to smile, to sing,
to hear, to ponder, to live, to breathe, are verbs. Or, any word
that will *conjugate,* is a verb. Thus, I run, thou runnest, he runs ;
I write, thou writest, he writes ; I smile, &c. But the words,
boy, lady, child, and world, will not make sense with *to* prefixed
—*to* boy, *to* lady, *to* world, is nonsense. Neither will they con-

---

S. Cardell has also rendered himself conspicuous in the philological field, by
taking a bolder stand than any of his predecessors. His view of the verb is
novel, and ingeniously supported. The following is the substance of his theory

OF THE VERB.

A VERB is a word which expresses *action ;* as, Man *exists ;*
Trees *grow ;* Waters *flow ;* Mountains *stand ;* I *am.*

All verbs are active, and have one object or more than one, expressed or
implied. The pillar *stands ;* that is, it *keeps itself* in an erect or standing
posture ; it *upholds* or *sustains itself* in that position. They *are ;* i. e. they
air themselves, or *breathe* air ; they *inspirit, vivify,* or *uphold* themselves by
inhaling air.

Many verbs whose objects are seldom expressed, always have a persona
or verbal one implied. The clouds *move ;* i. e. move *themselves* along. Th
troops *marched* twenty miles a day ; i. e. marched *themselves.* The moc'
shines :—The moon *shines* or *sheds* a shining, sheen, lustre, or brightness.
The sparrow *flies :*—*flies* or *takes* a *flight.* Talkers talk or speak *words* or
talk ; Walkers walk *walkings* or *walks ;* The rain rains *rain ;* Sitters sit or
hold *sittings* or *sessions.*

jugate—I lady, thou ladiest, &c. is worse than nonsense. Hence you perceive, that these words are *not* verbs. There are some exceptions to these rules, for verbs are sometimes used as nouns. This will be explained by and by.

To verbs belong *number, person, mood,* and *tense.*

At present I shall speak only of the number and person of erbs; but hereafter I will give you a full explanation of all their roperties. · And permit me to inform you, that I shall not lead you into the *intricacies* of the science, until, by gradual and easy progressions, you are enabled to comprehend the principles involved in them. Only such principles will be elucidated, as you are prepared to understand at the time they are unfolded before you. You must not be too anxious to get along *rapidly;* but endeavor to become thoroughly acquainted with one principle, before you undertake another. This lecture will qualify you for the next.

NUMBER AND PERSON OF VERBS. You recollect, that the nominative is the *actor* or *subject,* and the active verb is the *action* performed by the nominative. By this you perceive, that a very intimate connexion or relation exists between the nominative case and the verb. If, therefore, only *one* creature or thing acts, only *one* action, at the same instant, can be done; as, The *girl writes.* The nominative *girl* is here of the singular number, because it signifies but one person; and the verb *writes* denotes but one action, which the girl performs; therefore the verb *writes* is of the

---

To prove that there is no such thing as a neuter verb, the following appear to be the strongest arguments adduced.

1. No portion of matter is ever in a state of perfect quiescence; but the component parts of every thing are at all times "influenced by different, active principles, tending to produce change." Hence, it follows, that no being or thing can be represented in a *neuter* or *non-acting state.*
This argument supposes the essential character of the verb to be identified with the primary laws of action, as unfolded by the principles of physical science. The correctness of this position may be doubted; but if it can be clearly demonstrated, that every particle of matter is always in motion, it does not, by any means, follow, that we cannot *speak of* things in a state of quiescence What is *false* in fact may be *correct* in grammar. *The point contested, is not whether things always* act, *but whether, when we assert or affirm something respecting them, we always* represent *them as acting.*

2. Verbs were *originally* used to express the motions or changes of things which produced obvious actions, and, by an easy transition, were afterward pplied. in the same way, to things whose actions were not apparent. This assumption is untenable, and altogether gratuitous.

3. Verbs called neuter are used in the imperative mood; and, as this mood commands some one to *do* something, any verb which adopts it, must be active. Thus, in the common place phrases, " *Be* there quickly; *Stand* out of my way; *Sit* or *lie* farther."

singular number, agreeing with its nominative *girl*. When the nominative case is *plural*, the verb must be *plural ;* as, *girls write.* Take notice, the *singular* verb ends in *s*, but the noun is generally *plural* when it ends in *s ;* thus, The girl *writes*—the *girls* write.

Person, strictly speaking, is a quality that belongs *not* to *verbs*, but to nouns and pronouns. We say, however, that the verb must agree with its nominative in *person*, as well as in number; that is, the verb must be spelled and spoken in such a manner as to correspond with the *first, second,* or *third* person of the noun or pronoun which is its nominative.

I will now show you how the verb is varied in order to agree with its nominative in number and person. I, Thou, He, She, It ; We, Ye or You, They, are *personal pronouns. I* is of the *first* person, and *singular* number ; *Thou* is *second* person, *sing.; He, She,* or *It,* is *third* per. *sing.; We* is *first* per. *plural; Ye* or *You* is *second* per. *plural; They* is *third* per. *plural.* These pronouns are the representatives of nouns, and perform the same office that the nouns would for which they stand. When placed before the verb, they are, therefore, the *nominatives* to the verb.

Notice particularly, the different variations or endings of the verb, as it is thus conjugated in the

INDICATIVE MOOD, PRESENT TENSE.

Singular.	*Plural.*
1. *Per.* I walk,	1. *Per.* We Walk,
2. *Per.* Thou walk*est*,	2. *Per.* Ye *or* you walk,
3. *Per.* He walk*s, or* the boy walk*s*, *or* walk*eth*.	3. *Per.* They walk, *or* the boys walk.

It is admitted that these verbs are here employed in an *active* sense; but it is certain, that they are not used according to their proper, *literal* meaning. When I tell a man, *literally,* to *stand, sit,* or *lie,* by *moving* he would disobey me ; but when I say, "*Stand* out of my way," I employ the neuter verb *stand*, instead of the active verb *move* or *go*, and in a 'correspondent sense. My meaning is, *Move* yourself out of my way ; or *take* your *stand* somewhere else. This, however, does not prove that *stand* is properly used. If we choose to overstep the bounds of custom, we can employ any *word* in the language as an active-transitive verb. *Be, sit,* and *lie,* may be explained in the same manner.

4. Neuter verbs are used in connexion with adverbs which express the manner of *action.* They must, therefore, be considered active verbs. The child *sleeps soundly ;* He *sits genteelly ;* They *live contentedly* and *happily* together. The class of verbs that are never employed as active, is small. By using adverbs in connexion with verbs, we can fairly prove that some verbs are *not* active. It is incorrect to say, I am *happily ;* They were *peacefully ;* She remains *quietly ;* The fields appear *greenly.* These verbs in their common acceptation, do not express *action ;* for which reason we say, I am *happy ;* They are *peaceful ;* &c. But in the expressions, The child sleeps *soundly ;*

This display of the verb shows you, that whenever it ends in *est*, it is of the *second* person *singular ;* but when the verb ends in *s*, or *eth*, it is of the *third* person singular. *Walkest, ridest, standest*, are of the second person singular ; and *walks* or *walketh, rides* or *rideth, stands* or *standeth*, are of the third person singular.

I have told you, that when the nominative is singular number, the verb must be ; when the nominative is plural, the verb must be ; and when the nominative is first, second, or third person, the verb must be of the same person.   If you look again at the fore-going conjugation of *walk*, you will notice that the verb varies its endings in the *singular*, in order to agree in *form* with the first, second, and third person of its nominative ; but in the *plural* it does not vary its endings from the first person singular. The verb, however, agrees in *sense* with its nominative in the plural, as well as in the singular.   Exercise a little mind, and you will perceive that *agreement* and *government* in language do not consist *merely* in the *form* of words.   Now, is it not clear, that when I say, I *walk*, the verb walk is *singular*, because it ex-presses but *one* action ?   And when I say, Two men *walk*, is it not equally apparent, that walk is *plural*, because it expresses *two* actions ?   In the sentence, Ten men *walk*, the verb *walk* denotes *ten* actions, for there are ten actors.   Common sense teaches you, that there must be as many *actions* as there are *actors ;* and that the verb, when it has *no form* or *ending* to show it, is as strictly plu-ral, as when it has.   So, in the phrase, *We* walk, the verb walk is *first* person, because it expresses the actions performed by the *speakers :* Ye or *you* walk, the verb is *second* person, denoting

She sits *gracefully ;* They live *happily* and *contentedly ;* we employ the verbs *sleeps, sits*, and *live*, in an active sense.   When no action is intended, we say, They live *happy* and *contented.*

If, on scientific principles, it can be proved that those verbs generally de-nominated neuter, *originally* expressed action, their present, accepted mean-ing will still oppose the theory, for the generality of mankind do not attach to them the idea of *action.*

Thus I have endeavored to present a brief but impartial abstract of the *modern* theory of the verb, leaving it with the reader to estimate it according to its value.

To give a satisfactory definition of the verb, or such a one as shall be found scientifically correct and unexceptionable, has hitherto baffled the skill, and transcended the learning, of our philosophical writers.   If its essential quali-ty, as is generally supposed, is made to consist in *expressing affirmation*, it remains still to be defined *when* a verb *expresses* affirmation.   In English, and in other languages, words appropriated to express affirmation, are often used without any such force ; our idea of affirmation, in such instances, being the mere *inference of custom.*

In the sentence,—" *Think, love*, and *hate*, denote moral actions," the words *think, love*, and *hate*, are nouns, because they are mere *names* of actions.   So, when I say, " John, *write* ———— is an irregular verb," the word *write* is a

the actions of the persons *spoken to ;* third person, *They* walk
The verb, then, when correctly written, always agrees, in *sense,*
with its nominative in number and person.

At present you are learning two parts of speech, neither
of which can be understood without a knowledge of the other.
It therefore becomes necessary to explain them both in the same
lecture. You have been already informed, that nouns have three
cases ; the nominative, the possessive, and the objective.

POSSESSIVE CASE.   The *possessive case* denotes the
possessor of something; as, This is *John's* horse.

This expression implies, that *John* is the *owner* or *possessor*
of the horse ; and, that horse is the *property* which he possesses.

When I say, These are the *men's,* and those, the *boys'* hats,
the two words, "boys' hats," plainly convey the idea, if they
have any meaning at all, that the boys *own* or *possess* the hats.
" Samuel Badger sells *boys'* hats."   Who *owns* the hats ?   Mr.
Badger.   How is that fact ascertained ?   Not by the words,
" boys' hats," which, taken by themselves, imply, not that they
are *Mr. Badger's* hats, nor that they are *for* boys, but that they
are hats *of,* or *belonging to,* or *possessed by* boys.   But we *infer*
from the *words connected* with the phrase, " boys' hats," that the
boys are not yet, as the phrase literally denotes, in the actual
possession of the hats.   The possession is anticipated.

In the phrases, *fine* hats, *coarse* hats, *high-crowned* hats, *broad-
brimmed* hats, *woollen, new, ten, some, these, many* hats, the words
in italics, are adjectives, because they restrict, qualify, or define
the term *hats ;* but the term *boys'* does not *describe* or limit the
meaning of *hats.   Boys,'* therefore, is not, as some suppose, an
adjective.

" The *slave's* master."   Does the slave possess the master ?
Yes.   The slave *has* a master.   If he *has* him, then, he *possesses*
him ;—he sustains that relation to him which we call possession.

---

noun ; but when I say, " John, *write* ——— your copy," *write* is called a verb.
Why is this word considered a noun in one construction, and a verb in the
other, when both constructions, until you pass beyond the word write, are
exactly alike ?   If write does not *express* action in the former sentence, neither does it in the latter, for, in both, it is introduced in the same manner.
On scientific principles, *write* must be considered a noun in the latter sen
tence, for it does not *express* action, or make an affirmation ; but it merely
names the action which I wish John to perform, and affirmation is the *inferential* meaning.

The verb in the infinitive, as well as in the imperative mood, is divested
of its affirmative or verbal force.   In both these moods, it is always presented in its *noun-state.*

If, after dinner, I say to a servant, " *Wine,*" he infers, that I wish him to

A noun in the possessive case, is always known by its having an apostrophe, and generally an *s* after it; thus, *John's.* hat; the *boy's* coat. When a plural noun in the possessive case, ends in *s*, the apostrophe is added, but no additional *s ;* as, " *Boys'* hats ; *Eagles'* wings." When a singular noun ends in *ss*, the apostrophe only is added; as, " For *goodness'* sake ; for *righteousness'* sake ;" except the word witness ; as, " The *witness's* testimony." When a noun in the possessive case ends in *ence*, the *s* is omitted, but the apostrophe is retained ; as, " For *conscience'* sake."

Now please to turn back, and read over this and the preceding lecture *three* times, and endeavor, not only to understand, but, also, to *remember*, what you read. In reading, proceed thus : read one sentence over slowly, and then look off the book, and repeat it two or three times over in your mind. After that, take another sentence and proceed in the same manner, and so on through the whole lecture. Do not presume to think, that these directions are of no real consequence to you ; for, unless you follow them strictly, you need not expect to make rapid progress. On the other hand, if you proceed according to my instructions, you will be sure to acquire a practical knowledge of grammar in a short time.—When you shall have complied with this requisition, you may commit the following *order of parsing a noun,* and *the order of parsing a verb ;* and then you will be prepared to parse or analyze the following examples.

ANALYSIS, OR PARSING.

Do you recollect the meaning of the word *analysis ?* If you do not, I will explain it : and first, I wish you to remember, that analysis is the reverse of synthesis. *Synthesis* is the act of combining simples so as to form a whole or compound. Thus, in

---

bring me wine; but all this is not said. If I say, *Bring* some *wine*, he, in like manner, understands, that I wish him to bring me wine ; but all that is expressed, is the *name* of the action, and of the object of the action. In fact, as much is done by *inference*, as by actual expression, in every branch of language, for thought is too quick to be wholly transmitted by words.

It is generally conceded, that the termination of our verbs, *est, eth, s, ed,* and, also, of the other parts of speech, were originally separate words of distinct meaning ; and that, although they have been contracted, and, by the refinement of language, have been made to coalesce with the words in connexion with which they are employed, yet, in their present character of terminations, they retain their primitive meaning and force. To denote that a verbal name was employed as a verb, the Saxons affixed to it a verbalizing adjunct ; thus, *the* (to take, hold) was the noun-state of the verb ; and when they used it as a verb, they added the termination *an* ; thus, *thean.* The termination added, was a sign that *affirmation* was intended. The same

putting together letters so as to form syllables, syllables so as to form words, words so as to form sentences, and sentences so as to form a discourse, the process is called synthetic. *Analysis*, on the contrary, is the act of decomposition; that is, the act of separating any thing compounded into its simple parts, and thereby exhibiting its elementary principles. Etymology treats of the analysis of language. To analyze a sentence, is to separate from one another and classify the different words of which it is composed; and to analyze or *parse* a word, means to enumerate and describe all its various properties, and its grammatical relations with respect to other words in a sentence, and trace it through all its inflections or changes. Perhaps, to you, this will, at first, appear to be of little importance; but, if you persevere, you will hereafter find it of great utility, for parsing will enable you to detect, and correct, errors in composition.

SYSTEMATIC ORDER OF PARSING.

The *order of parsing* a Noun, is—a noun, and why?—common, proper, or collective, and why?—gender, and why?—person, and why?—number, and why?—case, and why?—Rule:—decline it.

The order of parsing a Verb, is—a verb, and why?—active, passive, or neuter, and why?—if *active*—transitive or intransitive, and why?—if *passive*—how is it formed?—regular, irregular, or defective, and why?—mood, and why?—tense, and why?—person and number, and why?—with what does it agree?—Rule:—conjugate it.

I will now parse two nouns according to the order, and, in so doing, by applying the definitions and rules, I shall answer all those questions given in the order. If you have *perfectly com-*

procedure has been adopted, and, in many instances, is still practised, in our language. *An*, originally affixed to our verbs, in the progress of refinement, was changed to *en*, and finally dropped. A few centuries ago, the plural number of our verbs was denoted by the termination *en*; thus, they *weren*, they *loven*; but, as these terminations do not supersede the necessity of expressing the *subject* of affirmation, as is the case in the Latin and Greek verbs, they have been laid aside, as unnecessary excrescences. For the same reason, we might, without any disparagement to the language, dispense with the terminations of our verbs in the singular.

In support of the position, that these terminations were once separate words, we can trace many of them to their origin. To denote the feminine gender of some nouns, we affix *ess*; as, heire*ss*, instructre*ss*. *Ess* is a contraction of the Hebrew noun *essa*, a female. Of our verbs, the termination

mitted the order of parsing a noun and verb, you may proceed with me ; but, recollect, you cannot parse a verb *in full*, until you shall have had a more complete explanation of it.

John's hand trembles.

John's is a noun, [because it is] the name of **a** person—proper, the name of an individual—masculine gender, it denotes a male—third person, spoken of—singular number, it implies but one—and in the possessive case, it denotes possession—it is governed by the noun "hand," according to

RULE 12. *A noun or pronoun in the possessive case, is governed by the noun it possesses.*

Declined—Sing. nom. John, poss. John's, obj. John. Plural—nom. Johns, poss. Johns', obj. Johns.

Hand is a noun, the name of a thing—common, the name of a sort or species of things—neuter gender, it denotes a thing without sex—third person, spoken of—sing. number, it implies but one—and in the nominative case, it is the actor and subject of the verb "trembles," and governs it agreeably to

RULE 3. *The nominative case governs the verb :*—that is, the nominative determines the number and person of the verb.

Declined—Sing. nom. hand, poss. hand's, obj. hand. Plur. nom. hands, poss. hands', obj. hands.

Trembles is a verb, a word which signifies to do—active, it expresses action—third person, singular number, because the nominative "hand" is with which it agrees, according to

RULE 4. *The verb must agree with its nominative in number and person.*

You must not say that the verb is of the third person because *it is spoken of.* The verb is never spoken of; but it is of the third person, and singular or plural number, because its nominative is.

Conjugated—First pers. sing. I tremble, 2 pers. thou tremblest, 3 pers. he trembles, or, the hand trembles. Plural, 1 pers. we tremble, 2 pers. ye or you tremble, 3 pers. they or the hands tremble.

---

est is a contraction of *doest, eth,* of *doeth, s,* of *does.* We say, thou *dost* or *doest* love ; or thou lov*est* ; i. e. love-*dost,* or love-*doest.* Some believe these terminations to be contractions of *havest, haveth, has.* We affix *ed,* a contraction of *dede,* to the present tense of verbs to denote that the action named, is, *dede, did, doed,* or *done.*

To and *do,* from the Gothic noun *taui,* signifying *act* or *effect,* are, according to Horne Tooke, nearly alike in meaning and force ; and when the custom of affixing some more ancient verbalizing adjunct, began to be dropped, its place and meaning were generally supplied by prefixing one of these. When I say, "I am going *to walk,*" the verbal or affirmative force is conveyed by the use of *to,* meaning the same as *do ;* and *walk* is employed merely

Government, in language, consists in the power which one word has over another, in causing that other word to be in some *particular case, number, person, mood,* or *tense.*

ILLUSTRATION.

RULE 3.   *The nominative case governs the verb.*

If you employ the pronoun *I,* which is of the *first* person, singular number, as the nominative to a verb, the verb must be of the first pers. sing. thus, I *smile ;* and when your nominative is *second* pers. sing. your verb must be ; as, thou smil*est.* Why, in the latter instance, does the ending of the verb change to *est ?* Because the nominative changes. And if your nominative is *third* person, the verb will vary again ; thus, he smile*s,* the man smile*s.* How clear it is, then, that *the nominative governs the verb ;* that is, the nominative has power to change the *form* and *meaning* of the verb, in respect to num. and person. Government, thus far, is evinced in the *form* of the words, as well as in the sense.

RULE 4.   *The verb must agree with its nominative in number and person.*

It is improper to say, thou *hear,* the men *hears.* Why improper ? Because *hear* is *first* pers. and the nominative *thou* is *second* pers. *hears* is singular, and the nom. *men* is *plural.* Rule 4th says, *The verb must agree with its nominative.* The expressions should, therefore, be, thou hear*est,* the men *hear ;* and then the verb would *agree* with its nominatives. But *why* must the verb agree with its nominative ? Why must we say, thou talk*est,* the man talk*s,* men *talk ?* Because the genius of our language, and the common consent of those who speak it, *require* such a construction : and this *requisition* amounts to a *law* or *rule.* This *rule,* then, is founded in *the nature of things,* and sanctioned by *good usage.*

RULE 12.   *A noun or pronoun in the possessive case, is governed by the noun which it possesses.*

It is correct to say, The *man* eats, *he* eats ; but we cannot say, the *man* dog eats, *he* dog eats. Why not ? Because the man is

---

as a verbal name ; that is, I assert that I shall *do* the act which I name by the word *walk,* or the act of *walking.*

Perhaps such speculations as these will prove to be more curious than profitable. If it be made clearly to appear, that, on scientific principles, whenever the verbal name is unaccompanied by a verbalizing adjunct, it is in the *noun-state,* and does not express affirmation, still this theory would be very inconvenient in practice.

I shall resume this subject in Lecture XI.

here represented as the *possessor,* and *dog,* the *property,* or *thing possessed ;* and the genius of our language requires, that when we add to the possessor, the *thing* which he is represented as possessing, the possessor shall take a particular form to show its *case,* or *relation to the property ;* thus, The *man's* dog eats, *his* dog eats. You perceive, then, that the *added* noun, denoting the thing possessed, has power *to change the form* of the noun or pronoun denoting the possessor, according to RULE 12. thus, by adding dog in the preceding examples, *man* is changed to *man's,* and *he,* to *his.*

Now parse the sentence which I have parsed, until the manner is quite familiar to you ; and then you will be prepared to analyze correctly and *systematically,* the following exercises. When you parse, you may spread the Compendium before you ; and, if you have not already committed the definitions and rules, you may read them on that, as you apply them. This mode of procedure will enable you to learn *all* the definitions and rules by applying them to practice.

EXERCISES IN PARSING.

Rain descends—Rains descend—Snow falls—Snows fall—Thunder rolls—Thunders roll—Man's works decay—Men's labors cease—John's dog barks—Eliza's voice trembles—Julia's sister's child improves—Peter's cousin's horse limps.

In the next place, I will parse a noun and a *neuter* verb, which verb, you will notice, differs from an active only in one respect.

"*Birds repose* on the branches of trees. "

Birds is a noun, the name of a thing or creature—common, the name of a genus or class—masculine and feminine gender, it denotes both males and females—third person, spoken of—plural number, it implies more than one—and in the nominative case, it is the *subject* of the verb " repose," and governs it according to RULE 3. *The nominative case governs the verb.* Declined—Sing. nom. bird, poss. bird's, obj. bird. Plural, nom. birds, poss. birds', obj. birds.

Repose is a verb, a word that signifies to *be*—neuter, it express-s neither action nor passion, but a state of being—third person, plural number, because the nominative " birds" is with which it agrees, agreeably to RULE 4. *The verb must agree with its nomi native in number and person.*

Declined—1. pers. sing. I repose, 2. pers. thou reposest, 3. pers. he reposes, or the bird reposes. Plur. 1. pers. we repose, 2. pers. ye or you repose, 3. pers. they repose, or birds repose.

Now parse those nouns and neuter verbs that are distinguished by *italics*, in the following

EXERCISES IN PARSING.

The *book lies* on the desk—The *cloak hangs* on the wall—*Man's days are* few—*Cathmor's warriors sleep* in death—*Caltho reposes* in the narrow house—Jocund *day stands* tiptoe on the misty mountain tops. The *sunbeams rest* on the grave where her *beauty sleeps.*

You may parse these and the preceding exercises, and all that follow, *five or six times over,* if you please.

OBJECTIVE CASE.—ACTIVE-TRANSITIVE VERBS.

The *objective* case expresses the object of an action or of a relation. It generally follows a transitive verb, a participle, or a preposition.

A noun is in the objective case when it is the *object* of something. At present I shall explain this case only as the object of an *action ;* but when we shall have advanced as far as to the preposition, I will also illustrate it as the object of a *relation.*

An active verb is *transitive* when the action passes over from the subject or nominative to an object; as, Richard *strikes* John.

Transitive means *passing.* In this sentence the action of the verb *strikes* is *transitive,* because it *passes over* from the nominative Richard to the object John; and you know that the noun John is in the *objective* case, because it is *the object of the action* expressed by the active-transitive verb strikes. This matter is very plain. For example: Gallileo invented the telescope. Now it is evident, that Gallileo did not exert his powers of invention, without some object in view. In order to ascertain that object, put the question, Gallileo invented what? The telescope. *Telescope,* then, is the real object of the action, denoted by the transitive verb invented ; and, therefore, telescope is in the objective case. If I say, The horse *kicks* the servant—Carpenters *build* houses—Ossian *wrote* poems—Columbus *discovered* America—you readily perceive, that the verbs *kick, build, wrote,* and *discovered,* express transitive actions; and you cannot be at a loss to tell which nouns are in the objective case :—they are *servant, houses, poems,* and *America.*

The nominative and objective cases of nouns are generally known by the following rule : the nominative *does something ;* the-objective *has something done to it.* The nominative generally comes *before* the verb ; and the objective, *after* it. When I say, George struck the servant, *George* is in the nominative, and *servant* is in the objective case ; but, when I say, The servant struck George, *servant* is in the nominative case, and *George* is in the objective. Thus you perceive, that *Case* means the different state or situation of nouns with regard to other words.

It is sometimes very difficult to tell the case of a noun. I shall, therefore, take up this subject again, when I come to give you an explanation of the participle and preposition.

Besides the three cases already explained, nouns are sometimes in the nominative case *independent,* sometimes in the nominative case absolute, sometimes in apposition in the same case, and sometimes in the nominative or objective case after the neuter to *be,* or after an active-intransitive or passive verb. These cases are illustrated in Lecture X. and in the 21 and 22 rules of Syntax.

ACTIVE-INTRANSITIVE VERBS.

An active verb is *transitive,* when the action terminates on an object : but

An active verb is *intransitive,* when the action does *not* terminate on an object ; as, John *walks.*

You perceive that the verb *walks,* in this example, is *intransitive,* because the action does not pass over to an object ; that is, the action is confined to the agent John. The following *sign* will generally enable you to distinguish a *transitive* verb from an *intransitive.* Any verb that will make sense with the words *a thing,* or *a person,* after it, is *transitive.* Try these verbs by the sign, *love, help, conquer, reach, subdue, overcome.* Thus, you can say, I love *a person* or *thing*—I can help *a person* or *thing*—and so on. Hence you know that these verbs are transitive. But an intransitive verb will not make sense with this sign, which fact will be shown by the following examples : *smile, go, come, play, bark, walk, fly.* We cannot say, if we mean to speak English, I smile a *person* or *thing*—I go *a person* or *thing* :—hence you perceive that these verbs are not transitive, but intransitive.

If you reflect upon these examples for a few moments, you will have a clear conception of the nature of transitive and intransitive verbs. Before I close this subject, however, it is necessary farther to remark, that some transitive and intransitive verbs express what is called a *mental* or *moral* action ; and others, a *corporeal* or *physical* action. Verbs expressing the different affections or operations of the mind, denote moral actions ; as, Brutus *loved* his country ; James *hates* vice ; We *believe* the tale :—to *repent,* to *relent,* to *think,* to *reflect,* to *mourn,* to *muse.* Those expressing the actions produced by matter, denote physical actions ; as, The *dog hears* the bell ; Virgil *wrote* the Ænead ; Columbus *discovered* America ;—to *see,* to *feel,* to *taste,* to *smell,* to *run,* to *talk,* to *fly,* to *strike.* In the sentence, Charles *resembles* his father, the verb *resembles* does not appear to express any action at all; yet the construction of the sentence, and the office which the verb performs, are such, that we are obliged to parse it as an *active-transitive* verb, governing the noun *father* in the objective case. This you may easily reconcile in your mind, by reflecting, that the verb has a *direct reference* to its object. The following verbs are of this character : *Have, own, retain ;* as, I *have* a book.

Active *in*transitive verbs are frequently made *transitive.* When I say, The birds *fly,* the verb *fly* is *in*transitive ; but when I say, The boy *flies* the kite, the verb *fly* is *transitive,* and governs the noun *kite* in the objective case. Almost any active intransitive verb, and sometimes even neuter verbs, are used as transitive. The horse *walks* rapidly ; The boy *runs* swiftly ; My friend *lives* well ; The man *died* of a fever. In all these examples the verbs are *in*transitive ; in the following they are *transitive :* The man *walks* his horse ; The boy *ran* a race ; My friend *lives* a holy life ; Let me *die* the death of the righteous.

The foregoing development of the character of verbs, is deemed sufficiently critical for practical purposes ; but if we dip a little deeper into the verbal fountain, we shall discover qualities which do not appear on its surface. If we throw aside the veil which art has drawn over the real structure of speech, we shall find, that almost every verb has either a *personal* or a *verbal* object, expressed or implied. Verbal objects, which are the *effects* or *productions* resulting from the actions, being necessarily implied, are seldom expressed.

The fire *burns.* If the fire burns, it must burn *wood, coal, tallow,* or some other combustible substance. The man *laughs.* Laughs what ? Laughs *laughter* or *laugh.* They *walk ;* that is, They walk or take *walks.* Rivers flow (move or roll *themselves* or their *waters*) into the ocean.

"I *sing* the shady *regions* of the west."

"And *smile* the *wrinkles* from the brow of age."

The child *wept itself* sick ; and then, by taking (or *sleeping*) a short *nap,* it *slept itself* quiet and well again. "He will soon *sleep* his everlasting *sleep ;*" that is, "He will *sleep* the *sleep* of death."

Thinkers think *thoughts ;* Talkers talk or employ *words, talk,* or *speeches ;* The rain rains *rain.* "Upon Sodom and Gomorrah the Lord *rained fire* and *brimstone.*" "I must *go* the whole *length.*" "I shall soon *go* the *way* of all the earth."

Now please to turn back again, and peruse this lecture attentively ; after which you may parse, systematically, the following exercises containing nouns in the three cases, and active — tranitive verbs.

The printer *prints* books.

Prints is·a verb, a word that signifies to do—active, it express-es action—transitive, the action passes over from the nominative "printer" to the object "books"—third pers. sing. numb. be-cause the nominative printer is with which it agrees.

RULE 4. *The verb must agree with its nominative case in number and person.*

Declined—1. pers. sing. I print, 2. pers. thou printest, 3. pers. he prints, or the printer prints, and so on.

Books is a noun, the name of a thing—common, the name of a sort of things,—neut. gend. it denotes a thing without sex—third pers. spoken of—plur. num. it implies more than one—and in the objective case, it is the object of the action, expressed by the ac-tive-transitive verb "prints," and is governed by it according to

RULE 20. *Active-transitive verbs govern the objective case.*

The noun *books* is thus declined—Sing. nom. book, poss. book's, obj. book—Plur. nom. books, poss. books', obj. books.

RULE 20.´ Transitive verbs *govern* the objective case ; that is, they *require* the noun or pronoun following them to be in that case ; and this requisition is government. Pronouns have a par-ticular *form* to suit each case ; but nouns have not. We cannot say, She *struck he ;* I gave the book *to they.* Why not ? Be-cause the genius of our language requires the pronoun following a transitive verb or preposition (*to* is a preposition) to assume that *form* which we call the *objective* form or case. Accordingly, the construction should be, She struck *him ;* I gave the book to *them.* —Read, again, the illustration of "government" on page 52.

EXERCISES IN PARSING.

Nom. case.	Trans. verb.	Poss. case.	Obj. case.
Julius	prints	childrens'	primers.
Harriet	makes	ladies'	bonnets.
The servant	beats	the man's	horse.
The horse	kicks	the servant's	master.
The boy	struck	that man's	child.
The child	lost	those boys'	ball.
The tempest	sunk	those merchants'	vessels.

Nom. case.	Trans. verb.	Poss. case.	Obj. case.
The gale	sweeps	the mountain's	brow.
Pope	translated	Homer's	Illiad.
Cicero	procured	Milo's	release.
Alexander	conquered	Darius'	army.
Perry	met	the enemy's	fleet.
Washington	obtained	his country's	freedom.

NOTE 1. The words *the, that, those,* and *his,* you need not parse.

2. A noun in the possessive case, is sometimes governed by a noun under stood ; as, Julia's lesson is longer than John's [lesson.]

As you have been analyzing nouns in their three cases, it be. comes necessary to present, in the next place, the declension of nouns, for you must decline every noun you parse. *Declension* means putting a noun through the different cases : and you will notice, that the possessive case varies from the nominative in its termination, or ending, but the *objective* case ends like the nominative. The nominative and objective cases of nouns, must, therefore, be ascertained by their situation in the sentence, or by considering the office they perform.

DECLENSION OF NOUNS.

	SING.	PLUR.			SING.	PLUR.
Nom.	king	kings		*Nom.*	man	men
Poss.	king's	kings'		*Poss.*	man's	men's
Obj.	king.	kings.		*Obj.*	man.	men.

Now, if you have parsed every word in the preceding examples, (except *the, that, those,* and *his,*) you may proceed with me and parse the examples in the following exercises, in which are presented nouns and active-intransitive verbs.

" My *flock increases* yearly."

Flock is a noun, a name denoting animals—a noun of multitude, it signifies many in one collective body—masculine and feminine gender, denoting both sexes—third person, spoken of—singular number, it denotes but one flock—and in the nominative case, it is the active agent of the verb " increases," and governs it, according to RULE 3. *The nominative case governs the verb.* (Decline it.)

Increases is a verb, a word that signifies to do—active, it expresses action—intransitive, the action does not pass over to an object—of the third person, singular number, because its nominative " flock " conveys *unity* of idea ; and it agrees with " flock " agreeably to

RULE 10. *A noun of multitude conveying* unity *of idea, must have a verb or pronoun agreeing with it in the singular.*

" The divided *multitude* hastily *disperse.*"

Multitude is a noun, a name that denotes persons—a collective noun, or noun of multitude, it signifies many—masculine and feminine gender, it implies both sexes—third person, spoken of—singular number, it represents but one multitude, or collective body; (but in another sense, it is plural, as it conveys plurality of idea, and, also, implies more *individuals* than one;)—and in the nominative case, it is the actor and subject of the verb " disperse," which it governs, according to RULE 3. *The nom. case governs the verb.*—Declined.—Sing. nom. multitude, poss. multitude's, obj. multitude—Plur. nom. multitudes, poss. multitudes', obj. multitudes.

Disperse is a verb, a word that signifies to do—active, it expresses action—intransitive, the action does not terminate on an object—third person, plural number, because its nominative " multitude" conveys plurality of idea; and it agrees with "multitude" agreeably to

RULE 11. *A noun of multitude conveying plurality of idea, must have a verb or pronoun agreeing with it in the plural.*

Rules 10, and 11, rest on a sandy foundation. They appear not to be based on the principles of the language; and, therefore, it might, perhaps, be better to reject than to retain them. Their application is quite limited. In many instances, they will not apply to nouns of multitude. The existence of such a thing as " unity or plurality of idea," as applicable to nouns of this class, is *doubtful.* It is just as correct to say, " The *meeting was* divided in *its* sentiments," as to say, " The *meeting were* divided in *their* sentiments." Both are equally supported by the genius of the language, and by the power of custom. It is correct to say, either that, "The *fleet were* dispersed;" " The *council were* unanimous;" " The *council were* divided;" or that, " The *fleet was* dispersed;" " The *council was* unanimous;" " The *council was* divided." But, perhaps for the sake of euphony, in some instances, custom has decided in favor of a singular, and in others, of a plural construction, connected with words of this class. For example; custom gives a preference to the constructions, " My *people do* not consider;" " The *peasantry go* barefoot;" " The *flock is* his object;" instead of, " My *people doth* not consider;" " The *peasantry goes* barefoot;" " The *flock are* his object." In instances like these, the application of the foregoing rules *may* be of some use; but the constructions in which they do not apply, are probably more numerous than those in which they do.

EXERCISES IN PARSING.

Nom. case.	Intran. verb.	Nom. case.	Intran. verb.
Men	labor.	The sun	sets.
Armies	march.	The moon	rises.
Vessels	sail.	The stars	twinkle.
Birds	fly.	The rain	descends.
Clouds	move.	The river	flows.
Multitudes	perish.	The nation	mourns.

Your improvement in grammar depends, not on the number of words which you parse, but on the *attention* which you give the subject. *You may parse the same exercises several times over.*

For the gratification of those who prefer it, I here present another

DIVISION OF VERBS.

Verbs are of two kinds, transitive and intransitive.

A verb is transitive when the action affects an object; as, "Earthquakes *rock* kingdoms; thrones and palaces *are shaken* down; and potentates, princes, and subjects, *are buried* in one common grave."

The nominative to a passive verb, is the *object*, but not the *agent*, of the action.

A verb is intransitive when it has no object; as, "The waters *came* upon me;" "I *am* he who *was*, and *is*, and *is* to *come*."

As an exercise on what you have been studying, I will now put to you a few questions, all of which you ought to be able to answer before you proceed any farther.

QUESTIONS NOT ANSWERED IN PARSING.

With what two general divisions of grammar does the second lecture begin ?—Of what does Etymology treat ?—Of what does Syntax treat ?—On what is based the true principle of classification ?—How do you ascertain the part of speech to which a word belongs ?—What is meant by its *manner* of meaning ?—Name the ten parts of speech.—Which of these are considered the most important ?—By what sign may a noun be distinguished ?—How many kinds of nouns are there ?—What belong to nouns ?—What is gender ?—How many genders have nouns ?—What is person ?—How many persons have nouns ?—What is number ?—How many numbers have nouns ?—What is case ?—How many cases have nouns ?—Does case consist in the *inflections* of a noun ?—How many kinds of verbs are there ?—By what sign may a verb be known ?—What belong to verbs ?—What is synthesis ?—What is analysis ?—What is parsing ?—Repeat the order

of parsing the noun.—Repeat the order of parsing the verb.—
What rule do you apply in parsing a noun in the possessive
case ?—What rule, in parsing a noun in the nominative case ?—
What rule applies in parsing a verb ?—What is meant by government ?—Explain rules 3, 4, and 12.—By what rule are the
nominative and objective cases of nouns known ?—By what sign
can you distinguish a transitive from an intransitive verb ?—Do
transitive verbs ever express a *moral* action ?—Are intransitive and
neuter verbs ever used as transitive ?—Give some examples of
transitive verbs with *personal* and *verbal* objects.—What rule do
you apply in parsing a noun in the objective case ?—Explain rule
20.—In parsing a verb agreeing with a noun of multitude conveying *plurality* of idea, what rule do you apply ?

QUESTIONS ON THE NOTES.

Whether the learner be required to answer the following questions, or not,
is, of course, left *discretionary* with the teacher. The author takes the liberty to suggest the expediency of *not*, generally, enforcing such a requisition,
until the pupil goes through the book a second time.

Name some participial nouns.—What are abstract nouns ?—What is the
distinction between abstract nouns and adjectives ?—What are natural
nouns ?—Artificial nouns ?—What is the distinction between *material* and
immaterial nouns ?—Are nouns ever of the masculine and feminine gender ?—
Give examples.—When are nouns, naturally neuter, converted into the masculine or feminine gender ?—Give examples.—Speak some nouns that are
always in the singular number.—Some that are always plural.—Speak some
that are in the same form in both numbers.—Name *all* the various ways of
forming the plural number of nouns.—Of what number are the nouns *news,
means, alms,* and *amends ?*—Name the plurals to the following compound
nouns, *handful, cupful, spoonful, brother-in-law, court-martial.*

QUESTIONS ON THE PHILOSOPHICAL NOTES.

What has usually been the object of philosophical investigations of language ? (page 32.)—Do the syntactical dependances and connexions of words
depend on their *original* import ?—Is the power of association and custom
efficient in changing the radical meaning of some words ?—Have words intrinsically a signification of their own ; or is their meaning *inferential;* i. e.
such as *custom* has assigned to them ? (page 38.)—On what *fact* is based the
true, philosophical principle of classification ?—Define philosophical grammar.—Which is supposed to be the original part of speech ?—How were the
others formed from that ?—How many parts of speech may be recognised in
a scientific development and arrangement of the principles of our language ?—
Name them.—What testimony have we that many things do not act ? (page
43.)—Repeat some of the arguments in favor of, and against, the principle
which regards all verbs as *active.*—In what moods are verbs used in their
noun-state ? (page 48.)—Give examples.—What is said of the terminations
est, eth, s, and *en,* and of the words *to* and *do ?*

REMARKS ON VERBS AND NOUNS.

You have already been informed, that verbs are the most important part
of speech in our language ; and to convince you of their importance, I now
tell you, that you cannot express a *thought,* or communicate an *idea,* without

making use of a verb, either expressed or implied. Verbs express, not only *the state* or *manner of being*, but, likewise, all the different *actions* and *movements* of all creatures and things, whether animate or inanimate. As yet I have given you only a partial description of this sort of words; but when you are better prepared to comprehend the subject, I will explain all their properties, and show you the proper manner of using them.

A word that is generally a *noun*, sometimes becomes a *verb;* and a verb is frequently used as a *noun.* These changes depend on the sense which the word conveys; or, rather, on the office it performs in the sentence; that is the *manner* in which it is applied to things. For instance; *glory* is generally a noun; as, "The *glory* of God's throne." But if I say, I *glory* in religion; or, He *glories* in wickedness, the word *glory* becomes a verb. The *love* of man is inconstant. In this sentence, *love* is a *noun;* in the next, it is a *verb:* They *love* virtue. He *walks* swiftly; Scavengers *sweep* the streets; The ship *sails* well. In these phrases, the words *walks, sweep,* and *sails,* are verbs; in the following they are nouns: Those are pleasant *walks;* He takes a broad *sweep;* The ship lowered her *sails.*

Thus you see, it is impossible for you to become a grammarian without exercising your judgment. If you have sufficient resolution to do this, you will, in a short time, perfectly understand the nature and office of the different parts of speech, their various properties and relations, and the rules of syntax that apply to them; and, in a few weeks, be able to speak and write accurately. But you must not take things for granted, without examining their propriety and correctness. No. You are not a mere *automaton,* or *boy-machine;* but a rational being. You ought, therefore, to *think* methodically, to *reason* soundly, and to *investigate* every principle critically. Don't be afraid to *think for yourself.* You know not the high destiny that awaits you. You know not the height to which you may soar in the scale of intellectual existence. Go on, then, boldly, and with unyielding perseverance; and if you do not gain admittance into the temple of fame, strive, at all hazards, to drink of the fountain which gurgles from its base.

EXERCISES IN FALSE SYNTAX.

NOTE 1, TO RULE 12. A noun in the possessive case, should always be distinguished by the apostrophe, or mark of elision; as, The *nation's* glory.

That girls book is cleaner than those boys books.

Not correct, because the nouns *girls* and *boys* are both in the possessive case, and, therefore, require the apostrophe, by which they should be distinguished; thus, "*girl's, boys',*" according to the preceding NOTE. [Repeat the note.

Thy ancestors virtue is not thine.

If the writer of this sentence meant *one* ancestor, he should have inserted the apostrophe after *r,* thus, "*ancestor's;*" if more than one, after *s,* thus, "*ancestors'* virtue ;" but, by neglecting to place the apostrophe, he has left his meaning ambiguous, and we cannot ascertain it. This, and a thousand other mistakes you will often meet with, demonstrate the truth of my declaration, namely, that " without the knowledge and application of grammar rules, you will often speak and write in such a manner as not to be *understood*." You may now turn back and re-examine the " illustration" of Rules 3, 4, and 12, on page 52, and then correct the following examples about *five* times over.

A mothers tenderness and a fathers care, are natures gift's for mans advantage. Wisdoms precept's form the good mans interest and happiness. They suffer for conscience's sake. He is reading Cowpers poems. James bought Johnsons Dictionary.

RULE 4. A verb must agree with its nominative in number and person.

Those boys improves rapidly. The men labors in the field. Nothing delight some persons. Thou shuns the light. He dare not do it. They reads well.

I know you can correct these sentences without a rule, for they all have a harsh sound, which offends the ear. I wish you, however, to adopt the habit of correcting errors by applying rules ; for, by-and-by, you will meet with errors in composition which you cannot correct, if you are ignorant of the application of grammar rules.

Now let us clearly understand this 4th Rule. Recollect, it applies to the *verb*, and not to the noun ; therefore, in these examples the verb is ungrammatical. The noun *boys*, in the first sentence, is of the third person *plural*, and the verb *improves* is of the third person *singular ;* therefore, Rule 4th is violated, because the verb does not agree with its nominative in *number*. It should be, " boys *improve*." The verb would then be *plural*, and agree with its nominative according to the Rule. In the fourth sentence, the verb does not agree in *person* with its nominative. *Thou* is of the *second* person, and *shuns* is of the *third*. It should be, " thou *shunnest*," &c. You may correct the other sentences, and, likewise, the following exercises in

FALSE SYNTAX.

A variety of pleasing objects charm the eye. The number of inhabitants of the United States exceed nine millions. Nothing but vain and foolish pursuits delight some persons.

In vain our flocks and fields increase our store,
When our abundance make us wish for more.

While ever and anon, there falls
Huge heaps of hoary, moulder'd walls.

LECTURE III.

OF ARTICLES.

An article is a word prefixed to nouns to limit their signification; as, *a* man, *the* woman.

There are only two articles, *a* or *an*, and *the*. *A* or *an* is called the indefinite article. *The* is called the definite article.

The *indefinite article* limits the noun to one of a kind, but to no particular one; as, *a* house.

The *definite article* generally limits the noun to a particular object, or collection of objects; as, *the* house, *the* men.

The small claims of the article to a separate rank as a distinct part of speech, ought not to be admitted in a scientific classification of words. *A* and *the*, *this* and *that*, *ten*, *few*, and *fourth*, and many other words, are used to restrict, vary, or define the signification of the nouns to which they are joined. They might, therefore, with propriety, be ranked under the general head of *Restrictives*, *Indexes*, or *Defining Adjectives*. But, as there is a marked distinction in their particular meaning and application, each class requires a separate explanation. Hence, no practical advantage would be gained, by rejecting their established classification, as articles, numerals, and demonstratives, and by giving them *new* names. The character and application of *a* and *the* can be learned as soon when they are styled *articles*, as when they are denominated *specifying* or *defining adjectives*.[1]

The history of this part of speech is very brief. As there are but two articles, *a* or *an* and *the*, you will know them wherever they occur.

A noun used without an article, or any other restrictive, is taken in its *general* sense; as, "*Fruit* is abundant;" "*Gold* is heavy;" "*Man* is born to trouble." Here we mean, fruit and gold *in general;* and *all men*, or *mankind*.

When we wish to limit the meaning of the noun to *one* object, but to no *particular* one, we employ *a* or *an*. If I say, "Give me *a* pen;" "Bring me *an* apple;" you are at liberty to fetch *any* pen or *any* apple you please. *A* or *an*, then, is *indefinite*, because it leaves the meaning of the noun to which it is applied, as far as regards the person spoken to, *vague*, or *indeterminate;*

that is, *not definite*. But when reference is made to a *particular* object, we employ *the*, as, " Give me *the* pen ;" "Bring me *the* apple, or *the* apples." When such a requisition is made, you are not at liberty to bring any pen or apple you please, but you must fetch the *particular* pen or apple to which you know me to refer. *The* is, therefore, called the *definite* article.

"*A* star appears." Here, the star referred to, may be known as a *particular* star, *definite*, and distinguished from all others, in the mind of the *speaker ;* but to the *hearer*, it is left, among the thousands that bedeck the vault of heaven, *undistinguished* and *indefinite*. But when the star has previously been made the subject of discourse, it becomes, in the minds of both speaker and hearer a *definite* object, and he says, " *The* star appears ;" that is, that *particular* star about which we were discoursing.

"Solomon built *a* temple." Did he build *any* temple, *undetermined which ?* No ; it was a *particular* temple, pre-eminently distinguished from all others. But *how* does it become a definite object in the mind of the *hearer ?* Certainly, not by the phrase, " *a* temple," which indicates *any* temple, leaving it altogether *undetermined* which ; but supposing the person addressed was totally unacquainted with the fact asserted, and it becomes to him, *in one respect only*, a definite and particular temple, by means of the associated words, "Solomon built ;" that is, by the use of these words in connexion with the others, the hearer gets the idea of a temple distinguished as *the one erected by Solomon*. If the speaker were addressing one whom he supposed to be unacquainted with the fact related, he might make the temple referred to a still more definite object in the mind of the hearer by a farther explanation of it ; thus, "Solomon built *a* temple *on mount Zion ;* and that was *the* temple *to which the Jews resorted to worship*."

" *The* lunatic, *the* poet, and *the* lover,
" Are of imagination all compact."
" *The* horse is a noble animal ;" " *The* dog is a faithful crea-

---

PHILOSOPHICAL NOTES.

A, AN, THE.

In a scientific arrangement of grammatical principles, *a* and *the* belong to that class of adjectives denominated *definitives* or *restrictives*.

A, an, ane, or *one*, is the past participle of *ananad*, to add, to join. It denotes that the thing to which it is prefixed, is *added, united, aned, an-d, oned*, (*woned*,) or made *one*.

The and *that*. According to Horne Tooke, *the* is the imperative, and *that*, the past participle, of the Anglo-Saxon verb *thean*, to get, take, assume. *The* and *that* had, originally, the same meaning. The difference in their present application, is a modern refinement. Hence, *that*, as well as *the*, was formerly used, indifferently, before either a singular or a plural noun.

ture ;" " *The* wind blows ;" " *The* wolves were howling in *the* woods." In these examples, we do not refer to any particular lunatics, poets, lovers, horses, dogs, winds, wolves, and woods, but we refer to these *particular classes* of things, in contradistinction to other objects or classes. The phrase, " Neither *the* one nor *the* other," is an idiom of the language.

REMARKS.—This method of elucidating the articles, which is popular with Blair, Priestley, Lowth, Johnson, Harris, Beattie, Coote, Murray, and many other distinguished philologists, is discarded by some of our modern writers. But, by proving that this theory is exceptionable, they by no means make it appear, that it ought, therefore, to be rejected.

Exceptionable or not, they have not been able to supply its place with one that is more *convenient in practice.* Neither have they adopted one *less* exceptionable. The truth is, after all which can be done to render the definitions and rules of grammar comprehensive and accurate, they will still be found, when critically examined by men of learning and science, more or less exceptionable. These exceptions and imperfections are the unavoidable consequence of the imperfections of the language. Language, as well as every thing else of human invention, will always be *imperfect.* Consequently, a *perfect* system of grammatical principles, would not suit it. A *perfect* grammar will not be produced, until some *perfect* being writes it for a *perfect* language ; and a perfect language will not be constructed, until some *super-human* agency is employed in its production. All grammatical principles and systems which are not *perfect,* are *exceptionable.*

NOTES.

1. The article is *omitted* before nouns implying the different virtues, vices, passions, qualities, sciences, arts, metals, herbs, &c. ; as, " *Modesty* is becoming ; *Falsehood* is odious ; *Grammar* is useful," &c.

. 2. The article is not prefixed to proper nouns ; as, *Barron* killed *Decatur ;* except by way of eminence, or for the sake of distinguishing a particular family, or when some noun is understood ; as, " He is not *a* Franklin ; He is *a* Lee, or of the family of *the* Lees ; We sailed down *the* (river) Missouri."

3. An *adjective* is frequently placed between the article and the noun with which the article agrees ; as, " A *good* boy ; an *industrious* man." Sometimes the adjective precedes the article ; as, " As *great* a man as Alexander ; *Such* a shame."

4. In referring to many individuals, when we wish to bring each separately under consideration, the indefinite article is sometimes placed between the adjective *many* and a singular noun ; as, " Where *many a rosebud* rears its blushing head ;" " Full *many a flower* is born to blush unseen."

5. The definite article *the* is frequently applied to *adverbs* in the comparative or superlative degree ; as, " *The more* I examine it, *the better* I like it, I like this *the least* of any."

You may proceed and parse the following articles, when you shall have committed this

SYSTEMATIC ORDER OF PARSING

The order of parsing an Article, is—an article, and why ?—definite or indefinite, and, why ?—with what noun does it agree ?—RULE.

" He is *the* son of *a* king."

The is an article, a word prefixed to a noun to limit its signification—definite, it limits the noun to a particular object—it belongs to the noun " son," according to

RULE 2. *The definite article* the *belongs to nouns in the singular or plural number.*

A is an article, a word placed before a noun to limit its signication—indefinite, it limits the noun to one of a kind, but to no particular one—it agrees with "king," agreeably to

RULE 1. *The article a or an agrees with nouns in the singular number only.*

NOTE. By considering the original meaning of this article, the propriety of Rule 1, will appear. *A* or *an*, (formerly written *ane*,) being equivalent to *one*, *any one*, or *some one*, cannot be prefixed to nouns in the plural number. There is, however, an exception to this rule. *A* is placed before a plural noun when any of the following adjectives come between the article and the noun : *few, great, many, dozen, hundred, thousand, million ;* as, *a* few *men, a* thousand *houses, &c.*

After having parsed these articles several times over, please to read this third lecture *three* times. Then turn back, and examine the *second* lecture critically, observing to parse every example according to the directions previously given, which will prepare you to parse systematically, all the articles, nouns, and verbs in these subsequent

EXERCISES IN PARSING.

A bird sings. An eagle flies. Mountains stand. The multitude pursue pleasure. The reaper reaps the farmer's grain. Farmers mow the grass. Farmers' boys spread the hay. The clerk sells the merchant's goods. An ostrich outruns an Arab's horse. Cecrops founded Athens. Gallileo invented the telescope. James Macpherson translated Ossian's poems. Sir Francis Drake circumnavigated the globe. Doctor Benjamin Franklin invented the lightning-rod. Washington Irving wrote the Sketch-Book.

I will now offer a few remarks on the misapplication of the articles, which, with the exercise of your own discriminating powers, will enable you to use them with propriety. But, before you proceed, please to answer the following

QUESTIONS NOT ANSWERED IN PARSING.

How many articles are there ?—In what sense is a noun taken, when it has no article to limit it ?—Repeat the *order* of parsing an article.—What rule applies in parsing the *definite* article ?— What rule in parsing the *indefinite ?*

QUESTIONS ON THE NOTES.

Before what nouns is the article omitted?—Is the article *the* ever applied to adverbs?—Give examples.—What is the meaning of *a* or *an?*—When is *a* or *an* placed before a plural noun?—From what are *a, the,* and *that* derived?

EXERCISES IN FALSE SYNTAX.

Note to Rule 1. *An* is used before a vowel or silent *h*, and *a* before a consonant or *u* long, and also before the word *one*.

It is not only disagreeable to the ear, but, according to this note, improper to say, *a* apple, *a* humble suppliant, *an* hero, *an* university, because the word *apple* begins with a vowel, and *h* is not sounded in the word *humble*, for which reasons *a* should be *an* in the first two examples; but, as the *h* is sounded in *hero*, and the *u* is long in *university*, *a* ought to be prefixed to these words: thus, *an* apple, *an* humble suppliant: *a* hero, *a* university. You may correct the following

EXAMPLES.

A enemy, a inkstand, a hour, an horse, an herald, an heart, an heathen, an union, a umbrella, an useful book, many an one. This is an hard saying. They met with an heavy loss. He would not give an hat for an horse.

Note 1, to Rule 2. The articles are often properly omitted: when used they should be justly applied, according to their distinct character; as, " Gold is corrupting; *The* sea is green; *A* lion is bold." It would be improper to say, *The* gold is corrupting; Sea is green; Lion is bold.

The grass is good for horses, and the wheat for men. Grass is good for the horses, and wheat for the men. Grass looks well. Wheat is blighted.

In the first of these sentences, we are not speaking of any particular kind of *grass* or *wheat*, neither do we wish to limit the meaning to any particular crop or field of grass, or quantity of wheat; but we are speaking of grass and wheat generally, therefore the article *the* should be omitted. In the second sentence, we do not refer to any definite kind, quality, or number of *horses* or *men;* but to horses and men generally; that is, the terms are here used to denote *whole species*, therefore, the article should be omitted, and the sentence should read thus, " Grass is good for horses, and wheat for men."

In the third and fourth examples, we wish to limit our meaning to the crops of *grass* and *wheat* now on the ground, which, in contradistinction to the crops heretofore raised, are considered as *particular* objects; therefore we should say, " *The* grass looks well; *The* wheat is blighted."

Note 2. When a noun is used in its *general* sense, the article should be omitted; as, " *Poetry* is a pleasing art;" " *Oranges* grow in New Orleans."

FALSE SYNTAX.

Corn in the garden, grows well; but corn in the field, does not. How does the tobacco sell? The tobacco is dear. How do you like the study of the grammar? The grammar is a

/

pleasing study. ~ A candid temper is proper for the man. World is wide. The man is mortal. And I persecuted this way unto the death. The earth, the air, the fire, and the water, are the four elements of the old philosophers.

LECTURE IV.

OF ADJECTIVES.

An ADJECTIVE is a word added to a noun to express its quality or kind, or to restrict its meaning ; as, a good man, a *bad* man, a *free* man, an *unfortunate* man, *one* man, *forty* men.

In the phrases, a *good* apple, a *bad* apple, a *large* apple, a *small* apple, a *red* apple, a *white* apple, a *green* apple, a *sweet* apple, a *sour* apple, a *bitter* apple, a *round* apple, a *hard* apple, a *soft* apple, a *mellow* apple, a *fair* apple, a *May* apple, an *early* apple, a *late* apple, a *winter* apple, a *crab* apple, a *thorn* apple, a *well-tasted* apple, an *ill-looking* apple, a *water-cored* apple, you perceive that all those words in *italics* are adjectives, because each expresses some quality or property of the noun apple, or it shows what *kind* of an apple it is of which we are speaking.

The distinction between a *noun* and an *adjective* is very clear. A noun is the *name* of a thing ; but an adjective denotes simply the *quality* or *property* of a thing. This is *fine cloth*. In this example, the difference between the word denoting the *thing*, and that denoting the *quality* of it, is easily perceived. You certainly cannot be at a loss to know, that the word *cloth* expresses the *name*, and *fine*, the *quality*, of the *thing* ; consequently *fine* must be an *adjective*. If I say, He is a *wise* man, a *prudent* man, a *wicked* man, or an *ungrateful* man, the words in *italics* are adjec-

---

PHILOSOPHICAL NOTES.

ADNOUNS.

Adnoun or *Adjective*, comes from the Latin, *ad* and *jicio*, to *add to*.

Adnouns are a class of words added to nouns to vary their comprehension, or to determine their extension. Those which effect the former object, are called *adjectives*, or *attributes* ; and those which effect the latter, *restrictives*. It is not, in all cases, easy to determine to which of these classes an adnoun should be referred. Words which express simply the *qualities* of nouns, are adjectives ; and such as denote their *situation* or *number*, are restrictives.

Adjectives were originally nouns or verbs.

tives, because each expresses a *quality* of the noun man. And, if I say, He is a *tall* man, a *short* man, a *white* man, a *black* man, or a *persecuted* man, the words, *tall, short, white, black,* and *persecuted,* are also adjectives, because they tell what *kind* of a man he is of whom I am speaking, or they attribute to him some particular property.

Some adjectives *restrict* or *limit* the signification of the nouns to which they are joined, and are, therefore, sometimes called *definitives ;* as, *one* era, *seven* ages, the *first* man, the *whole* mass, *no* trouble, *those* men, *that* book, *all* regions.

Other adjectives *define* or *describe* nouns, or do both; as, *fine* silk, *blue* paper, a *heavy* shower, *pure* water, *green* mountains, *bland* breezes, *gurgling* rills, *glass* window, *window* glass, *beaver* hats, *chip* bonnets, *blackberry* ridge, *Monroe* garden, *Juniata* iron, *Cincinnati* steam-mill.

Some adjectives are *secondary,* and qualify other adjectives ; as, *pale* red lining, *dark* blue silk, *deep sea* green sash, *soft* iron blooms, *red hot* iron plate.

You will frequently find the adjective placed after the noun ; as, " Those *men* are *tall ;* A *lion* is *bold ;* The *weather* is *calm ;* The *tree* is three feet *thick.*"

Should you ever be at a loss to distinguish an adjective from the other parts of speech, the following sign will enable you to tell it. Any word that will make sense with the word *thing* added, or with any other noun following it, is an adjective ; as, a *high* thing, a *low* thing, a *hot* thing, a *cold* thing, an *unfinished* thing, a *new-fashioned* thing :—or, a *pleasant* prospect, a *long-deserted* dwelling, an *American* soldier, a *Greek* Testament. Are these words adjectives, *distant, yonder, peaceful, long-sided, double-headed ?* A distant *object* or *thing,* yonder *hill, &c.* They are. They will make sense with a noun after them. – Adjectives some-

---

Some consider the adjective, in its present application, *exactly* equivalent to a noun connected to another noun by means of juxtaposition, of a preposition, or of a corresponding flexion. "A *golden* cup," say they, "is the same as a *gold* cup, or a cup *of gold.*" But this principle appears to be exceptionable. "A cup *of gold,*" may mean either a cup-*full* of gold, or a cup *made* of gold. "An *oaken* cask," signifies an *oak* cask, or a cask *of oak ;* i. e. a cask *made* of oak ; but a *beer* cask, and a cask *of beer,* are two different things. A *virtuous* son ; a son *of virtue.*

The distinguishing characteristic of the adjective, appears to consist in its both *naming* a quality, and *attributing* that quality to some object.

The terminations *en, ed,* and *ig,* (our modern *y,*) signifying *give, add, join,* denote that the names of qualities to which they are postfixed, are to be attributed to other nouns possessing such qualities: wood-*en,* wood *y.* See page 37.

Left is the past participle of the verb *leave.* Horne Tooke defines *right*

times become adverbs. This matter will be explained in Lecture VI. In parsing, you may generally know an adjective by its *qualifying a noun or pronoun.*

Most words ending in *ing* are *present participles.* These are frequently used as adjectives; therefore, most participles will make sense with the addition of the word thing, or any other noun, after them; as, a *pleasing* thing, a *moving* spectacle, *mouldering* ruins.

In the Latin language, and many others, adjectives, like nouns, have gender, number, and case; but in the English language, they have neither gender, person, number, nor case. These properties belong to *creatures* and *things,* and not to their *qualities ;* therefore gender, person, number, and case, are the properties of *nouns,* and *not* of adjectives.

Adjectives are varied only to express the degrees of comparison. They have three degrees of comparison, the Positive, the Comparative, and the Superlative.

The *positive degree* expresses the quality of an object without any increase or diminution; as, *good, wise, great.*

The *comparative degree* increases or lessens the positive in signification; as, *better, wiser, greater, less wise.*

The *superlative degree* increases or lessens the positive to the highest or lowest degree; as, *best, wisest, greatest, least wise.*

---

to be that which is *ordered* or *directed.* The *right* hand is that which your parents and custom direct you to use in preference to the other. And when you employ that in preference, the other is the *leaved, leav'd,* or *left* hand; i. e. the one *leaved* or *left.* "The one shall be taken, and the other *(leaved) left.*"

Own. Formerly a man's *own* was what he *worked for, own* being a past participle of a verb signifying to *work.*

Restrictives. Some restrictives, in modern times, are applied only to singular nouns; such as *a* or *an, another, one, this, that, each, every, either.* Others, only to plural nouns; as, *these, those, two, three, few, several, all* But most restrictives, like adjectives, are applied to both singular and plural nouns : *first, second, last, the, former, latter, any, such, same, some, which, what.*

Numerals. All numeration was, doubtless, originally performed by the fingers; for the number of the fingers is still the utmost extent of its signification. *Ten* is the past participle of *tynan,* to close, to shut in. The hands *tyned, tened,* closed, or shut in, signified *ten;* for there numeration *closed.* To denote a number greater than ten, we must begin again, *ten* and *one, ten* and *two,* &c.

COMPARISON OF ADJECTIVES.

More and *most* form the comparative and superlative degrees by increasing the positive; and *less* and *least,* by diminishing it.

Comparison by increasing the positive

Pos.	*Comp.*	*Sup.*
great,	greater,	greatest.
wise,	wiser,	wisest.
holy,	more holy,	most holy.
frugal,	more frugal,	most frugal.

Comparison by diminishing the positive.

Pos.	*Comp.*	*Sup.*
wise,	less wise,	least wise.
holy,	less holy,	least holy.
frugal,	less frugal,	least frugal.

NUMERAL ADJECTIVES.

Words used in counting, are called *numeral adjectives* of the *cardinal* kind; as, *one, two, three, four, twenty, fifty,* &c.

Words used in numbering, are called *numeral adjectives* of the *ordinal* kind; as, *first, second, third, fourth, twentieth, fiftieth,* &c.

NOTE. The words *many, few,* and *several,* as they always refer to an indefinite number, may be properly called *numeral adjectives* of the indefinite kind.

NOTES.

1. The simple word, or Positive, becomes the Comparative by adding *r,* or *er;* and the Positive becomes the Superlative, by adding *st,* or *est,* to the end of it; as, Pos. wise, Com. wise*r,* Sup. wise*st;* rich, richer, richest; bold, bold*er,* bold*est.* The adverbs, *more* and *most, less* and *least,* when placed before the adjective, have the same effect; as, Pos. wise, Com. *more* wise, Sup. *most* wise; Pos. wise, Com. *less* wise, Sup. *least* wise.

Twain, twa-in, twa-ain, twa-ane, is a compound of *two* (*twa, twae, twee, twi, two* or *dwo* or *duo*) and *one* (*ane, ain, an.*) It signifies *two* units *joined, united, aned,* or *oned. Twenty* (*twa-ane-ten*) signifies *two tens aned, oned,* or *united.* Things *separated* into parcels of twenty each, are called *scores. Score* is the past participle of *shear,* to *separate.*

The Ordinals are formed like abstract nouns in *eth. Fifth, sixth,* or *tenth* is the number which *fiv-eth, six-eth, ten-eth,* or mak-*eth* up the number *five, six,* or *ten.*

Philosophical writers who limit our acceptation of words to that in which they were *originally* employed, and suppose that all the complicated, yet often definable, associations which the gradual progress of language and intellect has connected with words, are to be reduced to *the standard of our*

2. *Monosyllables* are generally compared by adding *er* and *est; dissyllables, trisyllables,* &c. by *more* and *most;* as, mild, milder, mildest; frugal, more frugal, most frugal; virtuous, more virtuous, most virtuous. Dissyllables ending in *y;* as, happy, lovely; and in *le* after a mute; as, able, ample; and dissyllables accented on the last syllable; as, discreet, polite; easily admit of *er* and *est;* as, happi*er,* happi*est;* polit*er,* polit*est.* Words of more than two syllables very seldom admit of these terminations.

3. When the positive ends in *d,* or *t,* preceded by a *single* vowel, the consonant is doubled in forming the comparative and superlative degrees; as red, *redder, reddest;* hot, *hotter, hottest.*

4. In some words the superlative is formed by adding *most* to the end of them; as, nethermost, uttermost or utmost, undermost, uppermost, foremost.

5. In English, as in most languages, there are some words of very common use, (in which the caprice of custom is apt to get the better of analogy,) that are irregular in forming the degrees of comparison; as, "Good, better, best; bad, worse, worst; little, less, least; much or many, more, most; near, nearer, nearest or next; late, later, latest or last; old, older or elder, oldest or eldest;" and a few others.

6. The following adjectives, and many others, are always in the *superlative* degree, because, by expressing a quality in the highest degree, they carry in themselves a superlative signification: *chief, extreme, perfect, right, wrong, honest, just, true, correct, sincere, vast, immense, ceaseless, infinite, endless, unparalleled, universal, supreme, unlimited, omnipotent, all-wise, eternal.*

7. Compound adjectives, and adjectives denoting qualities arising from the figure of bodies, do not admit of comparison; such as, *well-formed, frost-bitten, round, square, oblong, circular, quadrangular, conical,* &c.

8. The termination *ish* added to adjectives, expresses a slight degree of quality below the comparative; as, *black, blackish; salt, saltish. Very,* prefixed to the comparative, expresses a degree of quality, but not always a superlative degree.

Read this Lecture carefully, particularly the Notes; after which you may parse the following adjectives and neuter verb, and, likewise, the examples that follow. If you cannot repeat all the definitions and rules, spread the Compendium when you parse. But before you proceed, please to commit the .

SYSTEMATIC ORDER OF PARSING.

The order of parsing an Adjective, is—an adjective, and why?—compare it—degree of comparison, and why?—to what noun does it belong?—Rule.

---

forefathers; appear not to have sufficiently attended to the *changes* which this principle of association actually produces. As language is transmitted from generation to generation, many words become the representatives of ideas with which they were not originally associated; and thus they undergo a change, not only in the *mode* of their application, but also in their meaning. Words being the signs of things, their meaning must necessarily change as much, *at least,* as things themselves change; but this variation in their import more frequently depends on accidental circumstances. Among the ideas connected with a word that which was once of primary, becomes only of secondary importance; and sometimes, by degrees, it loses altogether its

That *great* nation *was* once *powerful;* but now it is *feeble.*

Great is an adjective, a word added to a noun to express its quality—pos. great, com. greater, sup. greatest—it is in the positive degree, it expresses the quality of an object without any increase or diminution, and belongs to the noun "nation," according to

RULE 18. *Adjectives belong to, and qualify, nouns expressed or understood.*

Was is a verb, a word that signifies to be—neuter, it expresses neither action nor passion, but being or a state of being—third person singular, because its nominative "nation" is a noun of multitude conveying *unity* of idea—it agrees with "nation," agreeably to

RULE 10. *A noun of multitude conveying* unity *of idea, may have a verb or pronoun agreeing with it in the* singular.

Powerful is an adjective belonging to "nation," according to Rule 18. *Feeble* belongs to "it," according to Note 1, under Rule 18. *Is* is a neuter verb agreeing with "it," agreeably to Rule 4.

"Bonaparte entered Russia with 400,000 men."

Four-hundred-thousand is a numeral adjective of the cardinal kind, it is a word used in counting, and belongs to the noun "men," according to Note 2, under Rule 18. *Numeral adjectives belong to nouns, which nouns must agree in number with their adjectives.*

If, in parsing the following examples, you find any words about which you are at a loss, you will please to turn back, and parse all the foregoing examples again. This course will enable you to proceed without any difficulty.

More is an adverb. *Of* and *to* are prepositions, governing the nouns that follow them in the objective case.

EXERCISES IN PARSING.

A benevolent man helps indigent beggars. Studious scholars learn many long lessons. Wealthy merchants own large ships. The heavy ships bear large burdens; the lighter ships carry less burdens. Just poets use figurative language. Ungrammatical expressions offend a true critic's ear. Weak critics magnify trifling errors. No composition is perfect. The rabble was tumul-

---

connexion with the word, giving place to others with which, from some accidental causes, it has been associated.

Two or three instances will illustrate the truth of these remarks. In an ancient English version of the New Testament, we find the following language: "I, Paul, a *rascal* of Jesus Christ, unto you Gentiles," &c. But who, in the present acceptation of the word, would dare to call "the great apostle of the Gentiles" a *rascal?* *Rascal* formerly meant a *servant:* one devoted to the interest of another; but now it is nearly synonymous with

tuous. The late-washed grass looks green. Shady trees form a delightful arbor. The setting sun makes a beautiful appearance; the variegated rainbow appears more beautiful. Epaminondas was the greatest of the Theban generals; Pelopidas was next to Epaminondas.

The first fleet contained three hundred men; the second contained four thousand. The earth contains one thousand million inhabitants. Many a cheering ray brightens the good man's pathway.

NOTE. *Like, Worth.* The adjective *like* is a contraction of the participle *likened*, and generally has the preposition *unto* understood after it. " She is *like* [*unto*] her brother;" " They are *unlike* [*to*] him." " The kingdom of heaven is *like* [*likened* or made *like*] *unto* a householder."

The noun *worth* has altogether dropped its associated words. " The cloth is *worth* ten dollars *a* yard;" that is, The cloth is *of the* worth *of* ten dollars *by the* yard, or *for a, one,* or *every yard.*

Some eminent philologists do not admit the propriety of supplying an ellipsis after *like, worth, ere, but, except,* and *than,* but consider them prepositious. See Anomalies, in the latter part of this work.

REMARKS ON ADJECTIVES AND NOUNS.

A critical analysis requires that the adjective when used without its noun, should be parsed as an adjective belonging to its noun understood; as, " The *virtuous* [*persons*] and the *sincere* [*persons*] are always respected;" " Providence rewards the *good* [*people,*] and punishes the *bad* [*people.*]"

" The *evil* [*deed* or *deeds*] that men do, lives after them;

" The *good* [*deed* or *deeds*] is oft interred with their bones."

But sometimes the adjective, by its *manner* of meaning, becomes a noun, and has another adjective joined to it; as, " the chief *good;*" " The vast *immense* [*immensity*] of space."

Various nouns placed before other nouns, assume the character of adjectives, according to their *manner* of meaning; as, " *Sea* fish, *iron* mortar, *wine* vessel, *gold* watch, *corn* field, *meadow* ground, *mountain* height."

The principle which recognises *custom* as the standard of grammatical accuracy, might rest for its support on the usage of only *six* words, and defy all the subtleties of innovating skeptics to gainsay it. If the genius and analogy of our language were the standard, it would be correct to observe this analogy, and say, " Good, good*er,* good*est;* bad, bad*der,* bad*dest;* little, littl*er,* littl*est;* much, much*er,* much*est.*" " By *this mean;*" " What *are* the *news.*" But such a criterion betrays only the weakness of those who attempt to establish it. Regardless of the dogmas and edicts of the philosophical umpire, the good sense of the people will cause them, in this instance, as well as in a thousand others, to yield to *custom,* and say, " Good,

---

villain. *Villain* once had none of the odium which is now associated with the term; but it signified one who, under the feudal system, rented or held lands of another. Thus, Henry the VIII. says to a vassal or tenant, " As you are an accomplished *villain,* I order that you receive £700 out of the public treasury ' The word *villain,* then, has given up its original idea, and become the representative of a new one, the word *tenant* having supplanted it. To prove that the meaning of words *changes,* a thousand examples could be adduced; but with the intelligent reader, proof is unnecessary.

better, best; bad, *worse, worst;* little, *less, least:* much, *more, most;*" " By *this means;*" " What *is* the *news?*"

With regard to the using of adjectives and other qualifying words, care must be taken, or your language will frequently amount to absurdity or nonsense. Let the following general remark, which is better than a dozen rules, put you on your guard. Whenever you utter a sentence, or put your pen on paper to write, weigh well in your mind *the meaning of the words* which you are about to employ. See that they convey precisely the ideas which you wish to express by them, and thus you will avoid innumerable errors. In speaking of a man, we may say, with propriety, he is *very* wicked, or *exceedingly* lavish, because the terms *wicked* and *lavish* are adjectives that admit of comparison; but, if we take the words in their literal acceptation, there is a solecism in calling a man *very* honest, or *exceedingly* just, for the words *honest* and *just,* literally admit of no comparison. In point of fact, a man is *honest* or *dishonest, just* or *unjust:* there can be no medium or excess in this respect. *Very* correct, *very* incorrect, *very* right, *very* wrong, are common expressions; but they are not *literally* proper. What is not *correct,* must be *incorrect;* and that which is not *incorrect,* must be *correct:* what is not *right,* must be *wrong;* and that which is not *wrong,* must be *right.* To avoid that circumlocution which must otherwise take place, our best speakers and writers, however, frequently compare adjectives which do not literally admit of comparison: " The *most established* practice;" " The *most uncertain* method;" " Irving, as a writer, is *far more accurate* than Addison;" " The metaphysical investigations of our philosophical grammars, are *still more incomprehensible* to the learner." Comparisons like these, should generally be avoided; but sometimes they are so convenient in practice, as to render them admissible. Such expressions can be reconciled with the principles of grammar, only by considering them as figurative.

Comparative members of sentences, should be set in *direct opposition* to each other; as, " Pope was *rich,* but Goldsmith was *poor.*" The following sentences are inaccurate: " Solomon was *wiser* than Cicero was *eloquent.*" " The principles of the reformation were *deeper* in the prince's mind than to be *easily eradicated.*" This latter sentence contains *no comparison* at all; neither does it literally convey *any meaning.* Again, if the Psalmist had said, " I am the wisest of my teachers," he would have spoken absurdly, because the phrase would imply, that he was one of his teachers. But in saying, " I am wiser *than* my teachers," he does not consider himself one of them, but places himself in contradistinction to them.

Before you proceed any farther, you may answer the following

QUESTIONS NOT ANSWERED IN PARSING.

What is the distinction between a noun and an adjective?—By what sign may an adjective be known?—Are participles ever used as adjectives?—Does gender, person, number, or case, belong to adjectives?—How are they varied?—Name the three degrees of comparison.—What effect have *less* and *least* in comparing adjectives?—Repeat the order of parsing an adjective.—What rule applies in parsing an adjective?—What rule in parsing a verb agreeing with a noun of multitude conveying *unity* of idea?—What Note should be applied in parsing an adjective which belongs to a pronoun?—What Note in parsing *numeral* adjectives?

QUESTIONS ON THE NOTES.

Repeat all the various ways of forming the degrees of comparison, mentioned in the first five NOTES:—Compare these adjectives; *ripe, frugal, mischievous, happy, able, good, little, much* or *many, near, late, old.*—Name some adjectives that are always in the superlative, and never compared.— Are compound adjectives compared?—What is said of the termination *ish,* and of the adverb *very?*—When does an adjective become a noun?—What character does a noun assume when placed before another noun?—How can you prove that *custom* is the standard of grammatical accuracy?

QUESTIONS ON THE PHILOSOPHICAL NOTES.

How are adnouns divided?—What constitutes the true character of an adjective?—What are the signification and denotement of the terminations, *en, ed,* and *ig?*—What do *left* and *own* signify?—Name the three ways in which restrictives are applied.—How was numeration originally performed? —What is said of *twain, twenty, score,* and the ordinal numbers?—What is said of the changes produced in the meaning of words, by the principle of association?

EXERCISES IN FALSE SYNTAX.

NOTE 9, under RULE 18. Double *Comparatives* and *Superlatives* should be avoided; such as, *worser, lesser, more* deeper, *more* wickeder, &c.: *chiefest, supremest, perfectest, rightest;* or *more* perfect, *most* perfect, *most* supreme, &c.

Virtue confers the most supreme dignity on man, and it should be his chiefest desire.

He made the greater light to rule the day, and the lesser light to rule the night.

The phrases "most supreme," and "chiefest," in the first sentence, are incorrect, because *supreme* and *chief* are in the superlative degree without having the superlative form superadded, which addition makes them double superlatives. They should be written, "confers supreme dignity," and "his chief desire."

We can say, one thing is *less* than another, or *smaller* than another, because the adjectives *less* and *smaller* are in the comparative degree; but the phrase "*lesser* light," in the second sentence, is inaccurate. *Lesser* is a double comparative, which, according to the preceding Note, should be avoided. *Lesser* is as incorrect as *badder, gooder, worser.* "The *smaller* light," would be less exceptionable. You can correct the following without my assistance. Correct them *four* times over.

The pleasures of the understanding are more preferable than those of imagination or sense.

The tongue is like a race-horse, which runs the faster the lesser weight it carries.

The nightingale's voice is the most sweetest in the grove.

The Most Highest hath created us for his glory.

He was admitted to the chiefest offices.

The first witness gave a strong proof of the fact; the next more stronger still; but the last witness, the most stronger of all.

He gave the fullest and the most sincere proof of the truer friendship.

LECTURE V.

OF PARTICIPLES.

A PARTICIPLE is a word derived from a verb, and partakes of the nature of a verb, and also of an adjec ive.

Verbs have three participles, the present or imper fect, the perfect, and the compound.

The *present* or *imperfect* participle denotes action or being continued, but not perfected. It always ends in *ing*; as, *ruling, being:* "I am *writing* a letter."

The *perfect* participle denotes action or being perfected or finished. When derived from a regular verb, it ends in *ed*, and corresponds with the imperfect tense; as, *ruled, smiled:* "The letter is *written*."

The *compound* participle implies action or being completed before the time referred to. It is formed by placing *having* before the perfect participle; as, *having ruled, having been ruled:* "*Having written* the letter, he mailed it."

The term *Participle* comes from the Latin word *participio,* which signifies to *partake ;* and this name is given to this part of speech, because it *partakes* of the nature of the verb and of the adjective.

PHILOSOPHICAL NOTES.

Participles are formed by adding to the verb the termination *ing, ed,* or *en.* *Ing* signifies the same as the noun *being.* When postfixed to the noun-state of the verb, the compound word thus formed, expresses a continued state of the verbal denotement. It implies that what is meant by the verb, is *being* continued. *En* is an alteration of *an,* the Saxon verbalizing adjunct; *ed* is a contraction of *dede;* and the terminations *d* and *t,* are a contraction of *ed.* Participles ending in *ed* or *en,* usually denote the *dodo, dede, doed, did, done,* or *finished* state of what is meant by the verb. The book is *printed.* It is a *print-ed* or *print-done* book, or such a one as the *done* act of *printing* has made it. The book is *written ;* i. e. it has received the *done* or *finish-ed* act of *writ-ing* it.

Participles bear the same relation to verbs, that adnouns do to nouns. They might, therefore, be styled *verbal adjectives.* But that theory which ranks them with adnouns, appears to rest on a sandy foundation. In classi-

By many writers, the participle is classed with the verb, and treated as a part of it; but, as it has no nominative, partakes of the nature of an adjective, requires many syntactical rules which apply not to the verb, and, in some other respects, has properties peculiar to itself, it is believed that its character is sufficiently distinct from the verb, to entitle it to the rank of a separate part of speech. It is, in fact, the connecting link between, not only he adjective and the verb, but also the noun and the verb.

All participles are compound in their meaning and office. Like verbs, they express action and being, and denote time; and, like adjectives, they describe the nouns of which they denote the action or being. In the sentences, The boatman is *crossing* the river; I see a man *laboring* in the field; Charles is *standing ;* you perceive that the participles *crossing* and *laboring* express the actions of the boatman and the man, and *standing* the state of being of Charles. In these respects, then, they partake of the nature of verbs. You also notice, that they *describe* the several nouns associated with them, like describing adjectives; and that, in this respect, they participate the properties of adjectives. And, furthermore, you observe they denote actions which are still going on; that is, *incomplete* or *unfinished* actions; for which reason we call them *imperfect* participles.

Perhaps I can illustrate their character more clearly. When the imperfect or present and perfect participles are placed before nouns, they become defining or describing adjectives, and are denominated *participial adjectives ;* as, A *loving* companion; The *rippling* stream; *Roaring* winds; A *wilted* leaf; An *accomplished* scholar. Here the words *loving, rippling, roaring, wilted,* and *accomplished,* describe or define the nouns with which they are associated. And where the participles are placed after their nouns, they have, also, this descriptive quality. If I say, I see

---

fying words, we ought to be guided more by their *manner* of meaning, and their *inferential* meaning, than by their primitive, essential signification.

"I have a *broken* plate ;" i. e. I have a plate—*broken ;* "I have *broken* a plate." If there is no difference in the *essential* meaning of the word *broken,* in these two constructions, it cannot be denied, that there is a wide difference in the meaning *inferred* by custom; which difference depends on the *manner* in which the term is applied. The former construction denotes, that I *possess* a plate which was *broken,* (whether with or without my agency, is not intimated,) perhaps, one hundred or one thousand years ago; whereas, the meaning of the latter is, that I *performed the act* of reducing the plate from a whole to a *broken* state; and it is not intimated whether I possess it, or some one else. It appears reasonable, that, in a practical grammar, at least, any word which occurs in constructions differing so widely, may properly be classed with different parts of speech. This illustration likewise establishes the propriety of retaining what we call the *perfect tense* of the verb.

the moon *rising ;* The horse is *running* a race ; The dog is *beaten ;*
I describe the several objects, as a *rising* moon, a *running* horse,
and a *beaten* dog, as well as when I place these participles before
the nouns.   The same word is a participle or a participial adjective, according to its manner of meaning.   The preceding illustration, however, shows that this distinction is founded on a very
slight shade of difference in the meaning of the two.   The fol
lowing examples will enable you to distinguish the one from th
other.

Participles.	*Participial adjectives.*
See the sun *setting.*	See the *setting* sun.
See the moon *rising.*	See the *rising* moon.
The wind is *roaring.*	Hear the *roaring* wind.
The twig is *broken.*	The *broken* twig fell.
The vessel *anchored* in the bay, lost her mast.	The *anchored* vessel spreads her sail.

The *present* or *imperfect* participle is known by its ending in
ing ; as, float*ing,* rid*ing,* hear*ing,* see*ing.*   These are derived from
the verbs, *float, ride, hear,* and *see.*   But some words ending in
ing are not participles ; such as *evening, morning, hireling, sap-
ling, uninteresting, unbelieving, uncontrolling.*   When you parse
a word ending in *ing,* you should always consider whether it
comes from a verb or not.   There is such a verb as *interest,* hence
you know that the word *interesting* is a participle ; but there is
no such verb as *uninterest,* consequently, *uninteresting* can *not* be
a participle : but it is an adjective ; as, an *uninteresting* story.
You will be able very easily to distinguish the participle from the
other parts of speech, when you shall have acquired a more
extensive knowledge of the verb.

Speak the participles from each of these verbs, learn, walk,
shun, smile, sail, conquer, manage, reduce, relate, discover, over-
rate, disengage.   Thus, Pres. *learning,* Perf. *learned,* Comp.
having learned.   Pres. *walking,* Perf. *walked,* Compound, *having
walked,* and so on.

You may now commit the *order* of parsing a participle, and
then proceed with me.

SYSTEMATIC ORDER OF PARSING.

The *order of parsing* a PARTICIPLE, is—a partici
ple, and why ?—from what verb is it derived ?—speak
the three—present, perfect, or compound, and why ?
—to what does it refer or belong ?—RULE.

"I saw a vessel *sailing*."

Sailing is a participle, a word derived from a verb, and partakes of the nature of a verb, and also of an adjective—it comes from the verb to sail—pres. sailing, perf. sailed, comp. having sailed—it is a present or imperfect participle, because it denotes the continuance of an unfinished action—and refers to the noun ' vessel " for its subject, according to

RULE 27. *The present participle refers to some noun or pronoun denoting the subject or actor.*

" Not a breath disturbs the *sleeping* billow."

Sleeping is a participial adjective, a word added to a noun to express its quality—it cannot, with propriety, be compared—it belongs to the noun " billow," agreeably to

RULE 18. *Adjectives belong to, and qualify, nouns expressed or understood.*

You will please to parse these two words several times over, and, by a little reflection, you will perfectly understand the 27th RULE. Recollect, the participle never varies its termination to *agree* with a noun or pronoun, for, as it has no *nominative*, it has no agreement; but it simply *refers* to an actor. Examples: I see a *vessel* sailing ; or, I see three *vessels* sailing. You perceive that the participle *sailing* refers to a singular noun in the first example, and to a plural noun in the second ; and yet the participle is in the same form in both examples. The noun *vessel* is in the objective case, and governed by the transitive verb *see*. But when a verb follows a noun, the ending of the verb generally varies in order to agree with the noun which is its nominative ; as, the vessel *sails;* the vessels *sail.*

In this place it may not be improper to notice another Rule that relates to the participle. In the sentence, " The man is *beating* his horse," the noun *horse* is in the objective case, because it is the object of the action expressed by the active-transitive participle " beating," and it is governed by the participle beating, according to

RULE 26. *Participles have the same government as the verbs have from which they are derived.*

The principle upon which this rule is founded, is quite apparent. As a participle derived from a transitive verb, expresses the same kind of action as its verb, it necessarily follows, that the participle must govern the same case as the verb from which it is derived.

When you shall have studied this lecture attentively, you may proceed and parse the following exercises, containing five parts of speech. If, in analyzing these examples, you find any words which you cannot parse correctly and *systematically* by referring to your Compend for definitions and rules, you will please to turn back and read over again the whole *five* lectures. You must exercise a little patience; and, for your encouragement, permit me to remind you, that when you shall have acquired a thorough knowledge of these five parts of speech, only *five* more will remain for you to learn. Be ambitious to excel. Be thorough in your investigations. Give your reasoning powers free scope By studying these lectures with attention, you will acquire more grammatical knowledge in *three* months, than is commonly obtained in *two* years.

In the following examples, the words *purling, crusted, slumber·ing,* and *twinkling,* are participial adjectives. *There* and *its* you may omit.

EXERCISES IN PARSING.

Orlando left the herd grazing. The hunters heard the young dog barking. The old fox heard the sportsman's horn sounding. Deep rivers float long rafts. Purling streams moisten the earth's surface. The sun approaching, melts the crusted snow. The slumbering seas calmed the grave old hermit's mind. Pale Cynthia declining, clips the horizon. Man beholds the twinkling stars adorning night's blue arch. The stranger saw the desert thistle bending there its lowly head.

REMARKS ON PARTICIPLES.

Participles frequently become nouns; as, " A good *understanding;* Excellent *writing;* He made a good *beginning,* but a bad *ending.*"

Constructions like the following, have long been sanctioned by the best authorities: " The goods are *selling;*" " The house is *building;*" " The work is now *publishing.*" A modern innovation, however, is likely to supersede this mode of expression: thus, " The goods are *being sold;*" " The house is *being built;*" " The work is now *being published.*"

You may now answer these

QUESTIONS NOT ANSWERED IN PARSING.

How many kinds of participles are there ?—What is the ending of a present participle ?—What does a perfect participle denote ?—With what does the perfect participle of a regular verb correspond ?—What is a compound participle ?—From what word is the term participle derived ?—Why is this part of speech thus named ?—Wherein does this part of speech partake of the nature of a verb ?—Do all participles participate the properties of adjectives ?—In what respect ?—When are participles called *participial adjectives ?*—Give examples.—How may a present participle be known ?—Repeat the order of parsing a participle.—What rule applies in parsing a *present* participle ?—What Rule in parsing a participial adjective ?—Do participles vary in their terminations in order to agree with their subject or actor ?—What Rule applies in parsing a noun in the *objective case*, governed by a participle ?—Do participles ever become nouns ?—Give examples.

QUESTIONS ON THE PHILOSOPHICAL NOTES.

How are participles formed ?—What does the imperfect part. express ?—What do perfect participles denote ?

LECTURE VI.

OF ADVERBS.

An ADVERB is a word used to modify the sense of a *verb*, a *participle*, an *adjective*, or another *adverb*.

Recollect, an adverb never qualifies a *noun*. It qualifies any of the four parts of speech abovenamed, and none others.

To *modify* or *qualify*, you know, means to produce some *change*. The adverb modifies. If I say, Wirt's style *excels* Irving's, the proposition is affirmative, and the verb *excels* expresses the affirmation. But when I say, Wirt's style *excels not* Irving's, the assertion is changed to a negative. What is it that thus modifies or changes the meaning of the verb *excels ?* You perceive that it is the little word *not*. This word has power to reverse the meaning of the sentence. *Not*, then, is a modifier, qualifier, or negative adverb.

When an adverb is used to modify the sense of a verb or participle, it generally expresses the manner, time, or place, in which the action is performed, or some accidental circumstance respecting it. In the phrases, The man rides *gracefully, awkwardly,*

PHILOSOPHICAL NOTES.

As the happiness and increasing prosperity of a people essentially depend on their advancement in science and the arts, and as language, in all its sublime purposes and legitimate bearings, is strictly identified with these, it may naturally be supposed, that that nation which continues, through successive generations, steadily to progress in the former, will not be neglectful of the cultivation and refinement of the latter. The truth of this remark is illustrated by those who have, for many ages, employed the English language as their medium for the transmission of thought. Among its refinements may be ranked those procedures by which verbs and nouns have been so modified and contracted as to form what we call adverbs, distributives, conjunctions, and prepositions: for I presume it will be readily conceded,

badly, swiftly, slowly, &c. ; or, I saw the man riding *swiftly, slowly, leisurely, very fast,* &c., you perceive that the words *gracefully, awkwardly, very fast,*&c., are adverbs, qualifying the verb *rides,* or the participle *riding,* because they express the *manner* in which the action denoted by the verb and participle, is done.

In the phrases, The man rides *daily, weekly, seldom, frequently, often, sometimes, never ;* or, The man rode *yesterday, heretofore, long since, long ago, recently, lately, just now ;* or, The man wil ride *soon, presently, directly, immediately, by and by, to-day, here-after,* you perceive that all these words in *italics,* are adverbs, qualifying the meaning of the verb rides, because they express the *time* of the action denoted by the verb.

Again, if I say, The man lives *here, near by, yonder, remote, far off, somewhere, nowhere, everywhere,* &c., the words in *italics* are adverbs of *place,* because they tell where he lives.

Adverbs likewise qualify adjectives, and sometimes other adverbs ; as, *more* wise, *most* wise ; or *more wisely, most wisely.* When an adverb is joined to an adjective or adverb, it generally expresses the *degree* of comparison ; for adverbs, like adjectives, have degrees of comparison. Thus, in the phrase, A skilful artist, you know the adjective *skilful* is in the positive degree ; but, by placing the adverb *more* before the adjective, we increase the degree of quality denoted by the adjective to the comparative ; as, A *more* skilful artist : and *most* renders it superlative ; as, A *most* skilful artist. And if we place more and most before other adverbs, the effect is the same ; as, skilfully, *more* skilfully, *most* skilfully.

COMPARISON OF ADVERBS.

Positive.	*Comparative.*	*Superlative.*
soon,	sooner,	soonest.
often,	oftener,	oftenest.
much,	more,	most.
well,	better,	best.
far,	farther,	farthest.
wisely,	more wisely,	most wisely.
justly,	more justly,	most justly.
justly,	less justly,	least justly.

You will generally know an adverb at sight ; but sometimes

that conciseness, as well as copiousness and perspicuity in language, is the offspring of refinement. That an immense amount of time and breath is saved by the use of adverbs, the following development will clearly demonstrate. He who is successful in contracting one mode of expression that is daily used by thirty millions, doubtless does much for their benefit.

Most adverbs express in one word what would otherwise require two or

you will find it more difficult to be distinguished, than any other part of speech in the English language. I will, therefore, give you some *signs* which will assist you a little.

Most words ending in *ly* are adverbs; such as, *politely, gracefully, judiciously.* Any word or short phrase that will answer to any one of the questions, *how ? how much ? when ? or where ?* is an adverb; as, The river flows *rapidly ;* He walks *very fast ;* He has gone *far away ;* but he will *soon* return ; She sings *sweetly ;* They learn *none at all.* How, or in what manner does the river flow ? *Rapidly.* How does he walk ? *Very fast.* Where has he gone ? *Far away.* When will he return ? *Soon.* How does she sing ? *Sweetly.* How much do they learn ? *None at all.* From this illustration, you perceive, that, if you could not tell these adverbs by the sense, you would know them by their answering to the questions. However, your better way will be to distinguish adverbs by considering the office they perform in the sentence ; or by noticing their grammatical relation, or their situation, with respect to other words. To gain a thorough knowledge of their real character, is highly important. *Rapidly, fast, far away, soon, sweetly,* &c. are known to be adverbs by their qualifying the sense of verbs. " A *very* good pen writes *extremely well."* *Well,* in this sentence, is known to be an adverb by its qualifying the sense of the verb *writes ; extremely,* by its ending in *ly,* or by its being joined to the adverb *well* to qualify it ; and *very* is known as an adverb by its joining the adjective *good.*

Expressions like these, *none at all, a great deal, a few days ago, long since, at length, in vain,* when they are used to denote the *manner* or *time* of the action of verbs or participles, are generally termed *adverbial phrases.*

---

more words; as, " He did it *here,*" for, He did it *in this place ; there,* for, *in that place ; where,* for, *in what place ; now,* for, *at this time.* *Why* means *for what reason ; how*—*in what mind, mood, mode,* or *manner ; exceedingly*—*to a great degree ; very*—*in an eminent degree ; often* and *seldom* signify *many times, few times.*

The procedures by which words have been contracted, modified and combined, to form this class of words, have been various. The most prolific family of this illegitimate race, are those in *ly,* a contraction of *like. Gentleman-ly,* means *gentleman-like, like* a gentleman. We do not yet say, *ladily,* but *lady-like.* The north Britons still say, *wiselike, manlike,* instead of, *wise ly, manly.*

Quick comes from *gwick,* the past part. of the Anglo-Saxon verb *gwiccian,* to vivify, give life. *Quick-ly* or *live-ly,* means, in a *quick-like* or *life-like* manner ; in the manner of a creature that has *life. Rapid-ly*—*rapid-like, like* a *rapid ;* a *quick-ly* or *swift-ly* running place in a stream.

Al-ways, contraction of *in all ways.* By a slight transition, it means *in* or

Adverbs, though very numerous, may, for the sake of practical convenience, be reduced to particular classes.

1. *Of Number ;* as, Once, twice, thrice, &c.
2. *Of Order ;* as, First, secondly, lastly, finally, &c.
3. *Of Place ;* as, Here, there, where, elsewhere, anywhere, somewhere, nowhere, herein, whither, hither, thither, upward, downward, forward, backward, whence, thence, whithersoever, &c.
4. *Of Time.*
   Present ; as, Now, to-day, &c.
   Past ; as, Already, before, lately, yesterday, heretofore, hitherto, long since, long ago, &c.
   Future ; as, To-morrow, not yet, hereafter, henceforth, henceforward, by and by, instantly, presently, immediately, ere long, straightways, &c.
   Time indefinite ; as, Oft, often, oft-times, often-times, sometimes, soon, seldom, daily, weekly, monthly, yearly, always, when, then, ever, never, again, &c.
5. *Of Quantity ;* as, Much, little, sufficiently, how much, how great, enough, abundantly, &c.
6. *Of Manner* or *quality ;* as, Wisely, foolishly, justly, unjustly, quickly, slowly, &c. Adverbs of quality are the most numerous kind; and they are generally formed by adding the termination *ly* to an adjective or a participle, or by changing *le* into *ly ;* as, Bad, badly ; cheerful, cheerfully ; able, ably ; admirable, admirably.
7. *Of Doubt ;* as, Haply, perhaps, peradventure, possibly, perchance.
8. *Of Affirmation;* as, Verily, truly, undoubtedly, doubtless, certainly, yea, yes, surely, indeed, really, &c.
9. *Of Negation ;* as, Nay, no, not, by no means, not at all, in no wise, &c.
10. *Of Interrogation ;* as, How, why, wherefore, whither, &c., and sometimes when, whence, where.

---

at all times. Al-one, contraction of *all-one. On-ly—one-like. Al-so—all the same* (thing.) *Ever—an age.* For *ever* and *ever—*for *ages* and *ages.* Ever is not synonymous with always. *Never—ne ever.* It signifies *no age, no period of time. No,* contraction of *not. Not,* a modification of *no-thing, noth-ing, naught.* " He is *not* greater"—is greater *in naught—in no thing.*

Adrift is the past part. *adrifed, adrif'd, adrift ;* from the Saxon *drifan,* or *adrifan,* to drive. *Ago,* formerly written *ygo, gon, agon, gone, agone,* is the past part. of the verb *to go.* It refers to time *gone by. Asunder,* the Saxon past part. *asundren,* from the verb *sondrian* or *asondrian,* to separate. *Aloft—on the loft, on luft, on lyft ; lyft* being the Anglo-Saxon word for *air* or *clouds. Astray,* the part. of *straegan,* to stray. *Awry,* part. of *wrythan,* to writhe.

Needs—need-is ; anciently, *nedes, nede is.*

11. *Of Comparison ;* as, More, most, better, best, worse, worst, less, least, very, almost, little, alike, &c.

NOTES.

1. This catalogue contains but a small portion of the adverbs in our language. Many adverbs are formed by a combination of prepositions with the adverbs of place, *here, there, where;* as, Hereof, thereof, whereof; hereto, thereto, whereto; hereby, thereby, whereby; herewith, therewith, wherewith; herein, therein, wherein; therefore, (i. e. there-for,) wherefore, (i. e where-for,) hereupon, hereon, thereupon, thereon, whereupon, whereon, &c.

2. Some adverbs are composed of nouns or verbs and the letter *a,* used instead of *at, on,* &c.; as, Aside, athirst, afoot, asleep, aboard, ashore, abed, aground, afloat, adrift, aghast, ago, askance, away, asunder, astray, &c.

You will now please to read this lecture *four* times over, and read slowly and carefully, for unless you understand well the nature and character of this part of speech, you will be frequently at a loss to distinguish it from others in composition. Now do you notice, that, in this sentence which you have just read, the words *slowly, carefully, well,* and *frequently,* are adverbs? And do you again observe, that, in the question I have just put to you, the words *now* and *just* are adverbs? Exercise a little sober thought. Fifteen minutes spent in reflection, are worth whole days occupied in careless reading.

In the following exercises six parts of speech are presented, namely, Nouns, Verbs, Articles, Adjectives, Participles, and Adverbs; and I believe you are now prepared to parse them all agreeably to the systematic order, *four* times over. Those words in *italics* are adverbs.

SYSTEMATIC ORDER OF PARSING.

The order of parsing an ADVERB, is—an adverb, and why?—what sort?—what does it qualify?— RULE.

" My friend has returned *again ;* but his health is *not very* good."
Again, is an adverb, a word used to modify the sense of a verb—of time indefinite, it expresses a period of time not precisely defined—it qualifies the verb "has returned," according to

---

To-*wit,* the infinitive of *witan,* to know. It means, *to be known.*
Ay or *yea* signifies *have it, enjoy it. Yes* is *ay-es,* have, possess, enjoy *that.* Our corrupt *o-yes* of the crier, is the French imperative, *oyez,* hear, listen.
Straight way—by a straight way. *While*—*wheel;* period in which some thing *whiles* or *wheels* itself round. *Till*—to while.
Per, Latin,—the English *by.* Perhaps—per haps, per chance.
These examples of derivation are given with the view to invite the attention of the intelligent pupil to the " Diversions of Purley, by John Horne Tooke."

RULE 29. *Adverbs qualify verbs, participles, adjectives, and other adverbs.*

Not is an adverb, a word used to modify the sense of an adverb—of negation, it makes the assertion negative; that is, it changes the proposition from an affirmative to a negative—and it qualifies the adverb "very," agreeably to RULE 29. *Adverbs qualify verbs, &c.*

Very is an adverb, a word used to qualify the sense of an adjective—of comparison, it compares the adjective "good," and qualifies it according to RULE 29. *Adverbs qualify adjectives, &c.*

EXERCISES IN PARSING.

The traveller described a lofty castle decaying *gradually.* *Very* few literary men *ever* became distinguished poets. The great Milton excels *not* Homer. The Roman women, *once voluntarily* contributed their *most* precious jewels to save the city.

Many small streams uniting, form *very* large rivers. The river Funza falling *perpendicularly* forms a vast cataract. Attentive servants *always* drive horses *very carefully;* negligent servants *often* drive horses *very carelessly.* Assiduous scholars improve *very fast;* idle scholars learn *none at all.* Friendship *often* ends in love; but love in friendship, *never.*

NOTE. Several adverbs frequently qualify one verb. Have you walked? *Not yet quite far enough, perhaps. Not, yet, far,* and *enough,* qualify " have walked" understood; *perhaps* qualifies *not;* and *quite* qualifies *far.* The adverbs *always* and *carefully* both qualify the verb "drive :" the former expresses *time,* and the latter, *manner.* *Once* and *voluntarily* qualify the verb "contributed ;" the former expresses *number,* and the latter, *manner.* The word *their* you need not parse. The active verb *to save* has no nominative. The nouns *love* and *friendship,* following *in,* are in the objective case, and governed by that preposition.

REMARKS ON ADVERBS.

When the words *therefore, consequently, accordingly,* and the like, are used in connexion with other conjunctions, they are *adverbs;* but when they appear single, they are commonly considered *conjunctions.*

The words *when* and *where,* and all others of the same nature, such as *whence, whither, whenever, wherever, till, until, before, otherwise, while, wherefore,* &c. may be properly called *adverbial conjunctions,* because they participate the nature both of adverbs and conjunctions; of adverbs, as they denote the attributes either of *time* or *place;* of conjunctions, as they *conjoin sentences.*

There are many words that are sometimes used as adjectives, and sometimes as adverbs; as, " *More* men than women were there ; I am *more* diligent than he." In the former sentence *more* is evidently an adjective, for it is joined to a noun to qualify it; in the latter it is an adverb, because it qualifies an adjective. There are others that are sometimes used as nouns, and sometimes as adverbs; as, " *to-day's* lesson is longer than *yesterday's.*" In this example, *to-day* and *yesterday* are nouns in the possessive case ; but in

phrases like the following, they are generally considered adverbs of time:
" He came [*to his*] *home yesterday,* and will set out again *to-day.*" Here
they are nouns, if we supply *on* before them.

" Where *much* [*wealth, talent,* or something else] is given, *much* [*increase,
improvement*] will be required ; *Much* money has been expended ; It is *much*
better to write than starve." In the first two of these examples, *much* is an
adjective, because it qualifies a noun ; in the last, an adverb, because it
qualifies the adjective *better.* In short, you must determine to what part of
speech a word belongs, by its *sense,* or by considering the *manner* in whic
it is associated with other words.

An adjective may, in general, be distinguished from an *adverb* by this rule
when a word qualifies a *noun* or *pronoun,* it is an adjective, but when it
qualifies a *verb, participle, adjective,* or *adverb,* it is an adverb.

Prepositions are sometimes erroneously called adverbs, when their nouns
are understood. " He rides *about ;*" that is, about the *town, country,* or
some-*thing* else. " She was *near* [the *act* or *misfortune of*] falling ;" " But
do not *after* [that *time* or *event*] lay the blame on me." " He came *down*
[the *ascent*] from the hill ;" " They lifted him *up* [the *ascent*] out of the pit."
" The angels *above ;*"—above *us*—" Above these lower *heavens,* to us invisi
ble, or dimly seen."

Before you proceed to correct the following exercises in false
Syntax, you may answer these

QUESTIONS NOT ANSWERED IN PARSING.

Does an adverb ever qualify a noun ?—What parts of speech
does it qualify ?—When an adverb qualifies a verb or participle,
what does it express ?—When an adverb qualifies an adjective
or adverb, what does it generally express ?—Compare some adverbs.—By what signs may an adverb be known ?—Give examples.—Repeat some *adverbial phrases.*—Name the different
classes of adverbs.—Repeat some of each class.—Repeat the
order of parsing an adverb.—What rule do you apply in parsing
an adverb ?

QUESTIONS ON THE NOTES.

Repeat some adverbs that are formed by combining prepositions with adverbs of place.—Repeat some that are composed of the article *a* and nouns.
—What part of speech are the words, *therefore, consequently,* &c. ?—What
words are styled *adverbial conjunctions ?*—Why are they so called ?—Is the
same word sometimes used as an adjective, and sometimes as an adverb ?—
Give examples.—What is said of *much ?*—By what rule can you distinguish
an adjective from an adverb ?—Do prepositions ever become adverbs ?

QUESTIONS ON THE PHILOSOPHICAL NOTES.

How does the use of adverbs contribute to the conciseness of language ?—
Illustrate the fact.—What is said of *ly, like,* and *quick ?*—How are the following words composed, *always, alone, only, also ?*—What is the meaning
of *ever, never, not, adrift, ago, asunder, aloft, astray, awry ?*—Give the signification of *needs, to-wit, ye, yes, o-yes, straightway, while, till,* and *per.*

NOTE. Learners need not answer the questions on the Philosophical Notes,
in this or any other Lecture, unless the teacher deem it expedient.

EXERCISES IN FALSE SYNTAX.

NOTE 3, TO RULE 29. Adjectives are sometimes improperly applied as adverbs; as, indifferent honest; excellent well; miserable poor :—She writes elegant; He is walking slow.

The adjectives *indifferent, excellent,* and *miserable,* are here improperly used, because adjectives do not express the degree of adjectives or adverbs, but such modifications are denoted by adverbs. The phrases should, therefore, be, " *indifferently* honest, *excellently* well, *miserably* poor." *Elegant* and *slow* are also inaccurate, for it is not the office of the adjective to express the manner, time, or place of the action of verbs and participles, but it is *the office* of the adverb. The constructions should be, " She writes *elegantly;* He is walking *slowly.*"

You may correct the following examples several times over, and explain the principles that are violated.

FALSE SYNTAX.

He speaks fluent, and reasons coherent.

She reads proper, and writes very neat.

They once lived tolerable well, but now they are miserable poor.

The lowering clouds are moving slow.

He behaved himself submissive, and was exceeding careful not to give offence.

NOTE 4, TO RULE 29. Adverbs are sometimes improperly used instead of adjectives; as, " The tutor addressed him in terms rather warm, but *suitably* to his offence."

The adverb *suitably* is incorrect. It does not express the manner of the action of the verb " addressed," but it denotes the *quality* of the noun *terms* understood; for which reason it should be an adjective, *suitable.*

FALSE SYNTAX.

The man was slowly wandering about, *solitarily* and distressed.

He lived in a manner *agreeably* to his condition.

The study of Syntax should be *previously* to that of Punctuation.

He introduced himself in a manner very *abruptly.*

Conformably to their vehemence of thought, was their vehemence of gesture.

I saw him *previously* to his arrival.

LECTURE VII.

OF PREPOSITIONS.

A PREPOSITION is a word which serves to connect words, and show the relation between them.

The term *preposition* is derived from the two Latin words, *pre*, which signifies *before*, and *pono*, *to place*. Prepositions are so called, because they are mostly placed before the nouns and pronouns which they govern in the objective case.

The principal prepositions are presented in the following list, which you may now commit to memory, and thus you will be enabled to distinguish them from other parts of speech whenever you see them in composition.

A LIST OF THE PREPOSITIONS.

of	over	at	after	betwixt
to	under	near	about	beside
for	through	up	against	athwart
by	above	down	unto	towards
with	below	before	across	notwithstanding
in	between	behind	around	out of
into	beneath	off	amidst	instead of
within	from	on upon	throughout	over against
without	beyond	among	underneath	according to

This list contains many words that are sometimes used as conjunctions, and sometimes as adverbs ; but when you shall have become acquainted with the *nature* of the preposition, and of the conjunction and adverb too, you will find no difficulty in ascertaining to which of these classes any word belongs.

By looking at the definition of a preposition, you will notice, that it performs a *double* office in a sentence, namely, it *connects* words, and also shows a *relation* between them. I will first show you the use and importance of this part of speech as a connective. When corn is ripe—October, it is gathered—the field—

PHILOSOPHICAL NOTES.

From, according to H. Tooke, is the Anglo-Saxon and Gothic noun *frum*, beginning, source, author. " He came *from (beginning)* Rochester." *Of* he supposes to be a fragment of the Gothic and Saxon noun *afora*, consequence, offspring, follower. " Solomon, the son *of (offspring)* David." *Of* or *off*, in its modern acceptation, signifies *disjoined, sundered:* A piece *of* (*off*) the loaf, is, a piece *disjoined*, or *separated* from the loaf. The fragrance *of* or *off* the rose.

For signifies *cause*. " I write *for* your satisfaction ;" i. e. your satisfaction being the *cause*. *By* or *be* is the imperative *byth*, of the Saxon *beon*, to be. *With*, the imperative of *withan*, to join ; or, when equivalent to *by*, of *wyr-*

men—who go—hill—hill—baskets,—which they put the ears.
You perceive, that in this sentence there is a total want of connexion and meaning; but let us fill up each vacancy with a
preposition, and the sense will be clear. "When corn is ripe, *in*
October, it is gathered *in* the field *by* men, who go *from* hill *to*
hill *with* baskets, *into* which they put the ears."

From this illustration you are convinced, no doubt, that our
language would be very deficient without prepositions to connect
the various words of which it is composed. It would, in fact,
amount to nothing but nonsense. There is, however, another part
of speech that performs this office, namely, the conjunction.
This will be explained in Lecture IX.; in which lecture you will
learn, that the nature of a preposition, as a connective particle,
is nearly allied to that of a conjunction. In the next place I
will show you how prepositions express a *relation* between
words.

The boy's hat is *under* his arm. In this expression, what
relation does the preposition *under* show? You know that *hat*
and *arm* are words used as signs of two objects, or ideas; but
under is *not* the sign of a thing you can think of: it is merely
the sign of the *relation* existing between the two objects. Hence
you may perceive, that since the word *under* is the sign of the
relation existing between particular *ideas*, it also expresses a relation existing between the words *hat* and *arm*, which words are the
representatives of those ideas.

The boy holds his hat *in* his hand. In this sentence the preposition *in* shows the relation existing between *hat* and *hand*, or the
situation, or relative position, each has in regard to the other. And,
if I say, The boy's hat is *on* his head, you perceive that *on* shows
the relation between *hat* and *head*. Again, in the expressions,
The boy threw his hat *up stairs*—*under* the bed—*behind* the
The boy threw his hat *up stairs*—*under* the bed—*behind* the table—*through* the window—*over* the house—*across* the street—*into*
the water—and so on, you perceive that the several prepositions ex-

---

than, to be. "I will go *with* him." "I, *join* him, will go." *In* comes from
the Gothic noun *inna,* the interior of the body; a cave or cell. *About,* from
boda, the first outward boundary. *Among* is the past part. of *gamaengan,*
to mingle. *Through* or *thorough* is the Gothic substantive *dauro,* or the
Teutonic *thuruh.* It means passage, gate, door.

Before—be-fore, be-hind, be-low, be-side, be-sides, be-neath are formed by
combining the imperative, *be,* with the nouns *fore, hind, low, side, neath.*
Neath—Saxon *neothan, neothe,* has the same signification as *nadir.* *Be-tween,*
be-twixt—be and *twain.* A dual preposition. *Be-yond*—be-passed. *Beyond*
a place, means, *be passed* that place.

Notwithstanding—not-stand-ing-with, not-withstanding. "Any order to
the contrary not-withstanding" (this order;) i. e. *not* effectually *withstanding*
or *opposing* it.

press the different relations existing between the *hat* and the other nouns, *stairs, bed, table, window, house, street,* and *water.*

A preposition tells *where* a thing is : thus, " The pear is *on* the ground, *under* the tree."

Prepositions govern the objective case, but they do *not* express an action done to some object, as an active-transitive verb or participle does. When a noun or pronoun follows a preposition, it s in the objective case, because it is the object of the *relation* expressed by the preposition, and *not* the object of an *action.*

I can now give you a more extensive explanation of the *objective case,* than that which was given in a former lecture. I have already informed you, that the objective case expresses the object of an action *or* of a relation ; and, also, that there are *three* parts of speech which govern nouns and pronouns in the objective case, namely, *active-transitive verbs, participles derived from transitive verbs,* and *prepositions.* A noun or pronoun in the objective case, cannot be, at the same time, the object of an action *and* of a relation. It must be either the object of an action *or* of a relation. And I wish you particularly to remember, that whenever a noun or pronoun is governed by a transitive verb or participle, it is the object of an *action ;* as, The tutor *instructs* his *pupils ;* or, The tutor is *instructing* his *pupils ;* but whenever a noun or pronoun is governed by a preposition, it is the object of a *relation ;* as, The tutor gives good instruction *to* his *pupils.*

Before you proceed to parse the following examples, please to review this lecture, and then the whole seven in the manner previously recommended, namely, read one or two sentences, and then look off your book and repeat them two or three times over in your mind. This course will enable you to retain the most important ideas advanced. If you wish to proceed with ease and advantage, you must have the subject-matter of the preceding lectures stored in your mind. Do not consider it an unpleasant task to comply with my requisitions, for when you shall have learned thus far, you will understand *seven* parts of speech ; and only *three* more will remain to be learned.

If you have complied with the foregoing request, you may commit the following *order,* and then proceed in parsing.

SYSTEMATIC ORDER OF PARSING.

The order of parsing a PREPOSITION, is—a preposition, and why ?—what does it connect ?—what relation does it show ?

"He saw an antelope *in* the *wilderness*."

In is a preposition, a word which serves to connect words, and show the relation between them—it connects the words "antelope" and "wilderness"—and shows the relation between them.

Wilderness is a noun, the name of a place—com. the name of a sort or species—neut. gend. it denotes a thing without sex—third pers. spoken of—sing. num. it implies but one—and in the objective case, it is the object of a *relation* expressed by the preposition "in," and governed by it, according to

RULE 31. *Prepositions govern the objective case.*

The genius of our language will not allow us to say, Stand before *he ;* Hand the paper to *they.* Prepositions *require* the pronoun following them to be in the objective form, position, or case ; and this requisition amounts to *government.* Hence we say, "Stand before *him ;*" "Hand the paper to *them.*" Every preposition expresses a relation, and every relation must have an *object :* consequently, every preposition must be followed by a noun or pronoun in the objective case.

EXERCISES IN PARSING.

The all-wise Creator bestowed the power of speech upon man, for the most excellent uses. Augustus heard the orator pleading the client's cause, in a flow of most powerful eloquence. Fair Cynthia smiles serenely over nature's soft repose. Life's varying schemes no more distract the laboring mind of man. Septimius stabbed Pompey standing on the shore of Egypt.

A beam of tranquillity often plays round the heart of the truly pious man. The thoughts of former years glide over my soul, like swift-shooting meteors over Ardven's gloomy vales.

At the approach of day, night's swift dragons cut the clouds full fast ; and ghosts, wandering here and there, troop home to church-yards.

> Love still pursues an ever devious race,
> True to the winding lineaments of grace.

NOTE.—The words *my* and *and* you need not parse. The noun "meteors," following the adverb "like," is in the objective case, and governed by *unto* understood, according to NOTE 2, under Rule 32. The noun "home" is governed by *to* understood, according to Rule 32.

REMARKS ON PREPOSITIONS AND VERBS.

A noun or pronoun in the objective case, is often governed by a preposition understood ; as, "Give *him* that book ;" that is, "Give that book *to* him ;" "Ortugrul was one *day* wandering," &c. that is, *on* one day. "Mercy gives *affliction* a grace ;" that is, Mercy gives a grace *to* affliction. See Note 1, under Rule 32.

To be able to make a proper use of prepositions, particular attention is requisite. There is a peculiar propriety to be observed in the use of *by* and *with;* as, " He walks *with* a staff *by* moonlight ;" " He was taken *by* strata gem, and killed *with* a sword." Put the one preposition for the other, and say, " He walks *by* a staff *with* moonlight ;" " He was taken *with* stratagem, and killed *by* a sword ;" and it will appear, that the latter expressions differ from the former in signification, more than one, at first view, would be apt to imagine.

Verbs are often compounded of a verb and a *preposition;* as, to *up*hold, to *with*stand, to *over*look; and this composition gives a new meaning to the verb ; as, to *under*stand, to *with*draw, to *for*give. But the preposition is more frequently placed after the verb, and separately from it, like an ad verb; in which situation it does not less affect the sense of the verb, and give it a new meaning ; and in all instances, whether the preposition is placed either before or after the verb, if it gives a new meaning to the verb, it may be considered as *a part of the verb.* Thus, *to cast* means *to throw;* but *to cast up* an account, signifies *to compute* it ; therefore *up* is a part of the verb. The phrases, *to fall on, to bear out, to give over,* convey very different mean ings from what they would if the prepositions *on, out,* and *over,* were not used. Verbs of this kind are called *compound* verbs.

You may now answer the following

QUESTIONS NOT ANSWERED IN PARSING.

From what words is the term *preposition* derived ?—Why is it thus named ?—Repeat the list of prepositions.—Name the three parts of speech that govern nouns and pronouns in the objective case.—When is a noun or pronoun in the objective case, the object of an action ?—When is it the object of a relation ?— Repeat the order of parsing a preposition.—What rule do you apply in parsing a noun or pronoun governed by a preposition ?— Does every preposition require an objective case after it ?—Is a noun or pronoun ever governed by a preposition understood ?— Give examples.—What is said of verbs compounded of a verb and preposition ?—Give the origin and meaning of the preposi tions explained in the Philosophical Notes.

LECTURE VIII.

OF PRONOUNS.

A PRONOUN is a word used instead of a noun, and generally to avoid the too frequent repetition of the same word. A pronoun is, likewise, sometimes a substitute for a sentence, or member of a sentence.

The word *pronoun* comes from the two Latin words, *pro,* which means *for,* or *instead of,* and *nomen,* a *name,* or *noun.* Hence you perceive, that *pronoun* means *for a noun,* or *instead of a noun.*

In the sentence, " The man is happy; *he* is benevolent; *he* is useful ;" you perceive, that the word *he* is used instead of the noun *man ;* consequently *he* must be a *pronoun.* You observe, too, that, by making use of the pronoun *he* in this sentence, we avoid the *repetition* of the *noun* man, for without the pronoun, the sentence would be rendered thus, " The man is happy ; *the man* is benevolent ; *the man* is useful."

By looking again at the definition, you will notice, that pro-nouns always *stand for* nouns, but they do not always *avoid the repetition* of nouns. *Repetition* means *repeating* or mentioning the same thing again. In the sentence, " I come to die for my country," the pronouns, *I* and *my, stand* for the name of the per-son who speaks ; but they do not *avoid the repetition* of that name, because the name or noun for which the pronouns are used, is not mentioned at all. Pronouns of the *third* person, generally avoid the repetition of the nouns for which they stand ; but pro-nouns of the *first* and *second* person, sometimes avoid the repeti-tion of nouns, and sometimes they do not.

A little farther illustration of the pronoun will show you its importance, and, also, that its nature is very easily comprehended. If we had no pronouns in our language, we should be obliged to express ourselves in this manner : " A woman went to a man, and told the man that the man was in danger of being murdered by a gang of robbers ; as a gang of robbers had made prepara-tions for attacking the man. The man thanked the woman for the woman's kindness, and, as the man was unable to defend the man's self, the man left the man's house, and went to a neighbor's."

This would be a laborious style indeed ; but, by the help of pronouns, we can express the same ideas with far greater ease and conciseness : " A woman went to a man, and told *him,* that *he* was in great danger of being murdered by a gang of robbers, *who* had made preparations for attacking *him. He* thanked *her* for *her* kindness, and, as *he* was unable to defend *himself, he* left *his* house and went to a neighbor's."

If you look at these examples a few moments, you cannot be at a loss to tell which words are pronouns ; and you will observe too, that they all stand for nouns.

Pronouns are generally divided into three kinds, the *Personal,* the *Adjective,* and the *Relative* pro-nouns. They are all known by the *lists.*

1. OF PERSONAL PRONOUNS.

PERSONAL PRONOUNS are distinguished from the relative, by their denoting the *person* of the nouns for which they stand. There are five of them; *I, thou, he, she, it ;* with their plurals, *We, ye* or *you, they.*

To pronouns belong gender, person, number, and case.

GENDER. When we speak of a *man*, we say, *he, his, him ;* when we speak of a *woman*, we say, *she, hers, her ;* and when we speak of a *thing*, we say *it.* Hence you perceive, that gender belongs to pronouns as well as to nouns. Example; " The general, in gratitude to the lady, offered *her his* hand ; but *she,* not knowing *him,* declined accepting *it.*" The pronouns *his* and *him,* in this sentence, personate or represent the noun *general ;* they are, therefore, of the masculine gender : *her* and *she* personate the *lady ;* therefore, they are feminine : and *it* represents *hand ;* for which reason it is of the neuter gender. This illustration shows you, then, that pronouns must be of the same gender as the nouns are for which they stand. But, as it relates to the variation of the pronouns to express the sex,

Gender has respect only to the third person singular of the pronouns, *he, she, it.* *He* is masculine ; *she* is feminine ; *it* is neuter.

You may naturally inquire, why pronouns of the first and second persons are not varied to denote the gender of their nouns, as well as of the third. The reason is obvious. The first person, that is, the person speaking, and the second person, or the person spoken to, being at the same time the subjects of the discourse, are supposed to be present ; from which, and other circumstances, their sex is commonly known, and, therefore, the pronouns that represent these persons, need not be marked by a distinction of gender ; but the third person, that is, the person or thing spoken of, being absent, and in many respects unknown, necessarily requires the pronoun that stands for it, to be marked by a distinction of gender.

In parsing, we sometimes apply gender to pronouns of the first and second person, and also to the plural number of the third person ; but these have no peculiar form to denote their gender ; therefore they have no agreement, in this respect, with the nouns which they represent.

PERSON.   Pronouns have three persons **in each** number.

I, is the first person

Thou, is the second person } Singular.

He, she, or *it*, is the third person

We, is the first person

Ye or *you*, is the second person } Plural.

They, is the third person

This account of persons will be very intelligible, when you reflect, that there are three persons who may be the subject of any discourse : first, the person who speaks, may speak of himself; secondly, he may speak of the person to whom he addresses himself; thirdly, he may speak of some other person ; and as the speakers, the persons spoken to, and the persons spoken of, may be many, so each of these persons must have a plural number.

Pronouns of the second and third person, always agree in person with the nouns they represent ; but pronouns of the first person, do not. Whenever a pronoun of the first person is used, it represents a noun ; but nouns are *never* of the first person, therefore these pronouns cannot agree in person with their nouns.

NUMBER.   Pronouns, like nouns, have two numbers, the singular and the plural; as, *I, thou, he ; we, ye* or *you, they.*

CASE.   Pronouns have three cases, the nominative, the possessive, and the objective.

In the next place I will present to you the *declension* of the personal pronouns, which declension you must commit to memory before you proceed any farther.

The advantages resulting from the committing of the following declension, are so great and diversified, that you cannot be too particular in your attention to it.   You recollect, that it is sometimes very difficult to distinguish the nominative case of a noun from the objective, because these cases of nouns are not marked by a difference in termination ; but this difficulty is removed in regard to the personal pronouns, for their cases are always known by their termination.   By studying the declension you will learn, not only the cases of the pronouns, but, also, their genders, persons, and numbers.

DECLENSION OF THE PERSONAL PRONOUNS.

FIRST PERSON.

Sing.	*Plur.*
Nom. I,	we,
Poss. my *or* mine,	our *or* ours,
Obj. me.	us.

SECOND PERSON.

Sing.	*Plur.*
Nom. thou,	ye *or* you,
Poss. thy *or* thine,	your *or* yours,
Obj. thee.	you.

THIRD PERSON.

Mas. Sing.	*Plur.*
Nom. he,	they,
Poss. his,	their *or* theirs,
Obj. him.	them.

THIRD PERSON.

Fem. Sing.	*Plur.*
Nom. she,	they,
Poss. her *or* hers,	their *or* theirs,
Obj. her.	them.

THIRD PERSON.

Neut. Sing.	*Plur.*
Nom. it,	they,
Poss. its,	their *or* theirs,
Obj. it.	them.

NOTES.

1. When *self* is added to the personal pronouns, as himself, myself, itself, themselves, &c. they are called *compound personal pronouns*, and are used in the nominative or objective case, but not in the possessive.

2. In order to avoid the disagreeable harshness of sound, occasioned by the frequent recurrence of the terminations *est, edst,* in the adaptation of our verbs to the nominative *thou*, a modern innovation which substitutes *you* for *thou*, in familiar style, has generally been adopted. This innovation contributes greatly to the harmony of our colloquial style. *You* was formerly restricted to the plural number; but now it is employed to represent either a singular or a plural noun. It ought to be recollected, however, that when used as the representative of a singular noun, this word retains its original *plural form;* and, therefore, the verb connected with it, should always be

plural. Inattention to this peculiarity, has betrayed some writers into the erroneous conclusion, that, because *you* implies unity when it represents a singular noun, it ought, when thus employed, to be followed by a singular verb; as, "When *was you* there ?" "How far *was you* from the parties ?" Such a construction, however, is not supported by *good* usage, nor by analogy. It is as manifest a solecism as to say, We *am*, or we *is*. Were it, in any case, admissible to connect a singular verb with *you*, the use of *was* would still be ungrammatical, for this form of the verb is confined to the first and third persons, and *you* is second person. *Wast* being second person, it would approximate nearer to correctness to say, you *wast*. We never use the singular of the present tense with you:—you *art*, you *is*; you *walkest*, you *walks*. Why, then, should any attempt be made to force a usage so unnatural and gratuitous as the connecting of the singular verb in the past tense with this pronoun ? In every point of view, the construction, "When *were* you there ?" "How far *were* you from the parties ?" is preferable to the other.

3. The words *my, thy, his, her, our, your, their*, are, by many, denominated *possessive adjective pronouns;* but they always *stand for* nouns in the possessive case. They ought, therefore, to be classed with the *personal* pronouns. That principle of classification which ranks them with the adjective pronouns, would also throw all nouns in the possessive case among the adjectives. Example : " The lady gave the gentleman *her* watch for *his* horse." In this sentence *her* personates, or stands for, the noun "lady," and *his* represents "gentleman." This fact is clearly shown by rendering the sentence thus, " The lady gave the gentleman the *lady's* watch for the *gentleman's* horse." If *lady's* and *gentleman's* are nouns, *her* and *his* must be personal pronouns. The same remarks apply to *my, thy, our, your, their,* and *its*. This view of these words may be objected to by those who speculate and refine upon the principles of grammar until they prove their non-existence, but it is believed, nevertheless, to be based on sound reason and common sense.

4. *Mine, thine, his, hers, ours, yours, theirs*, have, by many respectable grammarians, been considered merely the possessive cases of personal pronouns, whilst, by others, they have been denominated pronouns or nouns in the nominative or objective case. It is believed, however, that a little attention to the meaning and office of these words, will clearly show the impropriety of both these classifications. Those who pursue the former arrangement, allege, that, in the examples, "You may imagine what kind of faith *theirs* was; My pleasures are past; *hers* and *yours* are to come; they applauded his conduct, but condemned *hers* and *yours*," the words *theirs, hers,* and *yours*, are personal pronouns in the possessive case, and governed by their respective nouns understood. To prove this, they construct the sentence thus, "You may imagine what kind of faith *their faith* was ;—*her pleasures* and *your pleasures* are to come ;—but condemned *her conduct* and *your conduct;*" or thus, " You may imagine what kind of faith the faith of them was ;—the pleasures of her and the pleasures of you, are to come ;— but condemned the conduct of her and the conduct of you." But these constructions, (both of which are correct,) prove too much for their purpose ; for, as soon as we supply the nouns after these words, they are resolved into personal pronouns of kindred meaning, and the nouns which we supply: thus, *theirs* becomes, their faith : *hers*, her pleasures ; and *yours*, your pleasures. This evidently gives us two words instead of, and altogether distinct from, the first ; so that, in parsing, *their faith*, we are not, in reality, analyzing *theirs*, but two other words of which *theirs* is the proper representative. These remarks also prove, with equal force, the impropriety of calling these words merely simple pronouns or nouns in the nominative or objective case. Without attempting to develop the original or intrinsic meaning of

these pluralizing adjuncts, *ne* and *s*, which were, no doubt, formerly detached from the pronouns with which they now coalesce, for all practical purposes, it is sufficient for us to know, that, in the present application of these pronouns, they invariably stand for, not only the person possessing, but, also the thing possessed, which gives them a *compound* character. They may, therefore, be properly denominated Compound Personal Pronouns; and, as they always perform a double office in a sentence by representing two other words, and, consequently, including two cases, they should, like the compound relative *what*, be parsed as two words. Thus, in the example, "You may imagine what kind of faith theirs was," *theirs* is a compound personal pronoun, equivalent to *their faith*. *Their* is a pronoun, a word used instead of a noun; personal, it personates the persons spoken of, understood; third pers. plur. numb., &c.—and in the possessive case, and governed by "faith," according to Rule 12. *Faith* is a noun, the name of a thing, &c. &c.—and in the nominative case to "was," and governs it; Rule 3. Or, if we render the sentence thus, "You may imagine what kind of faith *the faith of them** was," *faith* would be in the nominative case to "was," and *them* would be in the objective case, and governed by "of:" Rule 31.

Objections to this method of treating these pronouns, will doubtless be preferred by those who assert, that a noun is understood after these words, and not represented by them. But this is assertion without proof; for, if a noun were understood, it might be supplied. If the question be put, whose book? and the answer be, *mine, ours, hers,* or *theirs,* the word book is included in such answer. Were it not included, we might supply it, thus, mine *book,* ours *book,* hers *book,* and so on. This, however, we cannot do, for it would be giving a *double* answer: but when the question is answered by a noun in the possessive case, the word book is not included, but implied; as, Whose book? John's, Richard's; that is, John's *book;* Richard's *book.*

This view of the subject, without a parallel, except in the compounds *what, whoever,* and *others,* is respectfully submitted to the public; believing, that those who approve of a critical analysis of words, will coincide with me. Should any still be disposed to treat these words so superficially as to rank them among the simple pronouns, let them answer the following interrogatory: If *what,* when compound, should be parsed as two words, why not *mine, thine, his, hers, ours, yours,* and *theirs?*

5. *Mine* and *thine,* instead of *my* and *thy,* are used in solemn style, before a word beginning with a vowel or silent *h;* as, "Blot out all *mine* iniquities;" and when thus used, they are not compound. *His* always has the same form, whether simple or compound; as, "Give John *his* book; That desk is *his.*" *Her,* when placed before a noun, is in the possessive case; as, Take *her* hat: when standing alone, it is in the objective case; as, Give the hat to *her.*

When you shall have studied this lecture attentively, and committed the *declension* of the personal pronouns, you may commit the following

SYSTEMATIC ORDER OF PARSING.

The order of parsing a Personal Pronoun, *is—a*

---

* In the note next preceding, it is asserted, that my, thy, his, her, our your, and their, are personal pronouns. What can more clearly demonstrate the correctness of that assertion, than this latter construction of the word theirs? All admit, that, in the construction, "The faith *of them,*" the word *them* is a personal pronoun: and for this conclusive reason:—it represents a

pronoun, and why?—personal, and why?—person, and why?—gender and number, and why?—RULE: case, and why?—RULE.—Decline it.

There are many peculiarities to be observed in parsing personal pronouns in their different persons; therefore, if you wish ever to parse them correctly, you must pay particular attention o the manner in which the following are analyzed. Now notice, particularly, and you will perceive that we apply only *one* rule in parsing *I* and *my*, and *two* in parsing *thou, him,* and *they.*

" I saw my friend."

I is a pronoun, a word used instead of a noun—personal, it represents the person speaking, understood—first person, it denotes the speaker—singular number, it implies but one—and in the nominative case, it represents the actor and subject of the verb "saw," and governs it, agreeably to RULE 3. *The nom. case gov. the verb.* Declined—first pers. sing. num. nom. I, poss. my or mine, obj. me. Plur. nom. we, poss. our or ours, obj. us.

My is a pronoun, a word used instead of a noun—personal, it personates the person speaking, understood—first pers. it denotes the speaker—sing. num. it implies but one—and in the possessive case, it denotes possession; it is governed by the noun " friend," agreeably to RULE 12. *A noun or pronoun in the possessive case, is governed by the noun it possesses.* Declined—first pers. sing. nom. I, poss. my or mine, obj. me. Plur. nom. we, poss. our or ours, obj. us.

" Young man, thou hast deserted thy companion, and left him in distress."

Thou is a pronoun, a word used instead of a noun—personal, it personates " man "—second person, it represents the person spoken to—mas. gend. sing. num. because the noun " man " is for which it stands, according to

RULE 13. *Personal pronouns must agree with the nouns for which they stand in gender and number.*

Thou is in the nom. case, it represents the actor and subject of the verb " hast deserted," and governs it agreeably to RULE 3. *The nom. case governs the verb.* Declined—sec. pers. sing. num. nom. thou, poss. thy or thine, obj. thee. Plur. nom. ye or you, poss. your or yours, obj. you.

Him is a pronoun, a word used instead of a noun—personal, it personates " companion "—third pers. it represents the person

<hr>

noun understood. What, then, is *their*, in the phrase, " their faith?" Is it not obvious, that, if *them* is a personal pronoun, *their* must be, also? for the latter represents the same noun as the former.

spoken of—mas. gend. sing. num. because the noun "companion" is for which it stands: RULE 13. *Pers. pro. &c.* (Repeat the Rule.)—*Him* is in the objective case, the object of the action expressed by the active-transitive verb " hast left," and gov. by it: RULE 20. *Active-trans. verbs gov. the obj. case.* Declined—third pers. mas. gend. sing. num. nom. he, poss. his, obj. him. Plur. nom. they, poss. their or theirs, obj. them.

" Thrice I raised my voice, and called the chiefs to combat, but *they* dreaded the force of my arm."

They is a pronoun, a word used instead of a noun—personal, it represents " chiefs"—third pers. it denotes the persons spoken of—mas. gend. plur. num. because the noun " chiefs" is for which it stands: RULE 13. *Pers. Pron. &c.* (Repeat the Rule.) It is the nom. case, it represents the actors and subject of the verb " dreaded," and governs it: RULE 3. *The nom. case, gov. the verb.* Declined—third pers. mas. gend. sing. num. nom. he, poss. his, obj. him. Plur. nom. they, poss. their or theirs, obj. them.

NOTE. We do not apply gender in parsing the personal pronouns, (excepting the third person singular,) if the nouns they represent are understood ; and therefore we do not, in such instances, apply Rule 13. But when the noun is expressed, gender should be applied, and *two* Rules.

EXERCISES IN PARSING.

I saw a man leading his horse slowly over the new bridge. My friends visit me very often at my father's office. We improve ourselves by close application. Horace, thou learnest many lessons. Charles, you, by your diligence, make easy work of the task given you by your preceptor. Young ladies, you run over your lessons very carelessly. The stranger drove his horses too far into the water, and, in so doing, he drowned them.

Gray morning rose in the east. A green narrow vale appeared before us: its winding stream murmured through the grove. The dark host of Rothmar stood on its banks. with their glittering spears. We fought along the vale. They fled. Rothmar sunk beneath my sword. Day was descending in the west, when I brought his arms to Crothar. The aged hero felt them with his hands: joy brightened his thoughts.

NOTE. *Horace, Charles,* and *ladies,* are of the second person, and nom. case *independent:* see RULE 5, and NOTE. The first *you* is used in the nom. poss. and obj. case.—It represents Charles, therefore it is *singular* in sense, although plural in form. In the next example, *you* personifies *ladies,* therefore it is *plural. Given* is a perfect participle. *You* following given, is governed by *to* understood, according to NOTE 1, under Rule 32. *Run over* is a compound verb. *And* is a conjunction. The first *its* personates vale ; the second *its* represents stream.

You may now parse the following examples three times over.

COMPOUND PERSONAL PRONOUNS.

"Juliet, retain her paper, and present *yours.*"

Yours is a compound personal pronoun, representing both the possessor and the thing possessed, and is equivalent to *your paper.* *Your* is a pronoun, a word used instead of a noun—personal, it personates "Juliet"—second person, it represents the person spoken to—fem. gender, sing. number, (singular in sense, but *plura,* in form,) because the noun Juliet is for which it stands: Rule 13. *Pers. Pron. &c.*—*Your* is in the possessive case, it denotes possession, and is governed by "paper," according to Rule 12. *A noun or pron. &c.* (Repeat the Rule, and decline the pronoun.) *Paper* is a noun, the name of a thing—common, the name of a sort of things—neuter gender, it denotes a thing without sex—third person, spoken of—sing. number, it implies but one—and in the obj. case, it is the object of the action expressed by the transitive verb "present," and governed by it: Rule 20. *Active-transitive verbs govern the obj. case.*

NOTE. Should it be objected, that *yours* does not mean *your paper,* any more than it means *your book, your house, your* any thing, let it be borne in mind, that pronouns have no *definite* meaning, like other words; but their *particular* signification is always determined by the nouns they represent.

EXERCISES IN PARSING.

Julia injured her book, and soiled mine: hers is better than mine. My friend sacrificed his fortune to secure yours: his deeds deserve reward; yours merit disgrace. Henry's labors are past; thine are to come. We leave your forests of beasts for ours of men. My sword and yours are kin.

NOTE. *She* understood, is nominative to *soiled,* in the first example; and the substantive part of *mine,* after than, is nom. to *is,* understood: Rule 35. The verbs *to secure* and *to come* have no nominative. The pronouns *mine, my, yours, thine, we, your, ours, my,* and *yours,* personate nouns understood.

REMARKS ON *IT.*

For the want of a proper knowledge of this little pronoun *it,* many grammarians have been greatly puzzled how to dispose of it, or how to account for its multiform, and, seemingly, contradictory characters. It is in great demand by writers of every description. They use it without ceremony; either in the nominative or objective case; either to represent one person or thing, or more than one. It is applied to nouns in the masculine, feminine, or neuter gender, and, very frequently, it represents a member of a sentence a whole sentence, or a number of sentences taken in a mass.

A little attention to its true character, will, at once, strip it of all its mystery. *It,* formerly written *hit,* according to H. Tooke, is the past participle of the Moeso-Gothic verb *haitan.* It means, *the said,* and, therefore, like its near relative *that,* meaning, *the assumed,* originally had no respect, in its application, to number, person, or gender. "*It* is a wholesome law;" i. e. *the said* (law) is a wholesome law ; or, *that* (law) is a wholesome law ;—*the assumed* (law) is a wholesome law. " *It* is the man; I believe *it* to be them :"—*the said* (man) is the man ; *that* (man) is the man : I believe *the said* (persons) to be them ; I believe *that* persons (according to the ancient application of *that*) to be them. " *It* happened on a summer's day, that many people were assembled," &c.—Many people were assembled : *it*, *that*, or *the said* (fact or circumstance) happened on a summer's day.

It, according to its accepted meaning in modern times, is not referred to a noun understood after it, but is considered a substitute. " How is *it* with you ?" that is, How is your *state* or *condition* ?" " *It* rains ; *It* freezes ; *It* is a hard winter ;"—*The rain* rains ; *The frost* frosts or freezes ; *The said* (winter) is a hard winter. " *It* is delightful to see brothers and sisters living in uninterrupted love to the end of their days." What is delightful ? *To see brothers and sisters living in uninterrupted love to the end of their days. It, this thing*, is delightful. *It*, then, stands for all that part of the sentence expressed in italics; and the sentence will admit of the following construction; " To see brothers living in uninterrupted love to the end of their days, is delightful."

OF ADJECTIVE PRONOUNS.

ADJECTIVE PRONOUNS, PRONOMINAL ADJECTIVES, or, more properly, SPECIFYING ADJECTIVES, are a kind of adjectives which point out nouns by some distinct specification.

Pronouns and adjectives are totally distinct in their character. The former *stand for* nouns, and never belong to them ; the latter *belong to* nouns, and never stand for them. Hence, such a thing as an *adjective-pronoun* cannot exist. *Each, every, either, this, that, some, other*, and the residue, are pure adjectives.

Those specifying adjectives commonly called Adjective Pronouns, may be divided into three sorts ; the *distributive*, the *demonstrative*, and the *indefinite*. They are all known by the *lists*.

I. The *distributive adjectives* are those that denote the persons or things that make up a number, each taken separately and singly. *List : each, every, either*, and sometimes *neither* ; as, " *Each* of his brothers is in a favorable situation;" " *Every* man must account for himself;" " *Neither* of them is industrious."

These distributives are words which are introduced into language in its refined state, in order to express the nicest shades and colors of thought. " *Man* must account for himself;" "*Mankind* must account for themselves ;" " *All men* must account for themselves ;" " *All men, women*, and *children*, must ac-

count for themselves;" "*Every man* must account for himself."
Each of these assertions conveys the same fact or truth.   But
the last, instead of presenting the whole human family for the
mind to contemplate in a mass, by the peculiar force of *every,*
distributes them, and presents each separately and singly ; and
whatever is affirmed of one individual, the mind instantaneously
transfers to the whole human race.

Each relates to two or more persons or things, and signifies either of the
two, or every one of any number taken separately.

Every relates to several persons or things, and signifies each one of them
all taken separately.

Either relates to *two* persons or things taken separately, and signifies the
one or the other. " *Either* of the *three,*" is an improper expression.   It
should be, " any of the three."

Neither imports *not either ;* that is, not one nor the other ; as, " *Neither* of
my friends was there."   When an allusion is made to more than *two, none*
should be used instead of *neither ;* as, " *None* of my friends was there."

II. The *demonstrative* are those which precisely
point out the subject to which they relate.   *List :*
this and *that,* and their plurals, *these* and *those,* and
former and *latter ;* as, " *This* is true charity; " *that*
is only its image."

There is but a slight shade of difference in the meaning and
application of *the* and *that.*   When reference is made to a particular book, we say, " Take *the* book ;" but when we wish to
be very pointed and precise, we say, " Take *that* book ;" or, if it
be near by, " Take *this* book."   You perceive, then, that these
demonstratives have all the force of the definite article, and a
little more.

This and *these* refer to the nearest persons or things, *that* and *those* to the
most distant; as, " *These* goods are superior to those."   *This* and *these* indi-
cate the latter, or last mentioned ; *that* and *those,* the former, or first mentioned ; as, " Both *wealth* and *poverty* are temptations; *that* tends to excite
pride, *this,* discontent."

　　　" *Some* place the bliss in action, *some* in ease ;
　　　Those call it pleasure, and contentment, *these.*"

They, those.   As it is the office of the personal *they* to represent a noun
previously introduced to our notice, there appears to be a slight departure
from analogy in the following application of it: " *They* who seek after wisdom, are sure to find her: *They* that sow in tears, sometimes reap in joy."
This usage, however, is well established, and *they,* in such constructions, is
generally employed in preference to *those.*

III. The *indefinite* are those which express their
subjects in an indefinite or general manner.   *List :*
some, other, any, one, all, such, both, same, another,

none. Of these, *one* and *other* are declined like nouns. *Another* is declined, but wants the plural.

The indefinite adjectives, like the indefinite article, leave the meaning unfixed, or, in some degree, vague. With a slight shade of difference in meaning, we say, Give me *a* paper, *one* paper, *any* paper, *some* paper, and so on. Though these words restrict the meaning of the noun, they do not fix it to a *particular* object. We therefore call them indefinite.

These adjectives, or adjective pronouns, frequently belong to nouns under-stood, in which situation they should be parsed accordingly; as, " You may take *either;* He is pleased with *this* book, but dislikes *that* (book;) *All* (men) have sinned, but *some* (men) have repented."

The words, *one*, *other*, and *none*, are used in both numbers ; and, when they *stand for* nouns, they are not adjectives, but indefinite *pronouns ;* as, " The great *ones* of the world have their failings ;" "Some men increase in wealth, while *others* decrease ;" " *None* escape."

The word " ones," in the preceding example, does not belong to a noun understood. If it did, we could supply the noun. The meaning is not " the great one men, nor ones men," therefore *one* is not an adjective pronoun ; but the meaning is, " The great *men* of the world," therefore *ones* is a pronoun of the indefinite kind, representing the noun *men* understood, and it ought to be parsed like a personal pronoun. The word *others*, in the next example, is a compound pronoun, equivalent to *other men ;* and should be parsed like *mine, thine, &c.* See Note 4th, page 100.

I will now parse two pronouns, and then present some examples for you to analyze. If, in parsing the following exercises, you should be at a loss for definitions and rules, please to refer to the compendium. But before you proceed, you may commit the following

SYSTEMATIC ORDER OF PARSING.

The order of parsing an ADJECTIVE PRONOUN, is—an adjective pronoun, and why ?—distributive, demonstrative, or indefinite, and why ?—to what noun does it belong, or with what does it agree ?—RULE.

" *One* man instructs many *others.*"
One is an adjective pronoun, or specifying adjective, it speci-

fically points out a noun—indefinite, it expresses its subject in an indefinite or general manner, and belongs to the noun " man," according to

RULE 19. *Adjective pronouns belong to nouns, expressed or understood.*

Others is a compound pronoun, including both an adjective pronoun and a noun, and is equivalent to *other men. Other* is an adjective pronoun, it is used specifically to describe its noun—indefinite, it expresses its subject in an indefinite manner, and belongs to *men :* Rule 19. (Repeat the rule.) *Men* is a noun, a name denoting persons—common, &c. (parse it in full ;) and in the objective case, it is the object of the action expressed by the transitive verb " instructs," and gov. by it : Rule 20. *Active-transitive verbs, &c.*

" *Those* books are *mine.*"

Those is an adjective pronoun, it specifies what noun is referred to—demonstrative, it precisely points out the subject to which it relates—and agrees with the noun " books" in the plural number, according to NOTE 1, under Rule 19. *Adjective pronouns must agree in number with their nouns.*

Mine is a compound personal pronoun, including both the possessor and the thing possessed, and is equivalent to *my books. My* is a pron. a word used instead of a noun—personal, it stands for the name of the person speaking—first person, it denotes the speaker—sing. number, it implies but one—and in the poss. case, it denotes possession, and is gov. by " books," according to Rule 12. (Repeat the rule, and decline the pronoun.) *Books* is a noun, the name of a thing—common, &c. (parse it in full ;)—and in the nominative case after " are," according to RULE 21. *The verb* to be *admits the same case after it as before it.*

EXERCISES IN PARSING.

Each individual fills a space in creation. Every man helps a little. These men rank among the great ones of the world. That book belongs to the tutor, this belongs to me. Some men labor, others labor not ; the former increase in wealth, the latter decrease. The boy wounded the old bird, and stole the young ones. None performs his duty too well. None of those poor wretches complain of their miserable lot.

NOTE. In parsing the distributive pronominal adjectives, NOTE 2, unde Rule 19, should be applied.

III. OF RELATIVE PRONOUNS.

RELATIVE PRONOUNS are such as relate, in general,

to some word or phrase going before, which is called the antecedent. They are *who, which,* and *that.*

The word *antecedent,* comes from the two Latin words, *ante, before,* and *cedo, to go.* Hence you perceive, that antecedent means going before; thus, "The *man* is happy *who* lives virtuously; This is the *lady who* relieved my wants; *Thou who* lovest wisdom, &c. *We who* speak from experience," &c. The relative who, in these sentences, relates to the several words, *man, lady, thou,* and *we,* which words, you observe, come before the relative: they are, therefore, properly called antecedents.

The relative is not varied on account of gender, person, or number, like a personal pronoun. When we use a personal pronoun, in speaking of a man, we say *he,* and of a woman, *she;* in speaking of one person or thing, we use a singular pronoun, of more than one, a plural, and so on; but there is no such variation of the relative. *Who,* in the first of the preceding examples, relates to an antecedent of the mas. gend. third pers. sing.; in the second, the antecedent is of the fem. gend.; in the third, it is of the second pers.; and in the fourth, it is of the first pers. plur. num.; and, yet, the relative is in the same form in each example. Hence you perceive, that the relative has no peculiar *form* to denote its gend. pers. and num., but it always agrees with its antecedent *in sense.* Thus, when I say, The *man who* writes, *who* is mas. gend. and sing.; but when I say, The *ladies who* write, *who* is feminine, and plural. In order to ascertain the gend. pers. and num. of the relative, you must always look at its antecedent.

Who, Which, and That.

Who is applied to *persons, which* to *things* and *brutes;* as, "He is a *friend who* is faithful in adversity; The *bird which* sung so sweetly, is flown; This is the *tree which* produces no fruit."

That is often used as a relative, to prevent the too frequent repetition of *who* and *which.* It is applied both to persons and things; as, "He *that* acts wisely, deserves praise; Modesty is a *quality that* highly adorns a woman."

NOTES.

1. *Who* should never be applied to animals. The following application of it is erroneous:—"He is like a *beast* of prey, *who* destroys without pity." It should be, *that* destroys, &c.

2. *Who* should not be applied to children. It is incorrect to say, The *child whom* we have just seen," &c. It should be, " The child *that* we have just seen."

3. *Which* may be applied to persons when we wish to distinguish one person of two, or a particular person among a number of others; as, " *Which* of the two? *Which* of them is he ?"

4. *That*, in preference to *who* or *which*, is applied to persons when they are qualified by an adjective in the superlative degree, or by the pronominal adjective *same;* as, " Charles XII., king of Sweden, was one of the *greatest* madmen *that* the world ever saw ;—He is the *same* man *that* we saw before."

5. *That* is employed after the interrogative *who*, in cases like the following; " Who *that* has any sense of religion, would have argued thus ?"

When the word *ever* or *soever* is annexed to a relative pronoun, the combination is called a *compound pronoun ;* as, *whoever* or *whosoever, whichever* or *whichsoever, whatever* or *whatsoever.*

DECLENSION OF THE RELATIVE PRONOUNS.
SINGULAR AND PLURAL.

Nom. who,	*Poss.* whose,	*Obj.* whom.
" whoever,	" whosever,	" whomever.
" whosoever,	" whosesoever,	" whomsoever.

Which and *that* are indeclinable, except that *whose* is some. times used as the possessive case of *which ;* as, "Is there any other doctrine *whose* followers are punished ;" that is, the followers *of which* are punished. The use of this license has obtained among our best writers ; but the construction is not to be recommended, for it is a departure from a plain principle of grammar, namely, who, whose, whom, in their applications, should be confined to rational beings.

That may be used as a pronoun, an adjective, and a conjunction, depending on the office which it performs in the sentence.

That is a relative only when it can be changed to *who* or *which* without destroying the sense; as, " They *that* (who) reprove us, may be our best friends ; From every thing *that* (which) you see, derive instruction." *That* is a demonstrative adjective, when it belongs to, or points out, some particular noun, either expressed or implied ; as, " Return *that* book ; *That* belongs to me ; Give me *that.*" When *that* is neither a relative nor an adjective pronoun, it is a conjunction ; as, " Take care *that* every day be well employed." The word *that*, in this last sentence, cannot be changed to *who* or *which* without destroying the sense, therefore you know it is not a relative pronoun ; neither does it point out any particular noun, for which reason you know it is not an adjective pronoun ; but it connects the sentence, therefore it is a conjunction.

If you pay particular attention to this elucidation of the word *that*, you will find no difficulty in parsing it. When it is a relative or an adjective pronoun, it may be known by the signs given; and whenever these signs will not apply to it, you know it is a conjunction.

Some writers are apt to make too free use of this word. I will give you one example of affronted *that*, which may serve as a caution. The tutor said, in speaking of the word that, that that that that lady parsed, was not the that that that gentleman requested her to analyze. This sentence, though rendered inelegant by a bad choice of words, is strictly grammatical. The first *that* is a noun; the second, a conjunction; the third, an adjective pronoun; the fourth, a noun; the fifth, a relative pronoun; the sixth, an adjective pronoun; the seventh, a noun; the eighth, a relative pronoun; the ninth, an adjective pronoun. The meaning of the sentence will be more obvious, if rendered thus; The tutor said, in speaking of the word that, that that that *which* that lady parsed, was not the that *which* that gentleman requested her to analyze.

WHAT.

What is generally a compound relative, including both the antecedent and the relative, and is equivalent to *that which;* as, "This is *what* I wanted;" that is, *that which,* or, *the thing which* I wanted.

What is compounded of *which that.* These words have been contracted and made to coalesce, a part of the orthography of both being still retained: *what—wh[ich—t]hat; (which-that.)* Anciently it appeared in the varying forms, *tha qua, qua tha, qu'tha, quthat, quhat, hwat,* and finally, *what.*

What may be used as three kinds of a pronoun, and as an interjection. When it is equivalent to *that which, the thing which, those things which,* it is a compound relative, because it includes both the antecedent and the relative; as, "I will try *what* (that which) can be found in female delicacy; *What* you recollect with most pleasure, are the virtuous actions of your past life;" that is, *those things which* you recollect, &c.

When *what* is a compound relative, you must always parse it as two words; that is, you must parse the antecedent part as a noun, and give it a case; the relative part you may analyze like any other relative, giving it a case likewise. In the first of the preceding examples, *that,* the antecedent part of *what,* is in the obj. case, governed by the verb "will try;" *which,* the relative part, is in the nom. case to "can be found." "I have heard *what* (i. e. *that which*, or *the thing which*) has been alleged."

Whoever and *whosoever* are also compound relatives, and should be parsed like the compound *what ;* as, " *Whoever* takes that oath, is bound to enforce the laws." In this sentence, *whoever* is equivalent to *he who*, or, *the man who ;* thus, " *He who* takes that oath, is bound," &c.

Who, which, and *what,* when used in asking questions, are called interrogative pronouns, or relatives of the interrogative kind ; as, " *Who* is he ? *Which* is the person ? *What* are you doing ? "

Interrogative pronouns have no ántecedent ; but they relate to the word or phrase which is the answer to the question, for their subsequent ; as, " *Whom* did you see ? The *preceptor. What* have you done ? *Nothing.*" Antecedent and subsequent are opposed to each other in signification. Antecedent means preceding, or going before ; and subsequent means following, or coming after. *What,* when used as an interrogative, is never compound.

What, which, and *that,* when joined to nouns, are specifying adjectives, or adjective pronouns, in which situation they have no case, but are parsed like adjective pronouns of the demonstrative or indefinite kind ; as, " Unto *which* promise our twelve tribes hope to come ;" " *What* misery the vicious endure ! *What* havock hast thou made, foul monster, sin ! "

What and *which,* when joined to nouns in asking questions, are denominated interrogative pronominal adjectives ; as, " *What man* is that ? *Which road* did he take ? "

What, whatever, and *whatsoever, which, whichever,* and *whichsoever,* in constructions like the following, are compound pronouns, but not compound relatives ; as, " In *what* character Butler was admitted, is unknown ; Give him *what* name you choose ; Nature's care largely endows *whatever* happy man will deign to use her treasures ; Let him take *which* course, or, *whichever* course he will." These sentences may be rendered thus ; " *That* character, or, *the* character in *which* Butler was admitted, is unknown ; Give him *that* name, or, *the* name *which* you choose ; Nature's care endows *that* happy man *who* will deign, &c. ; Let him take *that* course, or, *the* course *which* he will." A compound relative necessarily includes both an antecedent and a relative. These compounds, you will notice, do not include antecedents, the first part of each word being the article *the*, or the adjective pronoun, *that ;* therefore they cannot properly be denominated compound relatives.—With regard to the word *ever* annexed to these pronouns, it is a singular fact, that, as soon as we analyze the word to which it is subjoined, *ever* is entirely excluded from the sentence.

What is sometimes used as an interjection; as, " But *what!* is thy servant a dog, that he should do this? *What!* rob us of our right of suffrage, and then shut us up in dungeons!"

You have now come to the most formidable obstacle, or, if I may so speak, to the most rugged eminence in the path of grammatical science; but be not disheartened, for, if you can get safely over this, your future course will be interrupted with only here and there a gentle elevation. It will require close application, and a great deal of sober thinking, to gain a clear conception of the nature of the relative pronouns, particularly the compound relatives, which are not easily comprehended by the young learner. As this eighth lecture is a very important one, it becomes necessary for you to read it carefully four or five times over before you proceed to commit the following order. Whenever you parse, you may spread the Compendium before you, if you please.

SYSTEMATIC ORDER OF PARSING.

The order of parsing a RELATIVE PRONOUN, is— a pronoun, and why?—relative, and why?—gender, person, and number, and why?—RULE:—case, and why?—RULE.—Decline it.

" This is the man *whom* we saw."

Whom is a pronoun, a word used instead of a noun—relative, it relates to "man" for its antecedent—mas. gend. third pers. sing. num. because the antecedent "man" is with which it agrees, according to

RULE 14. *Relative pronouns agree with their antecedents in gender, person, and number.* *Whom* is in the objective case, the object of the action expressed by the active-transitive verb "saw," and governed by it, agreeably to

RULE 16. *When a nominative comes between the relative and the verb, the relative is governed by the following verb, or some other word in its own member of the sentence.*

Whom, in the objective case, is placed before the verb that governs it, according to NOTE 1, under Rule 16. (Repeat the Note, and decline *who*.)

" From *what* is recorded, he appears," &c.

What is a comp. rel. pron. including both the antecedent and the relative, and is equivalent to *that which*, or the *thing which*— *Thing*, the antecedent part of *what*, is a noun, the name of a

10*

thing—com. the name of a species—neuter gender, it has no sex—third person, spoken of—sing. number, it implies but one—and in the obj. case, it is the object of the relation expressed by the prep. " from," and gov. by it : RULE 31.   (Repeat the Rule, and every other Rule to which I refer.)   *Which*, the relative part of *what*, is a pronoun, a word used instead of a noun—relative, it relates to " thing" for its antecedent—neut. gender, third person, sing. number, because the antecedent " thing" is with which it agrees, according to RULE 14.   *Rel. pron.* &c.   *Which* is in the nom. case to the verb " is recorded," agreeably to

RULE 15.   *The relative is the nominative case to the verb, when no nominative comes between it and the verb.*

" *What* have you learned?   Nothing."

What is a pron. a word used, &c.—relative of the interrogative kind, because it is used in asking a question—it refers to the word " nothing" for its *subsequent*, according to

RULE 17.   *When the rel. pron. is of the interrog. kind, it refers to the word or phrase containing the answer to the question, for its subsequent, which subsequent must agree in case with the interrogative.*   *What* is of the neut. gend. third pers. sing. because the subsequent " nothing" is with which it agrees ; RULE 14.   *Rel. pron. agree*, &c.—It is in the obj. case, the object of the action, of the active-transitive verb " have learned," and gov. by it, agreeably to RULE 16.   *When a nom.* &c.   See NOTE 1, under the Rule.

NOTE. 1. You need not apply gend. pers. and numb. to the interrogative when the answer to the question is *not* expressed.

WHO, WHICH, WHAT.

Truth and simplicity are twin sisters, and generally go hand in hand.   The foregoing exposition of the "relative pronouns," is in accordance with the usual method of treating them ; but if they were unfolded according to their true character, they would be found to be very simple, and, *doubtless*, much labor and perplexity, on the part of the learner, would thereby be saved.

Of the words called " relatives," *who*, only, is a pronoun ; and this is strictly *personal ;* more so, indeed, if we except *I* and *we*, than any other word in our language, for it is always restricted to persons.   It ought to be classed with the personal pronouns. *I, thou, he, she, it, we, ye, you,* and *they, relate* to antecedents, as well as *who*.   *Which, that,* and *what,* are always adjectives. They never *stand for*, but always *belong* to nouns, either expressed or implied.   They *specify*, like many other adjectives, and *connect* sentences.

Who supplies the place of *which* or *what* and its *personal*

noun. *Who* came ? i. e. *what man, what woman, what person ;—which man, woman,* or *person,* came ? " They heard *what* I said"—they heard *that* (thing) *which* (thing) I said. " Take *what* (or *whichever*) course you please ;"—take *that* course *which* (course) you please to take. " *What* have you done ?" i. e. *what thing, act,* or *deed* have you done ? " *Which thing* I also did at Jerusalem." " *Which* will you take ?"—*which book, hat,* or something else ? " This is the tree *which* (tree) produces no fruit." " He *that* (man, or *which* man) acts wisely, deserves praise."

They who prefer this method of treating the " relatives," are at liberty to adopt it, and parse accordingly.

EXERCISES IN PARSING.

The man who instructs you, labors faithfully. The boy whom I instruct, learns well. The lady whose house we occupy, bestows many charities. That modesty which highly adorns a woman, she possesses. He that acts wisely deserves praise. This is the tree which produces no fruit. I believe what he says. He speaks what he knows. Whatever purifies the heart, also fortifies it. What doest* thou ? Nothing. What book have you ? A poem. Whose hat have you ? John's. Who does that work ? Henry. Whom seest thou ? To whom gave you the present ? Which pen did he take ? Whom ye ignorantly worship, him declare I unto you. I heard what he said. George, you may pursue whatever science suits your taste. Eliza, take whichever pattern pleases you best. Whoever lives to see this republic forsake her moral and literary institutiens, will behold her liberties prostrated. Whosoever, therefore, will be a friend of the world, is the enemy of God.

NOTE. The nominative case is frequently placed after the verb, and the objective case, before the verb that governs it. *Whom,* in every sentence except one, *house, modesty, book, hat, pen, him,* the third *what* and *which,* the relative part of the first *two whats,* are all in the *objective* case, and governed by the several verbs that follow them. See RULE 16, and NOTE 1. *Tree* is nom. after is, according to RULE 21. Thing, the antecedent part of *whatever,* is nom. to " fortifies ;" *which,* the relative part, is nom. to " purifies." *Nothing* is governed by *do,* and *poem,* by *have,* understood. *Henry* is nomina tive to *does,* understood. *Whose* and *John's* are governed according to RULE 12. *I, thou, you, him,* &c. represent nouns understood. *Him,* in the last sen tence but five, is governed by *declare,* and *I* is nominative to *declare. George* and *Eliza* are in the nominative case independent: Rule 5. " *Whatever* science," &c. is equivalent to, *that* science *which* suits your taste ;—" *whichever* pattern ;" i. e. *that* pattern *which* pleases you best. *Whoever* is a com-

---

* The second person singular of *do,* when used as a principal verb, is spelled with an *e ;* thus, " What thou *doest,* do quickly ;" but when employed as an auxiliary, the *e* should be omitted ; as, " *Dost* thou not *behold* a rock with its head of heath ?"

pound relative; *he*, the antecedent part, is nominative to "**will behold.**"
Take agrees with *you* understood. *Forsake* is in the infinitive mood after
" see :" Rule 25.

REMARKS ON RELATIVE PRONOUNS.

Which sometimes relates to a member of a sentence, or to a whole sentence, for its antecedent: as, " We are required to fear God and keep his
commandments, *which* is the whole duty of man." What is the whole duty
of man? " To fear God and keep his commandments:" therefore, this
phrase is the antecedent to *which*.

The conjunction *as*, when it follows *such, many,* or *same,* is frequently denominated a relative pronoun ; as, " I am pleased with *such as* have a refined
taste ;" that is, with *those who,* or *them who have,* &c. " Let *such as* presume
to advise others, look well to their own conduct ;" that is, Let *those,* or *them
who* presume, &c. " *As many as* were ordained to eternal life, believed ;" that
is, *they, those,* or *all who* were ordained, believed. " He exhibited the *same*
testimonials *as* were adduced on a former occasion ;" that is, *those* testimonials *which* were adduced, &c. But, in examples like these, if we supply the
ellipsis which a critical analysis requires us to do, *as* will be found to be a
conjunction ; thus, " I am pleased with *such persons, as those persons are who*
have a refined taste ; Let *such persons, as those persons are who* presume," &c.

QUESTIONS NOT ANSWERED IN PARSING.

From what words is the term pronoun derived ?—Do pronouns
always avoid the repetition of nouns ?—Name the three kinds of
pronouns.—What distinguishes the personal from the relative
pronouns ?—How many personal pronouns are there ?—Repeat
them.—What belong to pronouns ?—Is gender applied to all the
personal pronouns ?—To which of them is it applied ?—Which
of the personal pronouns have no peculiar termination to denote
their gender ?—How many persons have pronouns ?—Speak them
in their different persons.—How many numbers have pronouns ?—
How many cases ?—What are they ?—Decline all the personal
pronouns.—When *self* is added to the personal pronouns, what
are they called, and how are they used ?—When is *you* singular
in sense ?—Is it ever singular in form ?—Why are the words, *my,
thy, his, her, our, your, their,* called personal pronouns ?—Why
are the words, *mine, thine, his, hers, ours, yours, theirs,* denominated
compound pers. pron.?—How do you parse these compounds ?—
What is said of *others ?*—Repeat the order of parsing a personal
pronoun.—What rule do you apply in parsing a pronoun of the
first person, and in the nom. case ?—What rule when the pronoun is in the possessive case ?—What Rules apply in parsing
personal pronouns of the second and third person ?—What Rules
in parsing the compounds, *yours, ours, mine,* &c.?—What is said
of the pronoun *it ?*

What are adjective pronouns ?—Name the three kinds.—What
does *each* relate to ?—To what does *every* relate ?—To what does
either relate ?—What does *neither* import ?—To what do *this* and

these refer ?—Give examples.—To what do *that* and *those* refer ?—
Give examples.—Repeat all the adjective pronouns.—When adj.
pronouns belong to nouns understood, how are they parsed ?—
When they stand for, or represent nouns, what are they called ?—
Give examples.—Repeat the order of parsing an adj. pronoun.—
What Rule do you apply in parsing the indefinite adjective pro-
nouns ?—What Notes, in parsing the distributives and demon-
stratives ?

What are relative pronouns ?—Repeat them.—From what
words is the term antecedent derived ?—What does *antecedent*
mean ?—Are relatives varied on account of gender, person, or
number ?—To what are *who* and *which* applied ?—To what is
that applied ?—Should *who* ever be applied to irrational beings or
children ?—In what instances may *which* be applied to persons ?—
Decline the rel. pronouns.—Can *which* and *that* be declined ?—
Is *that* ever used as three parts of speech ?—Give examples.—
What part of speech is the word *what ?*—Is *what* ever used as
three kinds of a pronoun ?—Give examples.—What is said of
whoever?—What words are used as interrogative pronouns ?—
Give examples.—When are the words, *what, which,* and *that,*
called adj. pron.?—When are they called interrogative pronominal adjectives ?—What is said of *whatever* and *whichever ?*—Is
what ever used as an interjection ?—Give examples.—Repeat the
order of parsing a rel. pron.—What Rules do you apply in parsing a relative ?—What Rules in parsing a compound relative ?—
What Rules in parsing an interrogative ?—Does the relative
which ever relate to a sentence for its antecedent?—When does
the conjunction *as* become a relative ?—Give examples.

EXERCISES IN FALSE SYNTAX.

NOTE 1, to RULE 13.   When a noun or pronoun is the subject
of a verb, it must be in the nominative case.

Who will go ?   Him and I.   How does thee do ?   Is thee well ?

" Him and I ;" not proper, because the pronoun *him* is the subject of the
verb *will go* understood, therefore him should be in the nominative case, *he,*
according to the above NOTE. (Repeat the NOTE.) *Him* and *I* are connected by the conjunction *and,* and *him* is in the obj. case, and *I* in the nom.,
therefore RULE 33d, is violated. (Repeat the Rule.) In the second and
third examples, *thee* should be *thou,* according to the NOTE. The verbs, *does*
and *is,* are of the third person, and the nom. *thou* is second, for which reason
the verbs should be of the second person, *dost do* and *art,* agreeably to
RULE 4.   You may correct the other examples, *four* times over.

FALSE SYNTAX.

Him and me went to town yesterday.   Thee must be attentive.
Him who is careless, will not improve.   They can write as well

as me. This is the man whom was expected. Her and I deserve esteem. I have made greater proficiency than him. Whom,
of all my acquaintances, do you think was there? Whom, for
the sake of his important services, had an office of honor bestowed
upon him.

NOTE 2, to RULE 13. Personal pronouns being used to supply
the place of nouns, should not be employed in the same member
of the sentence with the noun which they represent.

FALSE SYNTAX.

The men they are there. I saw him the king. Our cause it
is just. Many words they darken speech. That noble general
who had gained so many victories, he died, at last, in prison.
Who, instead of going about doing good, they are continually
doing evil.

In each of the preceding examples, the personal pronoun should be omitted,
according to Note 2.

NOTE 3, to RULE 13. A personal pronoun in the objective
case, should not be used instead of *these* and *those*.

FALSE SYNTAX.

Remove them papers from the desk. Give me them books.
Give them men their discharge. Observe them three there.
Which of them two persons deserves most credit?

In all these examples, *those* should be used in place of *them*. The use of
the personal, *them*, in such constructions, presents two objectives after one
verb or preposition. This is a solecism which may be avoided by employing
an adjective pronoun in its stead.

LECTURE IX.

OF CONJUNCTIONS.

A CONJUNCTION is a part of speech that is chiefly
used to connect sentences, joining two or more simple sentences into one compound sentence: it sometimes connects only words; as, "Thou *and* he are
happy, *because* you are good."

Conjunctions are those parts of language, which, by joining
sentences in different ways, mark the connexions and various
dependances of human thought. They belong to language only
in its refined state.

The term Conjunction comes from the two Latin words, *con*, which signifies *together*, and *jungo*, to *join*. A conjunction, then, is a word that conjoins, or joins together something. Before you can fully comprehend the nature and office of this sort of words, it is requisite that you should know what is meant by a sentence, a simple sentence, and a compound sentence, for conjunctions are chiefly used to connect sentences.

A Sentence is an assemblage of words forming complete sense.

A Simple Sentence contains but one subject, or nominative, and one verb which agrees with that nominative; as, " *Wheat grows* in the field."

You perceive that this sentence contains several words besides the nominative and the verb, and you will often see a simple sentence containing many parts of speech; but, if it has only one nominative and one *finite* verb, (that is, a verb *not* in the infinitive mood,) it is a simple sentence, though it is longer than many compound sentences.

A Compound Sentence is composed of two or more simple sentences connected together; as, " *Wheat grows* in the field, and *men reap* it."

This sentence is compound, because it is formed of two simple sentences joined together by the word *and ;* which word, on account of its connecting power, is called a conjunction. If we write this sentence without the conjunction, it becomes two simple sentences: thus, " Wheat grows in the field. Men reap it."

The nature and importance of the conjunction, are easily illustrated. After expressing one thought or sentiment, you know we frequently wish to *add* another, or several others, which are closely connected with it. We generally effect this addition by means of the conjunction: thus, " The Georgians cultivate rice *and* cotton ;" that is, " They cultivate rice *add* cotton." This sentence is compound, and without the use of the conjunction, it would be written in two separate, simple sentences: thus, " The Georgians cultivate rice. They cultivate cotton." The conjunction, though chiefly used to connect sentences, sometimes connects only words; in which capacity it is nearly allied to the preposition; as, " The sun *and* (*add*) the planets constitute the solar system." In this, which is a simple sentence, *and* connects two *words*.

A few more examples will illustrate the nature, and exhibit

the use of this part of speech so clearly, as to enable you fully to comprehend it. The following simple sentences and members of sentences, have no relation to each other until they are connected by conjunctions. He labors harder—more successfully— I do. That man is healthy—he is temperate. By filling up the vacancies in these sentences with conjunctions, you will see the importance of this sort of words : thus, He labors harder *and* more successfully *than* I do. That man is healthy *because* he is temperate.

Conjunctions are divided into two sorts, the Copulative and Disjunctive.

I. The Conjunction *Copulative* serves to connect and continue a sentence by joining on a member which expresses an addition, a supposition, or a cause ; as, " Two *and* three are five ; I will go *if* he will accompany me ; You are happy *because* you are good."

In the first of these examples, *and* joins on a word that expresses an *addition ;* in the second, *if* connects a member that implies a *supposition* or *condition ;* and in the third, *because* connects a member that expresses a *cause.*

II. The Conjunction *Disjunctive* serves to connect and continue a sentence by joining on a member that expresses opposition of meaning ; as, " They came with her, *but* they went away without her."

But joins on a member of this sentence which expresses, not only something added, but, also, *opposition* of meaning.

The principal conjunctions may be known by the following *lists*, which you may now commit to memory. Some words in these lists, are, however, frequently used as adverbs, and sometimes as prepositions ; but if you study well the nature of all the different sorts of words, you cannot be at a loss to tell the part of speech of any word in the language.

PHILOSOPHICAL NOTES.

On scientific principles, our *connectives*, commonly denominated prepositions and conjunctions, are but one part of speech, the distinction between them being merely technical. Some conjunctions unite only words, and some prepositions connect sentences. They are derived from nouns and verbs ; and the time has been, when, perhaps, in our language, they did not perform the office of connectives.

" I wish you to believe, *that* I would not wilfully hurt a fly." Here, in the

LISTS OF THE CONJUNCTIONS.

Copulative. And, if, that, both, then, since, for, because, therefore, wherefore, provided, besides.

Disjunctive. But, or, nor, as, than, lest, though, unless, either, neither, yet, notwithstanding, nevertheless, except, whether, whereas, as well as.

Some conjunctions are followed by corresponding conjunctions, so that, in the subsequent member of the sentence, the latter answers to the former; as,

1. *Though—yet* or *nevertheless;* as, " *Though* he was rich, *yet* for our sakes he became poor."

2. *Whether—or;* as, " *Whether* he will go, *or* not, I cannot tell." It is improper to say, " Whether he will go or *no.*"

3. *Either—or;* as, " I will *either* send it, *or* bring it myself."

4. *Neither—nor;* as, " *Neither* thou *nor* I can comprehend it."

5. *As—as;* as, " She is *as* amiable *as* her sister."

6. *As—so;* as, " *As* the stars, *so* shall thy seed be."

7. *So—as;* as, " To see thy glory, *so as* I have seen thee in tne sanctuary."

8. *So—that;* as, " He became *so* vain, *that* every one disliked him."

NOTES.

1. Some conjunctions are used to connect simple *sentences* only, and form them into compound *sentences;* such as, further, again, besides, &c. Others are employed to connect simple *members* only, so as to make them compound *members;* such as, than, lest, unless, that, so that, if, though, yet, because, as well as, &c. But, and, therefore, or, nor, for, &c., connect either whole sentences, or simple members.

2. Relative pronouns, as well as conjunctions, serve to connect sentences; as, " Blessed is the man *who* feareth the Lord, *and* keepeth his commandments."

---

opinion of H. Tooke, our modern conjunction *that,* is merely a demonstrative adjective, in a disguised form; and he attempts to prove it by the following resolution: " I would not wilfully hurt a fly. I wish you to believe *that* [*assertion.*"] Now, if we admit, that *that* is an adjective in the latter construction, it does not necessarily follow, that it is the same part of speech, nor that its associated meaning is precisely the same, in the former construction. Instead of expressing our ideas in two detached sentences, by the former phraseology we have a quicker and closer transition of thought, and both the mode of employing *that,* and its *inferential* meaning, are changed. Moreover, if we examine the meaning of each of these constructions, taken as a whole, we shall find, that they do not both convey the same ideas. By the latter, I assert, positively, that " I would not wilfully hurt a fly;" whereas, by the former, I merely *wish you to believe* that " I would not wilfully hurt a fly;" but I do not *affirm* that as a fact.

That being the past part. of *thean,* to get, take, assume, by rendering it as

You will now please to turn back and read this lecture four or five times over ; and then, after committing the following order, you may parse the subsequent exercises.

SYSTEMATIC ORDER OF PARSING.

The order of parsing a CONJUNCTION, is—a conjunction, and why ?—copulative or disjunctive, and why ?—what does it connect?

"Wisdom *and* virtue *form* the good man's character."

And is a conjunction, a word that is chiefly used to connect sentences ; but in this example it connects only words—copulative, it serves to connect and continue the sentence by joining on a member which expresses an addition—it connects the words "wisdom and virtue."

Wisdom is a noun, the name of a thing—(You may parse it in full.)—*Wisdom* is one of the nominatives to the verb "form."

Virtue is a noun, the name, &c.—(Parse it in full :)—and in the nom. case to the verb "form," and connected to the noun "wisdom" by *and*, according to

RULE 33. *Conjunctions connect nouns and pronouns in the same case.*

Form is a verb, a word which signifies to do, &c.—of the third person, *plural*, because its two nominatives, "wisdom and virtue," are connected by a copulative conjunction, agreeably to

RULE 8. *Two or more nouns in the singular number, joined by copulative conjunctions, must have verbs, nouns, and pronouns agreeing with them in the* plural.

"Wisdom *or* folly *governs* us."

Or is a conjunction, a word that is chiefly used to connect sentences : it sometimes connects words—disjunctive, it serves not only to connect and continue the sentence, but also to join on a member which expresses opposition of meaning—it connects the nouns "wisdom and folly."

---

a *participle*, instead of an adjective, we should come nearer to its primitive character. Thus, " I would not wilfully hurt a fly. I wish you to believe the *assumed* [*fact* or *statement* ;] or, the fact *assumed* or *taken*."

If, (formerly written *gif, give, gin,*) as previously stated, is the imperative of the Anglo-Saxon verb *gifan*, to give. In imitation of Horne Tooke, some of our modern philosophical writers are inclined to teach pupils to render it as a verb. Thus, " I will go, *if* he will accompany me :"—" He will accompany me. *Grant—give* that [fact] I will go." For the purpose of ascertaining the *primitive* meaning of this word, I have no objection to such a resolution ; but, by it, do we get the exact meaning and force of *if* as it is applied in our modern, refined state of the language ? I *trow* not. But, admitting we do, does this prove that such a mode of resolving sentences can be

Governs is a verb, a word that signifies, &c.—of the third person, singular number, agreeing with "wisdom or folly," according to

RULE 9. *Two or more nouns singular, joined by* disjunctive *conjunctions, must have verbs, nouns, and pronouns agreeing with them in the* singular:

If you reflect, for a few moments, on the meaning of the last two Rules presented, you will see, at once, their propriety and importance. For example; in the sentence, "Orlando *and* Thomas, *who study their lessons, make* rapid progress," you notice that the two singular nouns, *Orlando* and *Thomas*, are connected by the copulative conjunction *and*, therefore the verb *make*, which agrees with them, is plural, because it expresses the action of *both* its nominatives or actors. And you observe, too, that the pronouns *who* and *their*, and the noun *lessons*, are *plural*, agreeing with the nouns *Orlando* and *Thomas*, according to RULE 8. The verb *study* is plural, agreeing with *who*, according to RULE 4.

But let us connect these two nouns by a disjunctive conjunction, and see how the sentence will read: "Orlando *or* Thomas, *who studies his lesson, makes* rapid progress." Now, you perceive, that a different construction takes place, for the latter expression does not imply, that Orlando and Thomas, *both* study and make rapid progress; but it asserts, that either the one *or* the other studies, and makes rapid progress. Hence the verb *makes* is singular, because it expresses the action of the one *or* the other of its nominatives. And you observe, too, that the pronouns *who* and *his*, and the noun *lesson*, are likewise in the singular, agreeing with Orlando *or* Thomas, agreeably to RULE 9. *Studies* is also singular, agreeing with *who*, according to RULE 4.

---

advantageously adopted by learners in common schools? I presume it can not be denied, that instead of teaching the learner to express himself correctly in modern English, such a resolution is merely making him familiar with an ancient and barbarous construction which modern refinement has rejected. Our forefathers, I admit, who were governed by those laws of necessity which compel all nations in the early and rude state of their language, to express themselves in short, detached sentences, employed *if* as a verb when they used the following circumlocution: " My son will reform. *Give that fact.* I will forgive him." But in the present, improved state of our language, by using *if* as a *conjunction*, (for I maintain that it is one,) we express the same thought more briefly ; and our modern mode of expression has, too, a decisive advantage over the ancient, not only in point of elegance, but also in perspicuity and force. In Scotland and the north of England, some people still make use of *gin*, a contraction of *given :* thus, " I will pardon my son, *gin* he reform." But who will contend, that they speak pure English ?

But perhaps the advocates of what *they* call a philosophical development of language, will say, that by their resolution of sentences, they merely sup-

EXERCISES IN PARSING.

Joseph and his brother reside in New York. , The sun, moon, and stars, admonish us of a superior and superintending Power. I respect my friend, because he is upright and obliging. Henry and William, who obey their teacher, improve rapidly. Henry or William, who obeys his teacher, improves very fast. Neither ank nor possession makes the guilty mind happy. Wisdom, irtue, and meekness, form the good man's happiness and interest : they support him in adversity, and comfort him in prosperity. Man is a little lower than the angels. The United States, as justly as Great Britain, can now boast of their literary institutions.

Note. The verb *form* is plural, and agrees with three nouns singular, connected by copulative conjunctions, according to Rule 8. The verb *comfort* agrees with *they* for its nominative. It is connected to *support* by the conjunction *and*, agreeably to Rule 34. *Angels* is nom. to *are* understood, and *Great Britain* is nom. to *can boast* understood, according to Rule 35.

REMARKS ON CONJUNCTIONS AND PREPOSITIONS.

The same word is occasionally employed, either as a conjunction, an adverb, or a preposition. " I submitted, *for* it was in vain to resist ;" in this example, *for* is a conjunction, because it connects the two members of a compound sentence. In the next it is a preposition, and governs *victory* in the objective case : " He contended *for* victory only."

In the first of the following sentences, *since* is a conjunction ; in the second, it is a preposition, and in the third, an adverb ; "*Since* we must part, let us do it peaceably ; I have not seen him *since* that time ; Our friendship commenced long *since*."

" He will repent *before* he dies ; Stand *before* me ; Why did you not return *before*" [that or this *time ;*] in the first of these three examples, *before* is an adverbial conjunction, because it expresses time and connects ; and in the second and third, it is a preposition.

As the words of a sentence are often transposed, so are also its members. Without attending to this circumstance, the learner may sometimes be at a loss to perceive the *connecting* power of a preposition or conjunction, for every preposition and every conjunction connects either words or phrases, sentences or members of sentences. Whenever a sentence begins with a preposition or conjunction, its members are transposed ; as, " *In* the days of Juram, king of Israel, flourished the prophet Elisha ;" " *If* thou seek the Lord, he will be found of thee ; but, *if* thou forsake him, he will cast thee off for ever."

---

ply an ellipsis. If, by an ellipsis, they mean such a one as is necessary to the grammatical construction, I cannot accede to their assumption. In teaching grammar, as well as in other things, we ought to avoid extremes :—we ought neither to pass superficially over an ellipsis necessary to the sense of a phrase, nor to put modern English to the blush, by adopting a mode of resolving sentences that would entirely change the character of our language, and carry the learner back to the Vandalic age.

But comes from the Saxon verb, *beon-utan*, to be-out. " All were well *but* (*be-out, leave-out*) the stranger." " Man is *but* a reed, floating on the current of time." Resolution : " Man is a reed, floating on the current of time ; *but* (*be-out* this fact) he is not a stable being."

And—aned, an'd, and, is the past part. of *ananad*, to add, join. *A, an, ane,*

" *When* coldness wraps this suffering clay,
" Ah, whither strays the immortal mind ?"

That the words *in*, *if*, and *when*, in these examples, connect the members of the respective sentences to which they are attached, will obviously appear if we restore.these sentences to their natural order, and bring these particles *between* the members which they connect : thus, " Elisha the prophet flourished *in* the days of Joram, king of Israel ;" " The Lord will be found of thee *if* thou seek him ; but he will cast thee off for ever *if* thou forsake him :"

" Ah, whither strays the immortal mind,
" *When* coldness wraps this suffering clay ?"

As an exercise on this lecture, you may now answer these

QUESTIONS NOT ANSWERED IN PARSING.

From what words is the term conjunction derivêd ?—What is a sentence ?—What is a simple sentence ?—What is a compound sentence ?—Give examples.—In what respect do conjunctions and prepositions agree in their nature ?—How many sorts of conjunctions are there ?—Repeat the lists of conjunctions.—Repeat some conjunctions with their corresponding conjunctions.—Do relative pronouns ever connect sentences ?—Repeat the order of parsing a conjunction.—Do you apply any Rule in parsing a conjunction ?—What Rule should be applied in parsing a noun or pronoun connected with another ?—What Rule in parsing a verb agreeing with two or more nouns singular, connected by a copulative conjunction ?—What Rule when the nouns are connected by a disjunctive ?—In parsing a verb connected to another by a conjunction, what Rule do you apply ?—Is a conjunction ever used as other parts of speech ?—Give examples.—What is said of the words *for*, *since*, and *before ?*—What is said of the transposition of sentences ?

---

or *one*, from the same verb, points out whatever is *aned*, *oned*, or made *one*. *And* also refers to the thing that is *joined* to, *added* to, or *made one* with, some other person or thing mentioned. " Julius *and* Harriet will make a happy pair." Resolution : " Julius, Harriet *joined*, *united*, or *aned*, will make a happy pair ;" i. e. Harriet *made one* with Julius; will make a happy pair.

For means *cause*.

Because—*be-cause*, is a compound of the verb *be*, and the noun *cause*. It retains the meaning of both ; as, " I believe the maxim, *for* I know it to be true ;"—" I believe the maxim, *be-cause* I know it to be true ;" i. e. the *cause* of my belief, *be*, or *is*, I know it to be true.

Nor is a contraction of *ne or*. *Ne* is a contraction of *not*, and *or*, of *other*. *Nor* is, *not other*-wise : *not* in the *other* way or manner.

Else is the imperative of *alesan*, *unless*, of *onlesan*, and *lest*, the past part. of *lesan*, all signifying to dismiss, release, loosen, set free. " He will be punished, *unless* he repent ;"—" *Unless, release, give up,* (the fact) he repents he will be punished."

Though is the imperative of the Saxon verb *thafigan*, to allow, and *yet*, of *getan*, to get. *Yet* is simply, *get* ; ancient *g* is our modern *y*. " *Though* he slay me, *yet* will I trust in him :—*Grant* or *allow* (the fact) he slay me, *yet*, or *retain* (the opposite fact) I will trust in him."

QUESTIONS ON THE PHILOSOPHICAL NOTES.

From what parts of speech are prepositions and conjunctions derived ?—What is Horne Tooke's opinion of that ?—From what is each of the following words derived, *that, if, but, and, because, nor, else, unless, lest, though,* and *yet ?*

LECTURE X.

OF INTERJECTIONS.—CASES OF NOUNS.

INTERJECTIONS are words which express the sudden emotions of the speaker; as, " *Alas !* I fear for life ;" " *O* death ! where is thy sting ? "

Interjections are not so much the signs of thought, as of feeling. Almost any word may be used as an interjection; but when so employed, it is not the representative of a *distinct* idea. A word which denotes a distinct conception of the mind, must necessarily belong to some other part of speech. They who wish to speak often, or rather, to make *noises*, when they have no useful information to communicate, are apt to use words very freely in this way ; such as the following expressions, *la, la me, my, O my, O dear, dear me, surprising, astonishing,* and the like.

Interjections not included in the following list, are generally known by their taking an exclamation point after them.

A LIST OF THE PRINCIPAL INTERJECTIONS.

1. Of *earnestness* or *grief ;* as, O! oh! ah! alas!
2. *Contempt ;* as, Pish ! tush !
3. *Wonder;* as, Heigh ! really ! strange !
4. *Calling ;* as, Hem ! ho ! halloo !
5. *Disgust* or *aversion ;* as, Foh ! fy ! fudge ! away !

PHILOSOPHICAL NOTES.

The term INTERJECTION is applied to those *inarticulate* sounds employed both by men and brutes, not to express distinct ideas, but emotions, passions, or feelings. The sounds employed by human beings in groaning, sighing, crying, screaming, shrieking, and laughing, by the dog in barking, growling, and whining, by the horse in snorting and neighing, by the sheep in bleating, by the cat in mewing, by the dove in cooing, by the duck in uacking, and by the goose in hissing, we sometimes attempt to represent y words ; but, as *written* words are the ocular representatives of *articulate* sounds, they cannot be made clearly to denote *inarticulate* or *indistinct* noises. Such indistinct utterances belong to natural language ; but they fall below the bounds of regulated speech. Hence, *real* interjections are not a part of written language.

6. *Attention ;* as, Lo! behold! hark!

7. *Requesting silence ;* as, Hush! hist!

8. *Salutation ;* as, Welcome! hail! all hail!

NOTE. We frequently meet with what some call an *interjective phrase ;* such as, Ungrateful wretch! impudence of hope! folly in the extreme! what ingratitude ! away with him!

As the interjection is the least important part of speech in the English language, it will require but little attention. You may, however, make yourself well acquainted with what has been said respecting it, and then commit the

SYSTEMATIC ORDER OF PARSING.

The order of parsing an INTERJECTION, *is—*an interjection, and why?

"O virtue! how amiable thou art!"

O is an interjection, a word used to express some passion or emotion of the speaker.

The ten parts of speech have now been unfolded and eluci-dated, although some of them have not been fully explained. Be-fore you proceed any farther, you will please to begin again at the first lecture, and read over, attentively, the whole, observing to parse every example in the exercises systematically. You will then be able to parse the following exercises, which contain all the parts of speech. If you study faithfully *six* hours in a day, and pursue the directions given, you may become, if not a critical, at least, a good, practical grammarian, in *six weeks ;* but if you study only *three* hours in a day, it will take you nearly *three months* to acquire the same knowledge.

EXERCISES IN PARSING.

True cheerfulness makes a man happy in himself, and pro-motes the happiness of all around him.

Modesty always appears graceful in youth : it doubles the lus-tre of every virtue which it seems to hide.

The meaning of those words commonly called interjections, is easily shown by tracing them to their roots.

Pish and *pshaw* are the Anglo-Saxon *paec, paeca ;* and are equivalent to *trumpery !* i. e. *tromperie,* from *tromper.*

Fy or *fie* is the imperative, *foe,* the past tense, and *foh* or *faugh,* the past part. of the Saxon verb *fian,* to hate.

Lo is the imperative of *look. Halt* is the imperative of *healden,* to hold *Farewell—fare-well,* is a compound of *faran,* to go, and the adverb *well.* It means, to *go well. Welcome—well-come,* signifies, it is *well* that you are *come. Adieu* comes from the French *a Dieu,* to God ; meaning, I commend you *to God.*

He who, every morning, plans the transactions of the day, and follows out that plan, carries on a thread that will guide him through the labyrinth of the most busy life.

The king gave me a generous reward for committing that barbarous act; but, alas! I fear the consequence.

<blockquote>
E'en now, where Alpine solitudes ascend,
I set me down a pensive hour to spend;
And, placed on high, above the storm's career,
Look downward where a hundred realms appear:—
</blockquote>

<blockquote>
Alas! the joys that fortune brings,
Are trifling, and decay;
And those who mind the paltry things,
More trifling still than they.
</blockquote>

Note. In the second sentence of the foregoing exercises, *which* is governed by the verb *to hide,* according to Rule 16. *He* is nom. to *carries; who* is nom. to *plans. Follows* agrees with *who* understood, and is connected to *plans* by *and;* Rule 34. What did the king give? A *reward to* me. Then *reward* is in the *obj.* case, gov. by *gave; Me* is gov. by *to* understood; Note 1, Rule 32. The phrase, *committing that barbarous act,* is gov. by *for;* Note 2, under Rule 28. *Hour* is in the *obj.* case, gov. by *to spend;* Rule 20. *Look* is connected to *set* by *and;* Rule 34. *Joys* is nom. to *are. That* is gov. by *brings;* Rule 16. *Those* is nom. to *are* understood. *They* is nom. to *are* understood; Rule 35.

CASES OF NOUNS.

In a former lecture, I promised to give you a more extensive explanation of the cases of nouns; and, as they are, in many situations, a little difficult to be ascertained, I will now offer some remarks on this subject. But before you proceed, I wish you to parse all the examples in the exercises just presented, observing to pay particular attention to the remarks in the subjoined Note. Those remarks will assist you much in analyzing.

A noun is sometimes nominative to a verb placed many lines after the noun. You must exercise your judgment in this matter. Look at the sentence in the preceding exercises beginning with, "He who, every morning," &c. and see if you can find the verb to which *he* is nominative. What does *he* do? He carries on a thread, &c. *He,* then, is nominative to the verb *carries.* What does *who* do? Who *plans,* and who *follows,* &c. Then *who* is nom. to *plans,* and *who* understood, is nominative to *follows.*

<blockquote>
" A soul without reflection, like a pile
" Without inhabitant, to ruin runs."
</blockquote>

In order to find the verb to which the noun *soul,* in this sentence, is the nominative, put the question; What does a *soul* without reflection do? Such a soul *runs* to ruin, like a pile without inhabitant. Thus you discover, that *soul* is nominative to *runs*.

When the words of a sentence are arranged according to their natural order, the nominative case, you recollect, is placed before the verb, and the objective, after it; but when the words of a sentence are transposed; that is, not arranged according to their natural order, it frequently happens, that the nominative comes *after*, and the objective, *before* the verb; especially in poetry, or when a question is asked: as, " Whence *arises* the *misery* of the present world?" " What good *thing shall* I *do* to inherit eternal life?" Put these expressions in the declarative form, and the nominative will *precede*, and the objective *follow* its verb: thus, " The *misery* of the present world *arises* whence; I *shall do* what good *thing* to inherit eternal life."

> " Now came still *evening* on, and twilight gray
> "Had, in her sober livery, all *things* clad."

> " Stern rugged nurse, thy rigid *lore*
> " With patience many a *year* she bore."

What did the *evening* do? The evening *came on*. Gray *twilight* had clad what? Twilight had clad all *things* in her sober livery. *Evening*, then, is nom. to *came*, and the noun *things* is in the objective case, and gov. by *had clad*: RULE 20. What did *she* bear? She bore thy rigid *lore* with patience, *for*, or *during*, many a year. Hence you find, that *lore* is in the objective case, and governed by *bore*, according to RULE 20. *Year* is gov. by *during* understood: RULE 32.

A noun is frequently nominative to a verb understood, or in the objective, and governed by a verb understood; as, " Lo, [*there is*] the poor *Indian!* whose untutored mind." " O, the *pain* [*there is!*] the *bliss* [*there is*] in dying!" " All were sunk, but the wakeful *nightingale* [*was not sunk.*"] " He thought as a *sage* [*thinks,*] though he felt as a *man* [*feels.*"] " His hopes, immortal, blow them by, as *dust* [*is blown by.*"] Rule 35 applies to these last three examples.

In the next place I will explain several cases of nouns and pronouns which have not yet come under our notice. Sometimes a noun or pronoun may be in the nominative case when it has no verb to agree with it.

OF THE NOMINATIVE CASE INDEPENDENT.

Whenever a direct address is made, the person or thing spoken *to*, is in the *nominative case independent;* as, " *James*, I desire you to study."

You notice that, in this expression, I address myself to *James*. that is, I speak to him; and you observe, too, that there is no verb, either expressed or implied, to which James can be the nominative; therefore you know that *James* is in the nom. case independent, according to Rule 5.   Recollect, that *whenever a noun is of the second person*, it is in the nom. case independent; that is, independent of any verb; as, *Selma*, thy halls are silent; Love and meekness, my *lord*, become a churchman, better than ambition; O *Jerusalem, Jerusalem*, how often would I have gathered thy children together, even as a hen gathereth her chickens under her wings, but ye would not!—For a farther illustration of this case, see Note 2, under the 5th Rule of Syntax.

NOTE.   When a pronoun of the *second* person is in apposition with a noun independent, it is in the same case; as, " *Thou traitor*, I detest thee."

QF THE NOMINATIVE CASE ABSOLUTE.

A noun or pronoun placed before a participle, without any verb to agree with it, is in the nominative case *absolute;* as, "The *sun being risen*, we pursued our journey."

Sun is here placed before the participle " being risen," and has no verb to agree with it; therefore it is in the nominative case absolute, according to RULE 6.

NOTE 1.   A noun or pronoun in the nominative case independent, is always of the *second* person; but, in the case absolute, it is generally of the *third* person.

2.   The case absolute is always nominative: the following sentence is therefore incorrect; " Whose top shall tremble, *him* descending," &c.; it should be, *he* descending.

OF NOUNS IN APPOSITION.

Two or more nouns or pronouns signifying the same person or thing, are put, by *apposition*, in the same case; as, " *Cicero*, the great *orator, philosopher*, and *statesman* of Rome, was murdered by Antony."

Apposition, in a grammatical sense, means something added, or names added, in order more fully to define or illustrate the sense of the first name mentioned.

You perceive that *Cicero*, in the preceding example, is merely the proper name of a man; but when I give him the three additional appellations, and call him a great *orator, philosopher*, and *statesman*, you understand what kind of a man he was; that is, by giving him these three additional names, his character and abilities as a man are more fully made known. And, surely, you cannot be at a loss to know that these four nouns must be in the same case, for they are all names given to the same person; therefore, if *Cicero* was murdered, the *orator* was murdered, and the *philosopher* was murdered, and the *statesman* was murdered, because they all mean one and the same person.

Nouns and pronouns in the objective case, are frequently in *apposition ;* as, He struck *Charles* the *student.* Now it is obvious, that, when he struck *Charles,* he struck the *student,* because Charles was the *student,* and the *student* was *Charles ;* therefore the noun *student* is in the objective case, governed by "struck," and put by apposition with Charles, according to RULE 7.

Please to examine this lecture very attentively. You will then be prepared to parse the following examples correctly and systematically.

PARSING.

"Weep on the rocks of roaring winds, O *maid* of Inistore."

Maid is a noun, the name of a person—com. the name of a sort—fem. gender, it denotes a female—second pers. spoken to—sing. num. it implies but one—and in the nominative case independent, because it is addressed, and has no verb to agree with it, according to

RULE 5. *When an address is made, the noun or pronoun addressed, is put in the nominative case independent.*

"The *general* being ransomed, the barbarians permitted him to depart."

General is a noun, the name, &c. (parse it in full :)—and in the nominative case absolute, because it is placed before the participle "being ransomed," and it has no verb to agree with it, agreeably to

RULE 6. *A noun or pronoun placed before a participle, and being independent of the rest of the sentence, is in the nominative case absolute.*

"*Thou man* of God, flee to the land of Judah."

Thou is a pronoun, a word used instead of a noun—personal it personates "man"—second pers. spoken to—mas. gender, sing. num. because the noun "man" is for which it stands; RULE 13 (Repeat the Rule.)—*Thou* is in the nominative case independent, and put by *apposition* with *man*, because it signifies the same thing, according to

RULE 7. *Two or more nouns, or nouns and pronouns, signifying the same thing, are put, by apposition, in the same case.*

Man is in the nominative case independent, according to Rule 5. *Flee* agrees with *thou* understood.

"Lo! *Newton, priest* of Nature, shines afar,
"Scans the wide world, and numbers every star."

Newton is a noun, (parse it in full,) and in the nominative case to "shines." RULE 3.

Priest is a noun, (parse it in full,) and in the nom. case, it is the actor and subject of the verb "shines," and put by apposition with "Newton," because it signifies the same thing, agreeably to Rule 7. (Repeat the Rule.)

EXERCISES IN PARSING.

Turn from your evil ways, O house of Israel! Ye fields of light, celestial plains, ye scenes divinely fair! proclaim your Maker's wondrous power. O king! *live* for ever. The murmur of thy streams, O Lora, brings back the memory of the past. The sound of thy woods, Garmallar, is lovely in my ear. Dost thou not behold, Malvina, a rock with its head of heath? Three aged pines bend from its face; green is the plain at its feet; there the flower of the mountain grows, and shakes its white head in the breeze.

The General being slain, the army was routed. Commerce having thus got into the legislative body, privilege must be done away. Jesus had conveyed himself away, a multitude being in that place. I being in great haste, he consented. The rain having ceased, the dark clouds rolled away. The Son of God, while clothed in flesh, was subject to all the frailties and inconveniences of human nature, sin excepted; (that is, sin being excepted.)

In the days of Joram, king of Israel, flourished the prophet Elisha. Paul the apostle suffered martyrdom. *Come*, peace of mind, delightful guest! and *dwell* with me. Friends, Romans, countrymen, *lend* me your ears.

Soul of the just, companion of the dead!
Where is thy home, and whither art thou fled?
Till Hymen brought his love-delighted hour,
There dwelt no joy in Eden's rosy bower:—
The world was sad, the garden was a wild,
And man the hermit sighed, till woman smiled.

NOTE. Those verbs in *italics*, in the preceding examples, are all in the imperative mood, and *second* person, agreeing with *thou, ye,* or *you,* understood. *House of Israel* is a noun of multitude. *Was routed* and *must be done* are passive verbs. *Art fled* is a neuter verb in a passive form. *Clothed* is a perfect participle. *Till* is an adverbial conjunction.

When you shall have analyzed, systematically, every word in the foregoing exercises, you may answer the following

QUESTIONS NOT ANSWERED IN PARSING.

Repeat the list of interjections.—Repeat some interjective phrases.—Repeat the order of parsing an interjection.—In order to find the verb to which a noun is nom. what question do you put ?—Give examples.—Is the nominative case ever placed after the verb ?—When ?—Give examples.—Does the objective case ever come before the verb ?—Give examples.—Is a noun ever nom. to a verb understood ?—Give examples.—When is a noun or pronoun in the nom. case independent ?—Give examples.—Are nouns of the *second* person always in the nom. case independent ?—When a pronoun is put by apposition with a noun independent, in what case is it ?—When is a noun or pronoun in the nom. case absolute ?—Give examples.—When are nouns or nouns and pronouns put, by apposition, in the same case ?—Give examples.—In parsing a noun or pronoun in the nom. case independent, what Rule should be applied ?—In parsing the nom. case absolute, what Rule ?—What Rule in parsing nouns or pronouns in apposition ?—Do real interjections belong to written language ?—(*Phil. Notes.*)—From what are the following words derived, *pish, fy, lo, halt, farewell, welcome, adieu!*

LECTURE XI.

OF THE MOODS AND TENSES OF VERBS.

You have now acquired a general, and, I may say, an extensive, knowledge of nine parts of speech ; but you know but little, as yet, respecting the most important one of all ; I mean the Verb. I will, therefore, commence this lecture by giving you an explanation of the Moods and Tenses of verbs. Have the goodness, however, first to turn back and read over Lecture II., and reflect well upon what is there said respecting the verb ; after which I will conduct you so smoothly through the moods and tenses, and the conjugation of verbs, that, instead of finding yourself involved in obscurities and deep intricacies, you will scarcely find an obstruction to impede your progress.

I. OF THE MOODS.

The MOOD or MODE of a verb means the *manner* in which its action, passion, or being, is represented.

When I wish to assert a thing, positively, I use the *declarative* or *indicative* mode; as, The man *walks ;* but sometimes the action or occurrence of which I wish to speak, is doubtful, and then I must not declare it positively, but I must adopt another *mode* of expression; thus, *If* the man *walk*, he will refresh himself with the bland breezes. This second mode or manner of representing the action, is called the *subjunctive* or *conditional* mode.

Again, we sometimes employ a verb when we do not wish to *declare* a thing, nor to represent the action in a *doubtful* or *conditional* manner; but we wish to *command* some one to act. We then use the *imperative* or *commanding* mode, and say, *Walk*, sir. And when we do not wish to command a man to act, we sometimes allude to his *power* or *ability* to act. This fourth mode of representing action, is called the *potential* mode; as, He *can walk ;* He *could walk*. The fifth and last mode, called the *infinitive* or *unlimited* mode, we employ in expressing action in an unlimited manner; that is, without confining it, in respect to number and person, to any particular agent; as, *To walk, to ride*. Thus you perceive, that the mood, mode, or manner of representing the action, passion, or being of a verb, must vary according to the different intentions of the mind.

Were we to assign a particular name to *every* change in the mode or manner of representing action or being, the number of moods in our language would amount to many hundreds. But this principle of division and arrangement, if followed out in detail, would lead to great perplexity, without producing any beneficial result. The division of Mr. Harris, in his Hermes, is much more curious than instructive. He has fourteen moods; his *interrogative, optative, hortative, promissive, precautive, requisitive, enunciative,* &c. But as far as philosophical accuracy and the convenience and advantage of the learner are concerned, it is believed that no arrangement is preferable to the following. I am not unaware that plausible objections may be raised against it; but what arrangement cannot be objected to ?   –

There are five moods of verbs, the Indicative, the Subjunctive, the Imperative, the Potential, and the Infinitive.

The INDICATIVE MOOD simply indicates or declares a thing; as, "He *writes :*" or it asks a question; as, "*Does* he *write ?* Who *wrote* that?"

The term *indicative,* comes from the Latin *indico,* to *declare.* Hence, the legitimate province of the indicative mood, is to *declare* things, whether positively or negatively; thus, *positively,* He *came* with me; *negatively,* He *came not* with me. But in order to avoid a multiplication of moods, we extend its meaning, and use the indicative mood in asking a question; as, Who *came* with you ?

The subjunctive mood being more analogous to the indicative in conjugation, than any other, it ought to be presented next in order. This mood, however, differs materially from the indicative in sense; therefore you ought to make yourself well acquainted with the nature of the indicative, before you commence with the subjunctive.

The Subjunctive Mood expresses action, passion, or being, in a doubtful or conditional manner · or,

When a verb is preceded by a word that expresses a condition, doubt, motive, wish, or supposition, it is in the Subjunctive Mood; as, "*If* he *study,* he will improve; I will respect him, *though* he *chide* me; He will not be pardoned, *unless* he *repent;* *Had* he *been* there, he would have conquered;" (that is, *if* he *had been* there.)

The conjunctions *if, though, unless,* in the preceding examples, express condition, doubt, &c.; therefore, the verbs *study, chide, repent,* and *had been,* are in the subjunctive mood.

Note 1. A verb in this mood is generally attended by another verb in some other mood. You observe, that each of the first three of the preceding examples, contains a verb in the indicative mood, and the fourth, a verb in the potential. .

2. Whenever the conjunctions *if, though, unless, except, whether, lest,* or any others, denote contingency or doubt, the verbs that follow them are in the subjunctive mood; as, "*If* he *ride* out every day, his health will probably improve;" that is, if he *shall* or *should* ride out hereafter. But when these conjunctions do not imply doubt, &c. the verbs that follow them are in the indicative, or some other mood; as, "*Though* he *rides* out daily, his health is no better." The conjunctive and indicative forms of this mood, are explained in the conjugation of the verb to *love.* See page 145.

The Imperative Mood is used for commanding, exhorting, entreating, or permitting; as, "*Depart*

thou; *Remember* my admonitions; *Tarry* awhile
longer; *Go* in peace."

The verb *depart* expresses a command; *remember* exhorts;
tarry expresses entreaty; and *go*, permission; therefore they are
all in the imperative mood.

The *imperative*, from *impero*, to command, is literally that mood
f the verb used in *commanding;* but its technical meaning in
grammar is extended to the use of the verb in exhorting, entreating, and permitting.

A verb in the imperative mood, is always of the second person,
though never varied in its terminations, agreeing with *thou, ye,* or
you, either expressed or implied. You may know a verb in this
mood by the sense; recollect, however, that the nominative is
always *second* person, and frequently understood; as, George,
give me my hat; that is, give thou, or give you. When the
nominative is expressed, it is generally placed after the verb;.
as, Go *thou;* Depart *ye;* or between the auxiliary and the verb;
as, Do *thou* go; Do *ye* depart. (*Do* is the auxiliary.)

The POTENTIAL MOOD implies possibility, liberty,
or necessity, power, will, or obligation; as, " It *may
rain;* He *may go* or *stay;* We *must eat* and *drink;*
I *can ride;* He *would walk;* They *should learn.*"

In the first of these examples, the auxiliary *may* implies possibility; in the second it implies liberty; that is, he is at liberty
to go or to stay; in the third, *must* denotes necessity; *can* denotes
power or ability; *would* implies will or inclination; that is, he
had a *mind* to walk; and *should* implies obligation. Hence you

---

PHILOSOPHICAL NOTES.

The changes in the termination of words, in all languages, have been
formed by the *coalescence* of words of appropriate meaning. This subject
was approached on page 49. It is again taken up for the purpose of showing, that the moods and tenses, as well as the number and person, of English verbs, do not solely depend on inflection.

The coalescing syllables which form the number and person of the Hebrew verb, are still considered pronouns; and, by those who have investi-
gated the subject, it is conceded, that the same plan has been adopted in the
formation of the Latin and Greek verbs, as in the Hebrew. Some languages
have carried this process to a very great extent. Ours is remarkable for the
small number of its inflections. But they who reject the passive verb, and
hose moods and tenses which are formed by employing what are called
" auxiliary verbs," *because they are formed of two or more verbs,* do not appear to reason soundly. It is inconsistent to admit, that walk-*eth,* and walk-
ed, are tenses, because each is but one word, and to reject *have* walked, and
will walk, as tenses, because each is composed of two words. *Eth,* as pre-

perceive, that the verbs, may rain, may go, must eat, must drink, can ride, would walk, and should learn, are in the *potential* mood.

Note 1. As a verb in the indicative mood is converted into the subjunctive when it is preceded by a conjunction expressing doubt, contingency, supposition, &c., so a verb in the potential mood, may, in like manner, be turned into the subjunctive; as, " *If* I *could deceive* him, I should abhor it ; *Though* he *should increase* in wealth, he would not be charitable." I *could deceive*, is in the potential; *If* I *could deceive*, is in the subjunctive mood.

2. The potential mood, as well as the indicative, is used in asking a ques tion; as, " May I go ? Could you understand him ? Must we die ?"

The INFINITIVE MOOD expresses action, passion, or being, in a general and unlimited manner, having no nominative, consequently, neither person nor number ; as, " *To speak, to walk.*"

Infinitive means *unconfined*, or *unlimited*. This mood is called the infinitive, because its verb is not confined or limited to a nominative. A verb in any other mood is limited ; that is, it must agree in number and person with its nominative ; but a verb in this mood has *no* nominative, therefore, it never changes its termination, except to form the perfect tense. Now you understand why all verbs are called *finite* or *limited*, excepting those in the infinitive mood.

Note. *To*, the sign of the infinitive mood, is often understood before the verb ; as, " Let me proceed ;" that is, Let me *to* proceed. See RULE 25. *To* is not a preposition when joined to a verb in this mood ; thus, *to* ride, *to* rule; but it should be parsed with the verb, and as a part of it.

If you study this lecture attentively, you will perceive, that when I say, I *write*, the verb is in the indicative mood ; but when I say, *if* I write, or, *unless* I write, &c. the verb is in the subjunctive mood ; *write* thou, or *write* ye or you, the imperative ; I *may write*, I *must write*, I *could write*, &c. the potential ; and

---

viously shown, is a contraction of *doeth*, or *haveth*, and *ed*, of *dede*, *dodo*, *doed*, or *did*; and, therefore, walk-*eth*; i. e. walk-*doeth*, or *doeth*-walk, and walk-*ed*; i. e. walk-*did*, or *doed* or *did*-walk, are, when analyzed, as strictly compound, as *will* walk, *shall* walk, and *have* walked. The only difference in the formation of these tenses, is, that in the two former, the associated verbs have been contracted and made to coalesce with the main verb, but in the two latter, they still maintain their ground as separate words. If it be said that *will walk* is composed of two words, each of which conveys a distinct idea, and, therefore, should be analyzed by itself, the same argument, with all its force, may be applied to walk-*eth*, walk-*ed*, walk-*did*, or *did* walk. The result of all the investigations of this subject, appears to settle down into the hackneyed truism, that the passive verbs, and the moods and tenses, of some languages, are formed by inflections, or terminations either prefixed or postfixed, and of other languages, by the association of auxiliary verbs, which have not yet been contracted and made to coalesce

to write, the infinitive. Any other verb (except the **defective**) may be employed in the same manner.

II. OF THE TENSES.

TENSE means time.

Verbs have six tenses, the Present, the Imperfect, the Perfect, the Pluperfect, and the First and Second Future tenses.

The PRESENT TENSE represents an action or event as taking place at the time in which it is mentioned; as, "I *smile;* I *see;* I *am seen.*"

NOTE 1. The present tense is also used in speaking of actions continued, with occasional intermissions, to the present time; as, "He *rides* out every morning."

2. This tense is sometimes applied to represent the actions of persons long since dead; as, "Seneca *reasons* and *moralizes* well; An honest man *is* the noblest work of God."

3. When the present tense is preceded by the words, *when, before, after, as soon as,* &c. it is sometimes used to point out the relative time of a future action; as, "*When* he *arrives* we shall hear the news."

The IMPERFECT TENSE denotes a past action or event, however distant; or,

The IMPERFECT TENSE represents an action or event as past and finished, but without defining the precise time of its completion; as, "I *loved* her for her modesty and virtue; They *were* travelling post when he *met* them."

In these examples, the verbs *loved* and *met* express past and *finished* actions, and therefore constitute a *perfect* tense as strictly as any form of the verb in our language; but, as they do not

---

as *terminations.* The auxiliary, when contracted into a *terminating syllable,* retains its distinct and intrinsic meaning, as much as when associated with a verb by juxtaposition: consequently, an "auxiliary verb" may form a part of a mood or tense, or passive verb, with as much propriety as a *terminating syllable.* They who contend for the ancient custom of keeping the auxiliaries distinct, and parsing them as primary verbs, are, by the same principle, bound to extend their dissecting-knife *to every compound word in the language.*

Having thus attempted briefly to prove the philosophical accuracy of the theory which recognises the tenses, moods, and passive verbs, formed by the aid of auxiliaries, I shall now offer one argument to show that this theory, and this *only,* will subserve the purposes of the practical grammarian.

As it is not so much the province of philology to instruct in the exact meaning of single and separate words, as it is to teach the student to combine and employ them properly in framing sentences, and as those *combinations* which go by the name of compound tenses and passive verbs, are necessary in writing and discourse, it follows, conclusively, that that theory

define the precise time of the completion of these actions, their tense may properly be denominated an *indefinite past.* By de-fining the present participle in conjunction with the verb, we have an *imperfect* tense in the expression, *were travelling.* . This course, however, would not be in accordance with the ordinary method of treating the participle. Hence it follows, that the terms *imperfect* and *perfect*, as applied to this and the next succeeding tense, are not altogether significant of their true character; but if you learn to apply these tenses *correctly*, the propriety or impropriety of their names is not a consideration of very great moment.

The PERFECT TENSE denotes past time, and also conveys an allusion to the present; as, "I *have* finished my letter."

The verb *have finished*, in this example, signifies that the action, though past, was perfectly finished at a point of time immediately preceding, or in the course of a period which comes to the present. Under this view of the subject, the term *perfect* may be properly applied to this tense, for it specifies, not only the completion of the action, but, also, alludes to the particular period of its accomplishment.

The PLUPERFECT TENSE represents a past action or event that transpired before some other past time specified; as, "I *had finished* my letter before my brother arrived."

You observe that the verb *had finished*, in this example, represents one *past* action, and the arrival of my brother, another *past* action; therefore *had finished* is in the pluperfect tense, because

which does not explain these verbs in their *combined* state, cannot teach the student the correct use and application of the verbs of our language. By such an arrangement, he cannot learn when it is proper to use the phrases, *shall have walked, might have gone, have seen,* instead of, *shall walk, might go,* and *saw;* because this theory has nothing to do with the combining of verbs. If it be alleged, that the speaker or writer's own good sense must guide him in combining these verbs, and, therefore, that the directions of the grammarian are unnecessary, it must be recollected, that such an argument would bear, equally, against every principle of grammar whatever. In short, the theory of the compound tenses, and of the passive verb, appears to be so firmly based in the genius of our language, and so practically important to the student, as to defy all the engines of the paralogistic speculator, and the philosophical quibbler, to batter it down.

But the most plausible objection to the old theory is, that it is encumbered with much useless technicality and tedious prolixity, which are avoided by the *simple* process of exploding the passive verb, and reducing the number of

the action took place prior to the taking place of the other past action specified in the same sentence.

The FIRST FUTURE TENSE denotes a future action or event; as "I *will finish;* I *shall finish* my letter."

The SECOND FUTURE TENSE represents a future action that will be fully accomplished, at or before the time of another future action or event; as, "I *shall have finished* my letter when my brother arrives."

This example clearly shows you the meaning and the proper use of the second future tense. The verb "shall have finished" implies a future action that will be completely finished, at or before the time of the other future event denoted by the phrase, "*when* my brother *arrives.*"

NOTE. What is sometimes called the *Inceptive* future, is expressed thus, "I am going *to write;*" "I am about *to write.*" Future time is also indicated by placing the infinitive present immediately after the indicative present of the verb *to be;* thus, "I am *to write;*" "Harrison is *to be,* or ought *to be,* commander in chief;" "Harrison is *to command* the army."

You may now read what is said respecting the moods and tenses several times over, and then you may learn to *conjugate* a verb. But, before you proceed to the conjugation of verbs, you will please to commit the following paragraph on the *Auxiliary* verbs, and, also, the *signs* of the moods and tenses; and, in conjugating, you must pay particular attention to the manner in which these signs are applied.

OF THE AUXILIARY VERBS.

AUXILIARY or HELPING VERBS are those by the help of which the English verbs are principally con-

---

the moods to three, and of the tenses to two. It is certain, however, that if we reject the *names* of the perfect, pluperfect, and future tenses, the *names* of the potential and subjunctive moods, and of the passive verb, in writing and discourse we must still employ those *verbal combinations* which form them; and it is equally certain, that the proper mode of employing such combinations, is as easily taught or learned by the old theory, which *names* them, as by the new, which gives them *no name.*

On philosophical principles, we might, perhaps, dispense with the *future* tenses of the verb, by analyzing each word separately; but, as illustrated on page 79, the combined words which form our perfect and pluperfect tenses have an *associated* meaning, which is destroyed by analyzing each word separately. That arrangement, therefore, which rejects these tenses, appears to be, not only *unphilosophical,* but inconsistent and inaccurate.

For the satisfaction of those teachers who prefer it, and for their adop-

jugated. *May, can, must, might, could, would, should,* and *shall,* are always auxiliaries; *do, be, have,* and *will,* are sometimes auxiliaries, and sometimes principal verbs.

The use of the auxiliaries is shown in the following conjugation.

SIGNS OF THE MOODS.

The *Indicative* Mood is known by the *sense,* or by its having *no sign,* except in asking a question; as, "Who *loves* you?"

The conjunctions *if, though, unless, except, whether,* and *lest,* are generally signs of the *Subjunctive;* as, "*If* I *love; unless* I *love,*" &c.

A verb is generally known to be in the *Imperative* Mood by its agreeing with *thou,* or *ye* or *you,* understood; as, "*Love* virtue, and *follow* her steps;" that is, love *thou,* or love *ye* or *you;* follow *thou,* &c.

May, can, and *must, might, could, would,* and *should,* are signs of the *Potential* Mood; as, "I *may* love; I *must* love; I *should* love," &c.

To is the sign of the *Infinitive;* as, "*To* love, *to* smile, *to* hate, *to* walk."

SIGNS OF THE TENSES.

The first form of the verb is the sign of the present tense; as, *love, smile, hate, walk.*

tion, too, a modernized *philosophical* theory of the moods and tenses is here presented. If it is not quite so convenient and useful as the old one, they need not hesitate to adopt it. It has the advantage of being *new;* and, moreover, it sounds *large,* and will make the *commonalty stare.* Let it be distinctly understood, that you teach "*philosophical grammar, founded on reason and common sense,*" and you will pass for a very learned man, and make all the good housewives wonder at the rapid march of intellect, and the vast improvements of the age.

MOOD.

Verbs have three moods, the indicative, (embracing what is commonly included under the *indicative,* the *subjunctive,* and the *potential,*) the imperative, and the infinitive.—For definitions, refer to the body of the work.

TENSE OR TIME.

Verbs have only two tenses, the present and the past.

A verb expressing action commenced and not completed, is in the present tense; as, "Religion *soars:* it *has* gained many victories: it *will* [to] *carry* its votaries to the blissful regions"

Ed—the imperfect tense of regular verbs; as, *loved, smiled, hated, walked.*

Have—the perfect; as, *have* loved.

Had—the pluperfect; as, *had* loved.

Shall or *will*—the first future; as, *shall* love, or *will* love; *shall* smile, *will* smile.

Shall or *will • have*—the second future; as, *shall have* loved, or *will have* loved.

NOTE. There are some exceptions to these signs, which you will notice by referring to the conjugation in the potential mood.

Now, I hope you will so far consult your own ease and advantage, as to commit, perfectly, the signs of the moods and tenses before you proceed farther than to the subjunctive mood. If you do, the supposed Herculean task of learning to conjugate verbs, will be transformed into a few hours of pleasant pastime.

The Indicative Mood has *six* tenses.

The Subjunctive has also *six* tenses.

The Imperative has only *one* tense.

The Potential has *four* tenses.

The Infinitive has *two* tenses.

CONJUGATION OF VERBS.

The CONJUGATION of a verb is the regular combination and arrangement of its several numbers, persons, moods, and tenses.

The Conjugation of an active verb, is styled the *active voice;* and that of a passive verb, the *passive voice.*

When a verb expresses finished action, it is in the past tense; as, " This page (the Bible) God *hung* out of heaven, and *retired.*"

A verb in the imperative and infinitive moods, is always in the *present* tense, high authorities to the contrary notwithstanding. The *command* must *necessarily* be given in time present, although its *fulfilment* must be future. John, what are you doing? Learning my task. Why do you learn it? Because my preceptor *commanded* me to do so. When *did* he command you? *Yesterday.*—Not *now,* of course.

That it is inconsistent with the nature of things for a command to be given in *future* time, and that the *fulfilment* of the command, though future, has nothing to do with the tense or time of the command itself, are truths so plain as to put to the blush the gross absurdity of those who identify the time of the fulfilment with that of the command.

Verbs are called Regular when they form their imperfect tense of the indicative mood, and their perfect participle, by adding to the present tense *ed*, or *d* only when the verb ends in *e ;* as,

Pres. Tense.	Imp. Tense.	Perf. Participle
I favor.	I favor*ed*.	favor*ed*.
I love.	I love*d*,	love*d*.

A Regular Verb is conjugated in the following manner.

To Love.—Indicative Mood.
Present Tense.

Singular.	*Plural.*
1. *Pers.* I love,	1. We love,
2. *Pers.* Thou lovest,	2. Ye *or* you love,
3. *Pers.* He, she, *or* it, loveth } *or* loves.	3. They love.

When we wish to express energy or positiveness, the auxiliary *do* should precede the verb in the present tense: thus,

Singular.	*Plural.*
1. I do love,	1. We do love,
2. Thou dost love,	2. Ye *or* you do love.
3. He doth *or* does love.	3. They do love.

Imperfect Tense.

Singular.	*Plural.*
1. I loved,	1. We loved,
2. Thou lovedst,	2. Ye *or* you loved,
3. He loved.	3. They loved.

Or by-prefixing *did* to the present: thus,

Singular.	*Plural.*
1. I did love	1. We did love,
2. Thou didst love,	2. Ye *or* you did love,
3. He did love.	3. They did love.

EXERCISES IN PARSING.
You *may read* the book which I *have printed.*

May, an irregular active verb, signifying " to have and to exercise might or strength," indic. mood, pres. tense, second pers. plur. agreeing with its nom. *you.* *Read,* an irregular verb active, infinitive mood, pres. tense, with the sign *to* understood, referring to *you* as its agent. *Have,* an active verb, signifying to *possess,* indic. present, and having for its object, book under stood after "which." *Printed,* a perf. participle, referring to book understood

Johnson, and Blair, and Lowth, *would have been laughed at, had* they *essayed* to *thrust* any thing like our modernized philosophical grammar down the throats of their cotemporaries.

Would, an active verb, signifying " to exercise volition," in the past tense of the indicative. *Have,* a verb, in the infinitive, *to* understood. *Been,* a per

Perfect Tense.

Singular.	*Plural.*
1. I have loved,	1. We have loved,
2. Thou hast loved,	2. Ye *or* you have loved,
3. He hath *or* has loved.	3. They have loved.

Pluperfect Tense.

Singular.	*Plural.*
1. I had loved,	1. We had loved,
2. Thou hadst loved,	2. Ye *or* you had loved,
3. He had loved.	3. They had loved.

First Future Tense.

Singular.	*Plural.*
1. I shall *or* will love,	1. We shall *or* will love,
2. Thou shalt *or* wilt love,	2. Ye *or* you shall *or* will love,
3. He shall *or* will love.	3. They shall *or* will love.

Second Future Tense.

Singular.	*Plural.*
1. I shall have loved,	1. We shall have loved,
2. Thou wilt have loved,	2. Ye *or* you will have loved,
3. He will have loved.	3. They will have loved.

Note. Tenses formed without auxiliaries, are called *simple* tenses; as, I *love*; I *loved*; but those formed by the help of auxiliaries, are denominated *compound* tenses; as, I *have loved*; I *had loved*, &c.

This display of the verb shows you, in the clearest light, the application of the *signs* of the *tenses*, which signs ought to be perfectly committed to memory before you proceed any farther. By looking again at the conjugation, you will notice, that *have*, placed before the perfect participle of any verb, forms the perfect tense; *had*, the pluperfect; *shall* or *will*, the first future, and so on.

Now speak each of the verbs, *love, hate, walk, smile, rule*, and *conquer*, in the first person of each tense in this mood, with the pronoun *I* before it; thus, indicative mood, pres. tense, first pers. sing. I love; imperf. I loved; perf. I have loved; and so on, through all the tenses. If you learn thoroughly the conjugation

---

fect part. of to *be*, referring to Johnson, Blair, and Lowth. *Laughed at*, perf. part. of to *laugh at*, referring to the same as *been*. *Had*, active verb, in the past tense of the indicative, agreeing with its nom. *they*. *Essayed*, perf. part. referring to they.

Call this "*philosophical* parsing, on reasoning principles, according to the original laws of nature and of thought," and the *pill* will be swallowed, by pedants and their dupes, with the greatest ease imaginable.

of the verb in the indicative mood, you will find no difficulty in conjugating it through those that follow, for in the conjugation through all the moods, there is a great similarity.

SUBJUNCTIVE MOOD.

Present Tense, or elliptical future.—*Conjunctive form.*

Singular.	*Plural.*
1. If I love,	1. If we love,
2. If thou love,	2. If ye *or* you love,
3. If he love.	3. If they love.

Look again at the conjugation in the indicative present, and you will observe, that the form of the verb differs from this form in the subjunctive. The verb in the present tense of this mood, does not vary its termination on account of number or person. This is called the *conjunctive* form of the verb; but sometimes the verb in the subjunctive mood, present tense, is conjugated in the same manner as it is in the indicative, with this exception, *if, though, unless,* or some other conjunction, is prefixed; as,

Indicative form.

Singular.	*Plural.*
1. If I love,	1. If we love,
2. If thou lovest,	2. If ye *or* you love,
3. If he loves.	3. If they love.

The following general rule will direct you when to use the *conjunctive* form of the verb, and when the *indicative.* When a verb in the subjunctive mood, present tense, has a *future* signification, or a reference to *future* time, the conjunctive form should be used; as, "If thou *prosper,* thou shouldst be thankful;" "He will maintain his principles, though he *lose* his estate;" that is, If thou *shalt* or *shouldst* prosper; though he *shall* or *should* lose, &c. But when a verb in the subjunctive mood, present tense, has *no* reference to future time, the indicative form ought to be used; as, "Unless he *means* what he says, he is doubly faithless." By this you perceive, that when a verb in the present tense of the subjunctive mood, has a future signification, an *auxiliary* is always understood before it, for which reason, in this construction, the termination of the principal verb never varies; as, "He will not become eminent, unless he *exert* himself;" that is, unless he *shall* exert, or *should* exert himself. This tense of the subjunctive mood ought to be called the *elliptical future.*

The imperfect, the perfect, the pluperfect, and the first future tenses of this mood, are conjugated, in every respect, like the same tenses of the indicative, with this exception; in the subjunctive mood, a conjunction implying doubt, &c. is prefixed to the verb.

In the second future tense of this mood, the verb is conjugated thus:

Second Future Tense.

Singular.	Plural.
1. If I shall have loved,	1. If we shall have loved,
2. If thou shalt have loved,	2. If you shall have loved,
3. If he shall have loved.	3. If they shall have loved.

Look at the same tense in the indicative mood, and you will readily perceive the distinction between the two conjugations.

IMPERATIVE MOOD.

Singular.	Plural.
2. Love, *or* love thou, *or* do thou love.	2. Love, *or* love ye *or* you, *or* do ye *or* you love.

NOTE. We cannot command, exhort, &c. either in *past* or *future* time; therefore a verb in this mood is always in the *present* tense.

POTENTIAL MOOD.

Present Tense.

Singular.	Plural.
1. I may, can, *or* must love,	1. We may, can, *or* must love,
2. Thou mayst, canst, *or* must love,	2. Ye *or* you may, can, *or* must love,
3. He may, can, *or* must love.	3. They may, can, *or* must love.

Imperfect Tense.

Singular.	Plural.
1. I might, could, would, *or* should love,	1. We might, could, would, *or* should love,
2. Thou mightst, couldst, wouldst, *or* shouldst love,	2. Ye *or* you might, could, would, *or* should love,
3. He might, could, would, *or* should love.	3. They might, could, would, *or* should love.

Perfect Tense.

Singular.	Plural.
1. I may, can, *or* must have loved,	1. We may, can, *or* must have loved,
2. Thou mayst, canst, *or* must have loved,	2. Ye *or* you may, can, *or* must have loved,
3 He may, can, *or* must have loved.	3. They may, can, *or* must have loved.

Pluperfect Tense.

Singular.	*Plural.*
1. I might, could, would, *or* should have loved,	1. We might, could, would, *or* should have loved,
2. Thou mightst, couldst, wouldst, *or* shouldst have loved,	2. Ye *or* you might, could, would, *or* should have loved, •
3. He might, could, would, *or* should have loved.	3. They might, could, would *or* should have loved.

By examining carefully the conjugation of the verb through this mood, you will find it very easy; thus, you will notice, that whenever any of the auxiliaries, *may, can,* or *must,* is placed before a verb, that verb is in the potential mood, *present* tense; *might, could, would,* or *should,* renders it in the potential mood, *imperfect* tense; *may, can,* or *must have,* the *perfect* tense; and *might, could, would,* or *should have,* the *pluperfect* tense.

Infinitive Mood.

Pres. Tense. To love.   Perf. Tense. To have loved.

Participles.

Present *or* imperfect,	Loving.
Perfect *or* passive,	Loved.
Compound,	Having loved.

Note. The perfect participle of a regular verb, corresponds exactly with the imperfect tense; yet the former may, at all times, be distinguished from the latter, by the following rule: In composition, the imperfect tense of a verb *always* has a nominative, either expressed or implied: the perfect participle *never* has.

For your encouragement, allow me to inform you, that when you shall have learned to conjugate the verb to *love,* you will be able to conjugate all the regular verbs in the English language, for they are all conjugated precisely in the same manner. By pursuing the following direction, you can, in a very short time, learn to conjugate any verb. Conjugate the verb *love* through all the moods and tenses, in the first person singular, with the pronoun *I* before it, and speak the Participles: thus, Indicative mood, pres. tense, first pers. sing. I *love,* imperf. tense, I *loved;* perf. tense, I *have loved:* and so on, through every mood and tense. Then conjugate it in the second pers. sing. with the pronoun *thou* before it, through all the moods and tenses; 'thus, Indic. mood, pres. tense, second pers. sing. thou *lovest;* imperf. tense, thou *lovedst:* and so on, through the whole. After that, conjugate it in the third pers. sing. with *he* before it; and then in the first pers. plural, with *we* before it, in like manner through all the moods and tenses. Although this mode of procedure may, at first, appear to be laborious, yet, as it is necessary, I trust you will not hesitate to adopt it.   My confidence in your perseverance, induces me to recommend any course which I know will tend to facilitate your progress.

When you shall have complied with my requisition, you may conjugate the following verbs in the same manner; which will enable you, hereafter, to tell the mood and tense of any verb without hesitation: *walk, hate, smile, rule, conquer, reduce, relate, melt, shun, fail.*

LECTURE XII.

OF IRREGULAR VERBS.

IRREGULAR verbs are those that do not form their imperfect tense and perfect participle by the addition of *d* or *ed* to the present tense; as,

Pres. Tense.	Imperf. Tense	Perf. or Pass. Part.
I write	I wrote	written
I begin	I began	begun
I go	I went	gone

The following is a list of the *irregular* verbs. Those marked with an R. are sometimes conjugated *regularly.*

Pres. Tense.	Imperf. Tense.	Perf. or Pass. Part.
Abide	abode	abode
Am	was	been
Arise	arose	arisen
Awake	awoke, R.	awaked
Bear, *to bring forth*	bare	born
Bear, *to carry*	bore	borne
Beat	beat	beaten, beat
Begin	began	begun
Bend	bent	bent
Bereave	bereft, R.	bereft, R.
Beseech	besought	besought
Bid	bade, bid	bidden, bid
Bind	bound	bound
Bite	bit	bitten, bit
Bleed	bled	bled
Blow	blew	blown
Break	broke	broken
Breed	bred	bred
Bring	brought	brought
Build	built	built
Burst	burst, R.	burst, R.
Buy	bought	bought

Pres. Tense.	Imperf. Tense.	Perf. or Pass. Part.
Cast	cast	cast
Catch	caught, R.	caught, R.
Chide	chid	chidden, chid
Choose	chose	chosen
Cleave, *to adhere*	clave, R.	cleaved
Cleave, *to split*	cleft *or* clove	cleft, cloven
Cling	clung	clung
Clothe	clothed	clad, R.
Come	came	come
Cost	cost	cost
Crow	crew, R.	crowed
Creep	crept	crept
Cut	cut	cut
Dare, *to venture*	durst	dared
Dare, *to challenge*	REGULAR	
Deal	dealt, R.	dealt, R.
Dig	dug, R.	dug, R.
Do	did	done
Draw	drew	drawn
Drive	drove	driven
Drink	drank	drunk, drank,*
Dwell	dwelt, R.	dwelt, R.
Eat	eat, ate	eaten
Fall	fell	fallen
Feed	fed	fed
Feel	felt	felt
Fight	fought	fought
Find	found	found
Flee	fled	fled
Fling	flung	flung
Fly	flew	flown
Forget	forgot	forgotten
Forsake	forsook	forsaken
Freeze	froze	frozen
Get	got	got †
Gild	gilt, R.	gilt, R.
Gird	girt, R.	girt, R.
Give	gave	given,
Go	went	gone
Grave	graved	graven, R.
Grind	ground	ground
Grow	grew	grown
Have	had	had
Hang	hung, R.	hung, R.
Hear	heard	heard
Hew	hewed	hewn, R.
Hide	hid	hidden, hid
Hit	hit	hit
Hold	held	held
Hurt	hurt	hurt
Keep	kept	kept
Knit	knit, R.	knit, R.

* The men were drunk; i. e. inebriated. The toasts were drank.
† Gotten is nearly obsolete. Its compound forgotten, is still in good use.

Pres. Tense	*Imperf Tense.*	*Perf. or Pass. Part.*
Know	knew	known
Lade	laded	laden
Lay	laid	laid
Lead	led	led
Leave	left	left
Lend	lent	lent
Let	let	let
Lie, *to lie down*	lay	lain
Load	loaded	laden, **R.**
Lose	lost	lost
Make	made	made
Meet	met	met
Mow	mowed	mown, **R.**
Pay	paid	paid
Put	put	put
Read	read	read
Rend	rent	rent
Rid	rid	rid
Ride	rode	rode, **ridden**[*]
Ring	rung, rang,	rung
Rise	rose	risen
Rive	rived	riven
Run	ran	run
Saw	sawed	sawn, R.
Say	said	said
See	saw	seen
Seek	sought	sought
Sell	sold	sold
Send	sent	sent
Set	set	set
Shake	shook	shaken
Shape	shaped	shaped, **shapen**
Shave	shaved	shaven, R.
Shear	sheared	shorn
Shed	shed	shed
Shine	shone, R	shone, R
Show	showed	shown
Shoe	shod	shod
Shoot	shot	shot
Shrink	shrunk	shrunk
Shred	shred	shred
Shut	shut	shut
Sing	sung, sang,[†]	sung
Sink	sunk, sank,[†]	sunk
Sit	sat	set
Slay	slew	slain
Sleep	slept	slept
Slide	slid	slidden
Sling	slung,	slung
Slink	slunk	slunk
Slit	slit, R.	slit.

[*] Ridden is nearly obsolete.
[†] Sang and sank should not be used in familiar style.

Pres. Tense.	Imperf. Tense.	Perf. or Pass. Part
Smite	smote	smitten
Sow	sowed	sown, R.
Speak	spoke	spoken
Speed	sped	sped
Spend	spent	spent
Spill	spilt, R.	spilt, R.
Spin	spun	spun
Spit	spit, spat	spit, spitten,*
Split	split	split
Spread	spread	spread
Spring	sprung, sprang	sprung
Stand	stood	stood
Steal	stole	stolen
Stick	stuck	stuck
Sting	stung	stung
Stink	stunk	stunk
Stride	strode, strid	stridden
Strike	struck	struck or stricken
String	strung	strung
Strive	strove	striven
Strow or strew	strowed or strewed	{ strown, strowed, or strewed
Sweat	swet, R.	swet, R.
Swear	swore	sworn
Swell	swelled	swollen, R.
Swim	swum, swam	swum
Swing	swung	swung
Take	took	taken
Teach	taught	taught
Tear	tore	torn
Tell	told	told
Think	thought	thought
Thrive	throve, R.	thriven
Throw	threw	thrown
Thrust	thrust	thrust
Tread	trod	trodden
Wax	waxed	waxen, R.
Wear	wore	worn
Weave	wove	woven
Wet	wet	wet, R.
Weep	wept	wept
Win	won	won
Wind	wound	wound
Work	wrought, worked	wrought, worked
Wring	wrung	wrung
Write	wrote	written.

In familiar writing and discourse, the following, and some other verbs, are often improperly terminated by *t* instead of *ed*; as, "learnt, spelt, spilt, s:opt, latcht." They should be, "learned, spelled, spilled, stopped, latched."

You may now conjugate the following irregular verbs, in a manner similar to the conjugation of regular verbs: *arise, begin, bind, do, go, grow, run, lend, teach, write.* Thus, to *arise*—Indicative

---

* Spitten is nearly obsolete.

mood, pres. tense, first person, sing. I arise ; imperf. tense, I arose ;
perf. tense, I have arisen, and so on, through all the moods, and
all the tenses of each mood ; and then speak the participles : thus,
pres. arising, perf. arisen, comp. having arisen. In the next
place, conjugate the same verb in the second person sing. through
all the moods and tenses ; and then in the third person sing. and
in the first pers. plural. After that, you may proceed in th
same manner with the words *begin, bind*, &c.

Now read the eleventh and twelfth lectures *four* or *five* times
over, and learn the order of parsing a verb. You will then be
prepared to parse the following verbs in full ; and I presume, all
the other parts of speech. Whenever you parse, you must refer
to the Compendium for definitions and rules, if you cannot repeat
them without. I will now parse a verb, and describe all its properties by applying the definitions and rules according to the
systematic order.

"We *could* not *accomplish* the business."

Could accomplish is a verb, a word which signifies to do—active,
it expresses action—transitive, the action passes over from the
nom. "we" to the object "business"—regular, it will form its
imperfect tense of the indic. mood and perf. part. in *ed*—potential mood, it implies possibility or power—imperfect tense, it denotes past time however distant—first pers. plural, because the
nom. "we" is with which it agrees, agreeably to RULE 4. *A
verb must agree*, &c. Conjugated—Indic. mood, present tense,
first pers. sing. I accomplish; imperfect tense, I accomplished;
perfect, I have accomplished ; pluperfect, I had accomplished; and
so on.—Speak it in the person of each tense through all the
moods, and conjugate, in the same manner, every verb you parse.

EXERCISES IN PARSING.

These exercises contain a complete variety of Moods and Tenses.

I learn my lesson well. Charles, thou learnest thy lesson
badly. John, do you write a good hand ? Those ladies wrote a
beautiful letter, but they did not despatch it. Have you seen the
gentleman to whom I gave the book ? He has gone. They had
received the news before the messenger arrived. When will
those persons return ? My friend shall receive his reward. He
will have visited me three times, if he come to-morrow.

If Eliza study diligently, she will improve. If Charles studies
he does not improve. Unless that man shall have accomplished
his work by midsummer, he will receive no wages. Orlando,
obey my precepts, unless you wish to injure yourself. Remember what is told you. The physician may administer the medi-

cine, but Providence only can bless it. I told him that **might** go, but he would not. He might have gone last week, had he conducted himself properly ; (that is, *if he had conducted*, &c.) Boys, prepare to recite your lessons. ' Young ladies, let me hear you repeat what you have learned. Study, diligently, whatever task may be allotted to you. To correct the spirit of discontent, l t us consider how little we deserve. To die for one's country, s glorious. How can we become wise ? To seek God is wisdom. What is true greatness ? Active benevolence. A good man is a great man.

Note 1. *Man*, following *great*, and *what*, in the last two examples, are· nom. after *is :* Rule 21. *To seek God*, and *to die for one's country*, are members of sentences, each put as the nom. case to *is* respectively : Rule 24. The verb *to correct* is the infinitive mood absolute : Note under Rule 23. *May be allotted* is a passive verb, agreeing with *which*, the relative. part of *whatever*. *That*, the first part of whatever, is an adj. pronoun, agreeing with *task ;* and *task* is governed by *study*. *Hear*, following *let*, and *repeat*, following *hear*, are in the infinitive mood without the sign *to*, according to Rule 25. *To recite* is governed by *prepare :* Rule 23. *Is told*, is a passive verb, agreeing with *which*, the relative part of *whatever ;* and *you*, following by *to* understood : Note 1, under Rule 32.

2. In parsing a pronoun, if the noun for which it stands is not expressed, you must say it represents some person or thing understood.

LECTURE XIII.

OF THE AUXILIARY, PASSIVE, AND DEFECTIVE VERBS.

I. AUXILIARY VERBS.

Before you attend to the following additional remarks on the Auxiliary Verbs, you will do well to read again what is said respecting them in Lecture XI. page 140. The short account there given, and their application in conjugating verbs, have already made them quite familiar to you ; and you have undoubtedly observed, that, without their help, we cannot conjugate any verb in any of the tenses, except the present and imperfect of the indicative and subjunctive moods, and the present of the imperative and infinitive. In the formation of all the other tenses, they are brought into requisition.

Most of the auxiliary verbs are defective in conjugation ; that is, they are used only in some of the moods and tenses ; and when unconnected with principal verbs, they are conjugated in t1e following manner:

MAY.

Pres.   { *Sing.* I may, thou mayst, he may
Tense   { *Plur.* We may, ye *or* you may, they **may.**

| Imperf. | *Sing.* I might, thou mightst, he might. |
| Tense. | *Plur.* We might, ye *or* you might, they **might.** |

CAN.

Pres.	*Sing.* I can, thou canst, he can.
Tense.	*Plur.* We can, ye *or* you can, they **can.**
Imperf.	*Sing.* I could, thou couldst, he could.
Tense.	*Plur.* We could, ye *or* you could, they **could.**

WILL.

Pres.	*Sing.* I will, thou wilt, he will.
Tense.	*Plur.* We will, ye *or* you will, they **will.**
Imperf	*Sing.* I would, thou wouldst, he would.
Tense.	*Plur.* We would, ye *or* you would, they **would**

SHALL.

Pres.	*Sing.* I shall, thou shalt, he shall.
Tense.	*Plur.* We shall, ye *or* you shall, they **shall.**
Imperf.	*Sing.* I should, thou shouldst, he should.
Tense.	*Plur.* We should, ye *or* you should, they **should.**

TO DO.

Pres.	*Sing.* I do, thou dost *or* doest, he doth *or* **does.**
Tense.	*Plur.* We do, ye *or* you do, they do.
Imperf.	*Sing.* I did, thou didst, he did.
Tense.	*Plur.* We did, ye *or* you did, they did.

Participles. Pres. doing. Perf. **done.**

TO BE.

Pres.	*Sing.* I am, thou art, he is.
Tense.	*Plur.* We are, ye *or* you are, they **are.**
Imperf.	*Sing.* I was, thou wast, he was.
Tense.	*Plur.* We were, ye *or* you were, they **were.**

Participles. Pres. being. Perf. been.

TO HAVE.

Pres.	*Sing.* I have, thou hast, he hath *or* has.
Tense.	*Plur.* We have, ye *or* you have, they **have.**
Imperf.	*Sing.* I had, thou hadst, he had.
Tense.	*Plur.* We had, ye *or* you had, they had.

Participles. Pres. having. Perf. had.

Do, be, have, and *will,* are sometimes used as principal verbs; and when employed as such, *do, be,* and *have,* may be conjugated, by the help of other auxiliaries, through all the moods and tenses.

Do. The different tenses of *do,* in the several moods, are thus formed: Indicative mood, pres. tense, first pers. sing. I do; imperfect tense, I did; perf. I have done; pluperfect, I had done; first future, I shall or will do; sec. fut. I shall have done. Subjunctive mood, pres. tense, If I do; imperf. if I did; and so on Imperative mood, do thou. Potential, pres. I may, can, or must do, &c. Infinitive, present, to do; perf. to have done. Participles, pres. doing; perf. done; compound, having done.

HAVE. *Have* is in great demand. No verb can be conjugated through all the moods and tenses without it. *Have*, when used as a principal verb, is doubled in some of the past tenses, and becomes an auxiliary to itself; thus, Indic. mood, pres. tense, first pers. sing. I have; imperf. tense, I had; perf. I have had; pluperf. I had had; first fut. I shall or will have; sec. fut. I shall have had. Subjunctive, present, if I have; imperf. if I had; perf. if I have had; pluperf. if I had had; first fut. if I shall or will have; sec. fut. if I shall have had. Imper. mood, have thou. Potential, present, I may, can, or must have; imperf. I might, could, would, or should have; perf. I may, can, or must have had; pluperf. I might, could, would, or should have had. Infinitive, present, to have; perf. to have had. Participles, pres. having; perf. had; compound, having had.

BE. In the next place I will present to you the conjugation of the irregular, neuter verb, *Be*, which is an auxiliary whenever it is placed before the perfect participle of another verb, but in every other situation, it is a *principal* verb.

To BE.—INDICATIVE MOOD.

Pres. Tense.	*Sing.*	I am, thou art, he, she, *or* it is.
	Plur.	We are, ye *or* you are, they are.
Imperf. Tense.	*Sing.*	I was, thou wast, he was.
	Plur.	We were, ye *or* you were, they were.
Perf. Tense.	*Sing.*	I have been, thou hast been, he hath *or* has been.
	Plur.	We have been, ye *or* you have been, they have been.
Plup. Tense.	*Sing.*	I had been, thou hadst been, he had been.
	Plur.	We had been, ye *or* you had been, they had been.
First Fut. T.	*Sing.*	I shall *or* will be, thou shalt *or* wilt be, he shall *or* will be.
	Plur.	We shall *or* will be, you shall *or* will be, they shall *or* will be.
Second Fut. T.	*Sing.*	I shall have been, thou wilt have been, he will have been.
	Plur.	We shall have been, you will have been, they will have been.

SUBJUNCTIVE MOOD.

Pres. Tense.	*Sing.*	If I be, if thou be, if he be.
	Plur.	If we be, if ye *or* you be, if they be.
Imperf. Tense.	*Sing.*	If I were, if thou wert, if he were.
	Plur.	If we were, if ye *or* you were, if they were.

The neuter verb to *be*, and all passive verbs, have two forms in the imperfect tense of this mood, as well as in the present; therefore, the following rule may serve to direct you in the proper use of each form. When the sentence implies doubt, supposition, &c. and the neuter verb *be*, or the passive verb, is used with a reference to present or future time, and is either followed or preceded by another verb in the imperfect of the potential mood, the *conjunctive* form of the imperfect tense must be employed; as, " *If* he *were* here, we *should* rejoice together;" "She *might* go, *were* she so disposed." But when there is no reference to present or future time, and the verb is neither followed nor preceded by another in the potential imperfect, the *indicative* form of the imperfect tense must be used ; as, " *If* he *was* ill, he did not make it known ; " " *Whether* he *was* absent or present, is a matter of no consequence." The general rule for using the conjunctive form of the verb, is presented on page 145. See, also, page 135.

The perfect, pluperfect, and first future tenses of the subjunctive mood, are conjugated in a manner similar to the correspondent tenses of the indicative. The second future is conjugated thus :

Second { *Sing.* If I shall have been, if thou shalt have been, if he shall. &c
Fut. T. { *Plur.* If we shall have been, if you shall have been, if they, &c.

IMPERATIVE MOOD.

Pres. { *Sing.* Be, *or* be thou, *or* do thou be.
Tense. { *Plur.* Be, *or* be ye *or* you, *or* do ye *or* you be.

POTENTIAL MOOD.

Pres. { *Sing.* I may, can, *or* must be, thou mayst, canst, *or* must be, he may, can, *or* must be.
Tense. { *Plur.* We may, can, *or* must be, ye *or* you may, can, *or* must be, they may, can, *or* must be.
Imperf. { *Sing.* I might, could, would, *or* should be, thou mightst, &c.
Tense. { *Plur.* We might, could, would, *or* should be, you might, &c.
Perf. { *Sing.* I may, can, *or* must have been, thou mayst, canst, &c.
Tense. { *Plur.* We may, can, *or* must have been, you may, can, *or* must, &c.
Pluper. { *Sing.* I might, could, would, *or* should have been, thou, &c.
Tense. { *Plur.* We might, could, would, *or* should have been, you, &c.

INFINITIVE MOOD.

Pres. Tense. To be.   Perf. Tense. To have been.

PARTICIPLES.

Pres. Being.   Perf. Been.   Compound, Having been.

This verb to be, though very irregular in its conjugation, is by far the most important verb in our language, for it is more frequently used than any other ; many rules of syntax depend on constructions associated with it, and, without its aid, no passive verb can be conjugated. You ought, therefore, to make yourself perfectly familiar with all its changes, before you proceed any farther.

II. PASSIVE VERBS.

The *cases of nouns* are a fruitful theme for investigation and discussion. In the progress of these lectures, this subject has frequently engaged our attention ; and, now, in introducing to your notice the passive verb, it will, perhaps, be found both interesting and profitable to present one more view of the nominative case.

Every sentence, you recollect, must have one *finite* verb, or more than one, and one *nominative*, either expressed or implied, for, without them, no sentence can exist.

The *nominative* is the *actor* or *subject* concerning which the verb makes an affirmation. There are three kinds of nominatives, *active, passive,* and *neuter.*

The nominative to an *active* verb, is *active,* because it *produces* an action, and the nominative to a *passive* verb, is *passive,* because it *receives* or *endures* the action expressed by the verb ; for,

A Passive Verb denotes action *received* or *endured* by the person or thing which is the nominative ; as, "The *boy is beaten* by his father."

You perceive, that the nominative *boy,* in this example, is not represented as the *actor,* but as the *object* of the action expressed by the verb *is beaten ;* that is, the boy *receives* or *endures* the action performed by his father; therefore *boy* is a *passive* nominative. And you observe, too, that the verb *is beaten,* denotes the *action* received or endured by the nominative; therefore *is beaten* is a *passive* verb.

If I say, John *kicked* the horse, John is an active nominative, because he performed or produced the action; but if I say, John *was kicked* by the horse, John is a passive nominative, because he received or endured the action.

The nominative to a *neuter* verb, is *neuter,* because it does not produce an action nor receive one; as, John *sits* in the chair. John is here connected with the neuter verb *sits,* which expresses simply the state of being of its nominative, therefore *John* is a neuter nominative.

I will now illustrate the active, passive, and neuter nominatives by a few examples.

I. Of ACTIVE NOMINATIVES ; as, "The *boy* beats the dog; The *lady* sings ; The *ball* rolls ; The *man* walks."

II. Of PASSIVE NOMINATIVES ; as, "The *boy* is beaten ; The *lady* is loved ; The *ball* is rolled ; The *man* was killed."

III. Of NEUTER NOMINATIVES ; as, "The *boy* remains idle ; The *lady* is beautiful ; The *ball* lies on the ground ; The *man* lives in town."

You may now proceed to the conjugation of passive verbs.

Passive Verbs are called *regular* when they end in *ed ;* as, was *loved ;* was *conquered.*

All Passive Verbs *are formed* by adding the *per-*

fect participle of an active-transitive verb, to the neuter verb *to be.*

If you place a perfect participle of an active-transitive verb after this neuter verb *be*, in any mood or tense, you will have a *passive* verb in the same mood and tense that the verb *be* would be in if the participle were not used ; as, I am *slighted ;* I was *slighted ;* He will be *slighted ;* If I be *slighted ;* I may, can, *or* must be *slighted, &c.* Hence you perceive, that when you shall have learned the conjugation of the verb *be*, you will be able to conjugate any passive verb in the English language.

The regular passive verb to *be loved*, which is formed by adding the perfect participle *loved* to the neuter verb to *be*, is conjugated in the following manner :

To Be Loved.—Indicative Mood.

Pres. Tense. *Sing.* I am loved, thou art loved, he is loved.
Plur. We are loved, ye *or* you are loved, they are loved.

Imperf. Tense. *Sing.* I was loved, thou wast loved, he was loved.
Plur. We were loved, ye *or* you were loved, they were loved.

Perfect Tense. *Sing.* I have been loved, thou hast been loved, he has been loved.
Plur. We have been loved, you have been loved, they have, &c.

Pluper. Tense. *Sing.* I had been loved, thou hadst been loved, he had been, &c.
Plur. We had been loved, you had been loved, they had been, &c.

First Future. *Sing.* I shall *or* will be loved, thou shalt *or* wilt be loved, he, &c.
Plur. We shall *or* will be loved, you shall *or* will be loved, they, &c.

Second Future. *Sing.* I shall have been loved, thou wilt have been loved, he, &c.
Plur. We shall have been loved, you will have been loved, &c.

Subjunctive Mood.

Pres. Tense. *Sing.* If I be loved, if thou be loved, if he be loved.
Plur. If we be loved, if ye *or* you be loved, if they be loved.

Imperf Tense *Sing.* If I were loved, if thou wert loved, if he were loved.
Plur. If we were loved, if you were loved, if they were loved.

This mood has six tenses :—See conjugation of the verb to *be.*

Imperative Mood.

Pres. Tense. *Sing.* Be thou loved, *or* do thou be loved.
Plur. Be ye *or* you loved, *or* do ye be loved.

Potential Mood.

Pres. Tense. *Sing.* I may, can, *or* must be loved, thou mayst, canst, *or* must, &c.
Plur. We may, can, *or* must be loved, you may, can, *or* must, &c.

Imperf. Tense. *Sing.* I might, could, would, *or* should be loved, thou mightst, &c.
Plur. We might, could, would, *or* should be loved, ye *or* you, &c.

Perfect Tense. *Sing.* I may, can, *or* must have been loved, thou mayst, canst, &c.
Plur. We may, can, *or* must have been loved, you may, can, &c.

Plup. Tense. *Sing.* I might, could, would, *or* should have been loved, thou mightst, couldst, wouldst, *or* shouldst have been loved, &c.
Plur. We might, could would, *or* should have been loved, you might, could, would, *or* should have been loved, they, &c.

INFINITIVE MOOD.

Pres. Tense. To be loved.   Perf. Tense.   To have been loved.

PARTICIPLES.

Present, Being loved.   Perfect or Passive, Loved.
Compound, Having been loved.

NOTE. This conjugation of the passive verb *to be loved*, is called the *passive voice* of the regular active-transitive verb *to love*.

Now conjugate the following passive verbs; that is, speak them in the first pers. sing. and plur. of each tense, through all the moods, and speak the participles; " to be loved, to be rejected, to be slighted, to be conquered, to be seen, to be beaten, to be sought, to be taken."

NOTE 1. When the perfect participle of an *intransitive* verb is joined to the neuter verb *to be*, the combination is not a passive verb, but a *neuter* verb in a *passive form*; as, " He *is gone*; The birds *are flown*; The boy *is grown*; My friend *is arrived*." The following mode of construction, is, in general, to be preferred; " He *has* gone; The birds *have* flown; The boy *has* grown; My friend *has* arrived."

2. Active and neuter verbs may be conjugated by adding their present participle to the auxiliary verb *to be*, through all its variations; as, instead of, I teach, thou teachest, he teaches, &c., we may say, I am teaching, thou art teaching, he is teaching, &c.; and, instead of, I taught, &c.; I was teaching, &c. This mode of conjugation expresses the continuation of an action or state of being; and has, on some occasions, a peculiar propriety, and contributes to the harmony and precision of language. When the present participle of an active verb is joined with the neuter verb to be, the two words united, are, by some grammarians, denominated an active verb, either transitive or intransitive, as the case may be; as, " I am writing a letter; He is walking:" and when the present participle of a neuter verb is thus employed, they term the combination a neuter verb; as, " I am sitting; He is standing." Others, in constructions like these, parse each word separately. Either mode may be adopted.

III. DEFECTIVE VERBS.

DEFECTIVE VERBS are those which are used only in some of the moods and tenses.

The principal of them are these.

Pres. Tense.	Imperf. Tense.	Perfect or Passive Participle is wanting.
May,	might.	———
Can,	could.	———
Will,	would.	———
Shall,	should.	———
Must,	must.	———
Ought,	ought.	———
———	quoth.	

NOTE. *Must* and *ought* are not varied. *Ought* and *quoth* are never used as auxiliaries. *Ought* is always followed by a verb in the infinitive mood, which verb determines its tense. *Ought* is in the *present* tense when the infinitive following it is in the present; as, " He *ought* to do it;" and *ought* is in the *imperfect* tense when followed by the perfect of the infinitive; as, " He *ought* to have done it."

Before you proceed to the analysis of the following examples, you may read over the last *three* lectures carefully and attentively; and as soon as you become acquainted with all that has been presented, you will understand nearly all the principles and regular constructions of our language. In parsing a verb, or any other part of speech, be careful to pursue the *systematic order*, and to conjugate every verb until you become familiar with all the moods and tenses.

'He *should have been punished* before he committed that atrocious deed."

Should have been punished is a verb, a word that signifies to do—passive, it denotes action received or endured by the nom.—it is formed by adding the perfect part. *punished* to the neuter verb to *be*—regular, the perf. part. ends in *ed*—potential mood, it implies obligation, &c.—pluperfect tense, it denotes a past act which was prior to the other past time specified by " committed"—third pers. sing. num. because the nom. " he" is with which it agrees: RULE 4. *The verb must agree*, &c.—Conjugated, Indic. mood, pres. tense, he is punished; imperf. tense, he was punished; perf. tense, he has been punished; and so on. Conjugate it through all the moods and tenses, and speak the participles.

EXERCISES IN PARSING.

Columbus discovered America. America was discovered by Columbus. The preceptor is writing a letter. The letter is written by the preceptor. The work can be done. The house would have been built ere this, had he fulfilled his promise. If I be beaten by that man, he will be punished. Young man, if you wish to be respected, you must be more assiduous. Being ridiculed and despised, he left the institution. He is reading Homer. They are talking. He may be respected, if he become more ingenuous. My worthy friend ought to be honored for his benevolent deeds. This ought ye to have done.

ADDITIONAL EXERCISES IN PARSING.

All the most important principles of the science, together with many of the rules, have now been presented and illustrated. But before you proceed to analyze the following exercises, you may turn over a few pages, and you will find all the rules presented in a body. Please to examine them critically, and parse the *examples* under each rule and note. The examples, you will notice, are given to illustrate the respective rules and notes under which they are placed; hence, by paying particular attention to them, you will be enabled fully and clearly to comprehend the meaning and application of all the rules and notes.

As soon as you become familiarly acquainted with all the *defi-nitions*, so that you can apply them with facility, you may omit them in parsing ; but you mus. always apply the rules of Syntax. When you parse without applying the definitions, you may proceed in the following manner :

"Mercy is the true badge of nobility."

Mercy is a noun common, of the neuter gender, third person, singular number, and in the nominative case to " is:" RULE 3. *The nominative case governs the verb.*

Is is an irregular neuter verb, indicative mood, present tense, third person, singular number, agreeing with " mercy," according to RULE 4. *The verb must agree, &c.*

The is a definite article, belonging to " badge," in the singular number : RULE 2. *The definite article the, &c.*

True is an adjective in the positive degree, and belongs to the noun " badge :" RULE 18. *Adjectives belong, &c.*

Badge is a noun com. neuter gender, third person, singular number, and in the nominative case *after* " is," and put by apposition with " mercy," according to RULE 21. *The verb to be may have the same case after it as before it.*

Of is a preposition, connecting ' badge" and " nobility," and showing the relation between them.

Nobility is a noun of multitude, mas. and fem. gender, third person, sing. and in the obj. case, and governed by " of:" RULE 31. *Prepositions govern the objective case.*

EXERCISES IN PARSING.

Learn to unlearn what you have learned amiss.

What I forfeit for myself is a trifle; that my indiscretions should reach my posterity, wounds me to the heart.

Lady Jane Gray fell a sacrifice to the wild ambition of the duke of Northumberland.

King Missipsi charged his sons to consider the senate and people of Rome as proprietors of the kingdom of Numidia.

Hazael smote the children of Israel in all their coasts; and from what is left on record of his actions, he plainly appears to have proved, what the prophet foresaw him to be, a man of violence, cruelty, and blood.

Heaven hides from brutes what men, from men what spirits know.

He.that formed the ear, can he not hear ?

He that hath ears to hear, let him hear.

NOTE 1. . *Learn*, in the first of the preceding examples, is a transitive verb, because the action passes over from the nom. *you* understood, to *the rest of the sentence* for its object : RULE 24. In the next example, *that my indiscre-*

tions should reach my posterity, is a part of a sentence put as the nominative to the verb *wounds*, according to the same Rule.

2. The noun *sacrifice*, in the third example, is nom. after the active-intransitive verb *fell*: RULE 22. The noun *proprietors*, in the next sentence, is in the objective case, and put by apposition with *senate* and *people*: RULE 7, or governed by *consider*, understood, according to RULE 35.

3. In the fifth example, *what*, following *proved*, is a compound relative. *Thing*, the antecedent part, is in the nom. case after *to be*, understood, and put by apposition with *he*, according to RULE 21, and NOTE. *Which*, the relative part, is in the obj. case after *to be* expressed, and put by apposition with *him*, according to the same RULE. *Man* is in the obj. case, put by apposition with *which*: RULE 7. The latter part of the sentence may be *literally* rendered thus: He plainly appears to have proved *to be that base character which* the prophet foresaw him to be, viz. a *man* of violence, cruelty, and blood. The antecedent part of the first *what*, in the next sentence, is governed by *hides*; and *which*, the relative part, is governed by *know* understood. The antecedent part of the second *what*, is governed by *hides* understood, and the relative part is governed by *know* expressed.

4. The first *he*, in the seventh example, is, in the opinion of some, nom to *can hear* understood; but Mr. N. R. Smith, a distinguished and acute grammarian, suggests the propriety of rendering the sentence thus; " He that formed the ear, *formed it to hear*; can he not hear ?" The first *he*, in the last example, is redundant; yet the construction is sometimes admissible, for the expression is more forcible than it would be to say, " Let him hear who hath ears to hear;" and if we adopt the ingenious method of Mr. Smith, the sentence is grammatical, and may be rendered thus; " He that hath ears, *hath ears* to hear; let him hear."

EXERCISES IN PARSING.

Idioms, anomalies, and intricacies.

1. " The wall is three *feet* high."
2. " His son is eight *years* old."
3. " My knife is worth a *shilling*."
4. " She is worth *him* and all his *connexions*."
5. " He has been there three *times*."
6. " The hat cost ten *dollars*."
7. " The load weighs a *tun*."
8. " The spar measures ninety *feet*."

REMARKS.—*Anomaly* is derived from the Greek, *a*, without, and *omales,* similar; that is, *without similarity*. Some give its derivation thus; *anomaly,* from the Latin, *ab*, from, or out of, and *norma*, a rule, or law, means an *outlaw;* a mode of expression that departs from the rules, laws, or *general* usages of the language; a construction in language peculiar to itself. Thus, it is a general rule of the language, that adjectives of one syllable are compared by adding *r*, or *er*, and *st*, or *est*, to the positive degree; but good, *better, best;* bad, *worse, worst*, are not compared according to the general rule. They are, therefore, anomalies. The plural number of nouns is generally formed by adding *s* to the singular: man, *men;* woman, *women;* child, *children;* penny, *pence*, are anomalies. The use of *news, means, alms,* and *amends*, in the singular, constitutes anomalies. Anomalous constructions are correct according to custom; but, as they are departures from general rules, by them they cannot be analyzed.

An *idiom*, Latin *idioma*, a construction peculiar to a language, may be an anomaly, or it may not. An idiomatical expression which is not an anomaly, can be analyzed.

Feet and *years*, in the 1st and 2d examples, are not in the nominative after *is*, according to Rule 21, because they are not in apposition with the respective nouns that precede the verb; but the constructions are anomalous; and, therefore, no rule can be applied to analyze them. The same ideas, however, can be conveyed by a legitimate construction which can be analyzed; thus, " The *height* of the wall is three *feet*;" " The *age* of my son is eight *years*."

An anomaly, when ascertained to be such, is easily disposed of; but sometimes it is very difficult to decide whether a construction is anomalous or not. The 3d, 4th, and 5th examples, are generally considered anomalies; but if we supply, as we are, perhaps, warranted in doing, the associated words which modern refinement has dropped, they will cease to be anomalies; thus, " My knife is *of the* worth *of* a shilling;" "—*of the* worth *of* him," &c. " He has been there *for* three times;" as we say, " I was unwell *for* three days, after I arrived;" or, " I was unwell three days." Thus it appears, that by tracing back, *for* a few centuries, what the merely modern English scholar supposes to be an anomaly, an ellipsis will frequently be discovered, which, when supplied, destroys the anomaly.

On extreme points, and peculiar and varying constructions in a living language, the most able philologists can never be agreed; because many usages will always be unsettled and fluctuating, and will, consequently, be disposed of according to the caprice of the grammarian. By some, a sentence may be treated as an anomaly; by others who contend for, and supply, an ellipsis, the same sentence may be analyzed according to the ellipsis supplied; whilst others, who deny both the elliptical and anomalous character of the sentence, construct a rule by which to analyze it, which rule has for its foundation the principle contained in that sentence only. This last mode of procedure, inasmuch as it requires us to make a rule for every peculiar construction in the language, appears to me to be the most exceptionable of the three. It appears to be multiplying rules beyond the bounds of utility.

The verbs, *cost, weighs*, and *measures*, in the 6th, 7th, and 8th examples, may be considered as transitive. See remarks on *resemble, have, own*, &c., page 56.

EXAMPLES.

1. " And God said, ' *Let* there be light,' and there was light." " Let us make man." " Let us bow before the Lord." " Let high-born seraphs tune the lyre."

2. " *Be it* enacted." " *Be it* remembered." " *Blessed be he* that blesseth thee; and *cursed be he* that curseth thee." " My soul, turn from them :—*turn we* to survey," &c.

3. " *Methinks* I see the portals of eternity wide open to receive him." " *Methought* I was incarcerated beneath the mighty deep." " I was there just thirty *years ago*."

4. " Their laws and their manners, generally *speaking*, were extremely rude." " *Considering* their means, they have effected much."

5. " Ah *me* ! nor hope nor life remains."
   " *Me* miserable ! which way shall I fly ?"

6. " O *happiness* ! our being's end and aim !
   Good, pleasure, ease, content ! whate'er thy name,
   That something still which prompts th' eternal sigh,
   For which we bear to live, or dare to die."—

The verb *let*, in the idiomatic examples under number 1, has no nominative specified, and is left applicable to a nominative of the first, second, or third person, and of either number. Every action necessarily depends on an agent or moving cause ; and hence it follows, that the verb, in such constructions, has a nominative understood ; but as that nominative is not particularly *pointed out*, the constructions may be considered anomalous.

Instead of saying, "*Let* it [*to*] be enacted ;" or, "It *is* or *shall* be enacted ;" "*Let* him [*to*] be blessed ;" or, "He *shall* be blessed ;" "*Let us* turn to survey," &c.; the verbs, *be enacted*, *be blessed*, *turn*, &c. according to an idiom of our language, or the poet's license, are used in the *imperative*, agreeing with a nominative of the first or third person.

The phrases, *methinks* and *methought*, are anomalies, in which the objective pronoun *me*, in the *first* person, is used in place of a nominative, and takes a verb after it in the *third* person. *Him* was anciently used in the same manner ; as, "*him thute*, him thought." There was a period when these constructions were not anomalies in our language. Formerly, what we call the *objective* cases of our pronouns, were employed in the same manner as our present *nominatives* are. *Ago* is a contraction of *agone*, the past part. of to *go*. Before this participle was contracted to an adverb, the noun *years* preceding it, was in the nominative case absolute ; but now the construction amounts to an anomaly. The expressions, " generally speaking," and " considering their means," under number 4, are idiomatical and anomalous, the subjects to the participles not being specified.

According to the genius of the English language, transitive verbs and prepositions require the *objective* case of a noun or pronoun after them ; and this requisition is all that is meant by government, when we say, that these parts of speech govern the objective case. See pages 52, 57, and 94. The same principle applies to the interjection. " Interjections require the *objective* case of a pronoun of the first person after them ; but the *nominative* of a noun or pronoun of the second or third person ; as, " Ah *me* ! Oh *thou* ! O my *country !*" To say, then, that interjections *require* particular cases after them, is synonymous with saying, that they *govern* those cases ; and this office of the interjection is in perfect accordance with that which it performs in the Latin and many other languages. In the examples under number 5, the first *me* is in the objective after " ah," and the second *me,* after *ah* understood ; thus, " Ah miserable me !" according to NOTE 2, under Rule 5.—*Happiness*, under number 6, is nom. independent ; Rule 5, or in the nom. after *O*, according to this Note. The principle contained in the note, proves that every noun of the second person is in the *nominative* case ; for, as the pronoun of the second person, in such a situation, is always nominative, which is shown by its *form*, it logically follows that the noun, under such circumstances, although it has *no form* to show its case, must necessarily be in the same case as the pronoun. " Good, pleasure, ease, content, *that*," the antecedent part of "*whatever*," and *which*, the relative part, are nom. after *art* understood : Rule 21, and *name* is nom. to *be* understood.

The second line may be rendered thus ; Whether thou art good, or whether thou art pleasure, &c. or *be* thy *name* that [thing] which [ever thing] it may be : putting *be* in the imperative, agreeing with *name* in the third person. *Something* is nominative after *art* understood.

EXAMPLES.

1. " All were well *but* the *stranger*." " I saw nobody but the *stranger*." " All had returned but he." " None but the *brave* deserve the fair." " The thing they can't *but* purpose, they postpone." " This life, at best, is *but* a dream." " It affords *but* a

scanty measure of enjoyment." "If he *but* touch the hills, they will smoke." " Man is *but* a reed, floating on the current of time."

2. " Notwithstanding his poverty, he is content."

3. " Open your hand *wide*." " The apples boil *soft*." " The purest clay is that which burns *white*." " Drink *deep*, or taste not the Pierian spring." .

4. " *What though* the swelling surge thou see ?" &c. "*What if* he foot, ordain'd the dust to tread ?" &c.

REMARKS.—According to the principle of analysis assumed by many of our most critical philologists, *but* is *always* a disjunctive conjunction ; and agreeably to the same authorities, to construe it, in any case, as a preposition, would lead to error. See false Syntax under Rule 35. They maintain, that its legitimate and undeviating office is, to join on a member of a sentence which *expresses opposition of meaning*, and thereby forms an exception to, or takes from the universality of, the proposition contained in the preceding member of the sentence. That it sustains its true character as a conjunction in all the examples under number 1, will be shown by the following resolution of them. —" All were well but the *stranger* [*was not well.*"] " I saw nobody but [*I saw*] the *stranger*." " None deserve the fair but the *brave* [*deserve the fair.*"] " They postpone the thing which [*they ought to do, and do not,*] *but* which [*thing*] they cannot avoid purposing to do." " This life, at best, [*is not a reality,*] *but* it is a dream. It [*affords not unbounded fruition*] *but* it affords a scanty measure of enjoyment." " If he *touch* the hills, *but exert no greater power upon them*, they will smoke ;"—"If *he exert no greater power upon the hills, but* [*be-out this fact*] if he touch them, they will smoke." " Man *is not a stable being, but* he is a reed, floating on the current of time." This method of analyzing sentences, however, if I mistake not, is too much on the plan of our pretended philosophical writers, who, in their rage for ancient constructions and combinations, often overlook the modern associated meaning and application of this word. It appears to me to be more consistent with the *modern* use of the word, to consider it an *adverb* in constructions like the following : " If he *but (only, merely)* touch the hills they will smoke."

Except and *near*, in examples like the following, are generally construed as prepositions : " All went *except him ;*" " She stands *near them.*" But many contend, that when we employ *but* instead of *except*, in such constructions, a *nominative* should follow : " All went *but he* [*did not go.*"] On this point and many others, *custom* is *variable ;* but the period will doubtless arrive, when *but, worth*, and *like*, will be considered prepositions, and, in constructions like the foregoing, invariably be followed by an objective case. This will not be the case, however, until the practice of supplying an ellipsis after these words is entirely dropped.

Poverty, under number 2, is governed by the preposition *notwithstanding*, Rule 31. The adjectives *wide, soft, white*, and *deep*, under number 3, not only express the quality of nouns, but also qualify verbs: Note 4, under Rule 18.—*What*, in the phrases " what though" and " what if," is an interrogative in the objective case, and governed by the verb *matters* understood, or by some other verb ; thus, " What matters it—what dost thou fear, though thou see the swelling surge ?" " What would you think, if the foot, which · is ordained to tread the dust, aspired to be the head ?"

In the following examples, the same word is used as several parts of speech. But by exercising judgment sufficient to com-

prehend the meaning, and by supplying what is understood, you
will be able to analyze them correctly.

EXERCISES IN PARSING.

I like what you dislike.

Every creature loves its like.

Anger, envy, and like passions, are sinful.

Charity, like the sun, brightens every object around it.

Thought flies swifter than light.

He thought as a sage, though he felt as a man.

Hail often proves destructive to vegetation.

I was happy to hail him as my friend.

Hail! beauteous stranger of the wood.

The more I examine the work, the better I like it.

Johnson is a better writer than Sterne.

Calm was the day, and the scene delightful.

We may expect a calm after a storm.

To prevent passion is easier than to calm it.

Damp air is unwholesome.

Guilt often casts a damp over our sprightliest hours.

Soft bodies damp the sound much more than hard ones.

Much money has been expended.

Of him to whom much is given, much will be required.

It is much better to give than to receive.

Still water runs deep.　　He labored to still the tumult.

Those two young profligates remain still in the wrong.

They wrong themselves as well as their friends.

I will now present to you a few examples in poetry. Parsing
in poetry, as it brings into requisition a higher degree of mental
exertion than parsing in prose, will be found a more delightful
and profitable exercise. In this kind of analysis, in order to
come at the meaning of the author, you will find it necessary to
transpose his language, and supply what is understood ; and then
you will have the literal meaning in prose.

EXERCISES IN PARSING.

APOSTROPHE TO HOPE.—CAMPBELL.

Eternal Hope! when yonder spheres sublime
Pealed their first notes to sound the march of time,
Thy joyous youth began :—but not to fade.—
When all the sister planets have decayed ;
When wrapt in flames the realms of ether glow,
And Heaven's last thunder shakes the world below ;
Thou, undismay'd, shalt o'er the ruins smile,
And light thy torch at Nature's funeral pile !

TRANSPOSED.

Eternal Hope! thy joyous youth began when yonder sublime
spheres pealed their first notes to sound the march of time:—
but it began not to fade.—Thou, undismayed, shalt smile over
the ruins, when all the sister planets shall have decayed; and
thou shalt light thy torch at Nature's funeral pile, when wrapt in
flames, the realms of ether glow, and Heaven's last thunder
shakes the world below.

ADDRESS TO ADVERSITY.—GRAY.

Daughter of heaven, relentless power,
Thou tamer of the human breast,
Whose iron scourge. and tort'ring hour,
The bad affright, afflict the best!
The gen'rous spark extinct revive;
Teach me to love and to forgive;
Exact my own defects to scan:
What others are to feel; and know myself a man.

TRANSPOSED.

Daughter of heaven, relentless power, thou tamer of the human
breast, whose iron scourge and torturing hour affright the bad,
and afflict the best! Revive thou in me the generous, extinct
spark; and teach thou me to love others, and to forgive them;
and teach thou me to scan my own defects exactly, or critically:
and teach thou me that which others are to feel; and make thou
me to know myself to be a man.

ADDRESS TO THE ALMIGHTY.—POPE.

What conscience dictates to be done,
  Or warns me not to do,
This teach me more than hell to shun,
  That more than heav'n pursue.

TRANSPOSED.

O God, teach thou me to pursue that (*the thing*) which conscience dictates to be done, more ardently than I pursue heaven;
and teach thou me to shun this (*the thing*) which conscience warns
me not to do, more cautiously than I would shun hell

TRIALS OF VIRTUE.—MERRICK.

For see, ah! see, while yet her ways
  With doubtful step I tread,
A hostile world its terrors raise,
  Its snares delusive spread.
O how shall I, with heart prepared,
  Those terrors learn to meet?
How, from the thousand snares to guard
  My unexperienced feet?

TRANSPOSED.

For see thou, ah! see thou a hostile world *to* raise its terrors, and see thou a hostile world *to* spread its delusive snares, while I yet tread her (*virtue's*) ways with doubtful steps.

O how shall I learn to meet those terrors with a prepared heart? How shall I learn to guard my unexperienced feet from the thousand snares of the world?

THE MORNING IN SUMMER.—THOMPSON.

Short is the doubtful empire of the night;
And soon, observant of approaching day,
The meek-eyed morn appears, mother of dews,
At first, faint gleaming in the dappled east,
Till far o'er ether spreads the wid'ning glow,
And from before the lustre of her face
White break the clouds away.

TRANSPOSED.

The doubtful empire of the night is short; and the meek-eyed morn, (*which is the*) mother of dews, observant of approaching day, soon appears, gleaming faintly, at first, in the dappled east, till the widening glow spreads far over ether, and the white clouds break away from before the lustre of her face.

NATURE BOUNTIFUL.—AKENSIDE.

——Nature's care, to all her children just,
With richest treasures, and an ample state,
Endows at large whatever happy man
Will deign to use them.

TRANSPOSED.

Nature's care, which is just to all her children, largely endows, with richest treasures and an ample state, that happy man who will deign to use them.

NOTE. *What,* in the second example, is a comp. rel. The antecedent part is gov. by *teach* understood; and the relative part by *to feel* expressed. *To shun* and *to pursue,* in the third example, are in the infinitive mood, gov. by *than,* according to a NOTE under Rule 23. *Faint* and *from,* in the 5th example, are adverbs. An adverb, in poetry, is often written in the form of an adjective. *Whatever,* in the last sentence, is a compound pronoun, and is equivalent to *that* and *who.* *That* is an adj. pron. belonging to " man;" *who* is nom. to " will deign;" and *ever* is excluded from the sentence in sense. See page 113. Parse these examples as they are transposed, and you will find the analysis very easy.

ADDITIONAL EXERCISES IN PARSING.

GOLD, NOT GENUINE WEALTH.

Where, thy true treasure? Gold says, "not in me;"
And, "not in me," the Diamond. Gold is poor.

TRANSPOSED.

Where is thy true treasure? Gold says, "It is not in me;" and the Diamond says, "It is not in me." Gold is poor.

SOURCE OF FRIENDSHIP.—DR. YOUNG.

Lorenzo, pride repress; nor hope to find
A friend, but what has found a friend in thee.

TRANSPOSED.

Lorenzo, repress thou pride; nor hope thou to find a friend, only in him who has already found a friend in thee.

TRUE GREATNESS.—POPE.

Who noble ends by noble means obtains,
Or, failing, smiles in exile or in chains,
Like good Aurelius let him reign, or bleed
Like Socrates, that man is great indeed.

TRANSPOSED.

That man is great indeed, let him to reign like unto good Aurelius, or let him to bleed like unto Socrates, who obtains noble ends by noble means; or that man is great indeed, who, failing to obtain noble ends by noble means, smiles in exile or in chains.

INVOCATION.—POLLOK.

Eternal Spirit! God of truth! to whom
All things seem as they are, inspire my song;
My eye unscale: me what is substance teach;
And shadow what, while I of things to come,
As past rehearsing, sing. Me thought and phrase
Severely sifting out the whole idea, grant.

TRANSPOSED.

Eternal Spirit! God of truth! to whom all things seem to be as they really are, inspire thou my song; and unscale thou my eyes: teach thou to me the thing which is substance; and teach thou to me the thing which is shadow, while I sing of things which are to come, as one sings of things which are past rehearsing. Grant thou to me thought and phraseology which shall severely sift out the whole idea.

THE VOYAGE OF LIFE.

How few, favored by ev'ry element,
With swelling sails make good the promised port,
With all their wishes freighted! Yet ev'n these,
Freighted with all their wishes, soon complain.
Free from misfortune, not from nature free,
They still are men; and when is man secure?
As fatal time, as storm. The rush of years
Beats down their strength; their numberless escapes

In ruin end : and, now, their proud success
But plants new terrors on the victor's brow.
What pain, to quit the world just made their **own**!
Their nests so deeply downed and built so high!—
Too low they build, who build beneath the stars.

TRANSPOSED.

How few persons, favored by every element, safely make the
promised port with swelling sails, and with all their wishes freighted! Yet even these few persons who do safely make the promised
port with all their wishes freighted, soon complain. Though they
are free from misfortunes, yet (*though* and *yet*, corresponding conjunctions, form only *one* connexion) they are not free from the
course of nature, for they still are men; and when is man
secure? Time is as fatal to him, as a storm is to the mariner.—
The rush of years beats down their strength ; (*that is, the strength
of these few ;*) and their numberless escapes end in ruin: and
then their proud success only plants new terrors on the victor's
brow. What pain it is to them to quit the world, just as they
have made it to be their own world ; when their nests are built
so high, and when they are downed so deeply!—They who build
beneath the stars, build too low for their own safety.

REFLECTIONS ON A SCULL.—LORD BYRON.

Remove yon scull from out the scattered heaps.
Is that a temple, where a God may dwell?
Why, ev'n the worm at last disdains her shattered cell!
Look on its broken arch, its ruined wall,
Its chambers desolate, and portals foul ;
Yes, this was once ambition's airy hall,
The dome of thought, the palace of the soul.
Behold, through each lack-lustre, eyeless hole,
The gay recess of wisdom and of wit,
And passion's host, that never brooked control.
Can all, saint, sage, or sophist ever writ,
People this lonely tower, this tenement refit?

TRANSPOSED.

Remove thou yonder scull out from the scattered heaps. Is
that a temple, where a God may dwell? Why, even the worm
at last disdains her shattered cell! Look thou on its broken
arch, and look thou on its ruined wall, and on its desolate chambers, and on its foul portals :—yes, this scull was once ambition's
airy hall ; (*it was*) the dome of thought, the palace of the soul.
Behold thou, through each lack-lustre, eyeless hole, the gay
recess of wisdom and of wit, and passion's host, which never

brooked control. Can all the works which saints, or sages, or sophists have ever written, repeople this lonely tower, or can they refit this tenement?

For your future exercises in parsing, you may select pieces from the English Reader, or any other grammatical work. I have already hinted, that parsing in poetry, as it brings more immediately into requisition the reasoning faculties, than parsing in prose, will necessarily tend more rapidly to facilitate your progress: therefore it is advisable that your future exercises in this way, be chiefly confined to the analysis of poetry. Previous to your attempting to parse a piece of poetry, you ought always to transpose it, in a manner similar to the examples just presented; and then it can be as easily analyzed as prose.

Before you proceed to correct the following exercises in false syntax, you may turn back and read over the whole thirteen lectures, unless you have the subject-matter already stored in your mind.

LECTURE XIV.

OF DERIVATION.

At the commencement of Lecture II., I informed you that Etymology treats, 3dly, of derivation. This branch of Etymology, important as it is, cannot be very extensively treated in an elementary work on grammar. In the course of the preceding lectures, it has been frequently agitated; and now I shall offer a few more remarks, which will doubtless be useful in illustrating some of the various methods in which one word is derived from another. Before you proceed, however, please to turn back and read again what is advanced on this subject on page 27, and in the PHILOSOPHICAL NOTES.

1. Nouns are derived from verbs.

2. Verbs are derived from nouns, adjectives, and sometimes from adverbs.

3. Adjectives are derived from nouns.

4. Nouns are derived from adjectives.

5. Adverbs are derived from adjectives.

1. Nouns are derived from verbs; as, from "to love," comes "lover;" from "to visit, visiter;" from "to survive, surviver," &c.

In the following instances, and in many others, it is difficult to

determine whether the verb was deduced from the noun, or the
noun from the verb, *viz.* "Love, to love; hate, to hate; fear, to
fear; sleep, to sleep; walk, to walk; ride, to ride; act, to act,"
&c.

2. Verbs are derived from nouns, adjectives, and sometimes
from adverbs; as, from the noun *salt*, comes "to salt;" from the
adjective *warm*, "to warm;" and from the adverb *forward*, "to
forward." Sometimes they are formed by lengthening the vowel,
or softening the consonant; as, from "grass, to graze;" sometimes
by adding *en;* as, from "length, to lengthen;" especially to adjectives; as, from "short, to shorten; bright, to brighten."

3. Adjectives are derived from nouns in the following manner:
adjectives denoting plenty are derived from nouns by adding *y;*
as, from "Health, healthy; wealth, wealthy; might, mighty," &c.

Adjectives denoting the matter out of which any thing is made,
are derived from nouns by adding *en;* as, from "Oak, oaken;
wood, wooden; wool, woollen," &c.

Adjectives denoting abundance are derived from nouns by adding *ful;* as, from "Joy, joyful; sin, sinful; fruit, fruitful," &c.

Adjectives denoting plenty, but with some kind of diminution,
are derived from nouns by adding *some;* as, from "Light, light-
some; trouble, troublesome; toil, toilsome," &c.

Adjectives denoting want are derived from nouns by adding
less; as, from "Worth, worthless;" from "care, careless; joy,
joyless," &c.

Adjectives denoting likeness are derived from nouns by adding
ly; as, from "Man, manly; earth, earthly; court, courtly," &c.

Some adjectives are derived from other adjectives, or from
nouns by adding *ish* to them; which termination when added to
adjectives, imports diminution, or lessening the quality; as,
"White, whitish;" i. e. somewhat white. When added to nouns,
it signifies similitude or tendency to a character; as, "Child,
childish; thief, thievish."

Some adjectives are formed from nouns or verbs by adding the
termination *able;* and those adjectives signify capacity; as,
"Answer, answerable; to change, changeable."

4. Nouns are derived from adjectives, sometimes by adding the
termination *ness;* as, "White, whiteness; swift, swiftness;" sometimes by adding *th* or *t*, and making a small change in some of
the letters; as, "Long, length; high, height."

5. Adverbs of quality are derived from adjectives, by adding
ly, or changing *le* into *ly;* and denote the same quality as the
adjectives from which they are derived; as, from "base," comes
"basely;" from "slow, slowly;" from "able, ably."

There are so many other ways of deriving words from one another, that it would be extremely difficult, if not impossible, to enumerate them. The primitive words of every language are very few; the derivatives form much the greater number. A few more instances only can be given here.

Some nouns are derived from other nouns, by adding the terminations *hood* or *head, ship, ery, wick, rick, dom, ian, ment,* and *age.*

Nouns ending in *hood* or *head*, are such as signify character or qualities; as, "Manhood, knighthood, falsehood," &c.

Nouns ending in *ship*, are those that signify office, employment, state, or condition; as, "Lordship, stewardship, partnership," &c. Some nouns in *ship* are derived from adjectives; as, "Hard, hardship," &c.

Nouns which end in *ery*, signify action or habit; as, "Slavery, foolery, prudery," &c. Some nouns of this sort come from adjectives; as, "Brave, bravery," &c.

Nouns ending in *wick, rick*, and *dom*, denote dominion, jurisdiction, or condition; as, "Bailiwick, bishopric, kingdom, dukedom, freedom," &c.

Nouns which end in *ian*, are those that signify profession; as, "Physician, musician," &c. Those that end in *ment* and *age*, come generally from the French, and commonly signify the act or habit; as, "Commandment," "usage."

Some nouns ending in *ard*, are derived from verbs or adjectives, and denote character or habit; as, "Drunk, drunkard; dote, dotard."

Some nouns have the form of diminutives; but these are not many. They are formed by adding the terminations *kin, ling, ing, ock, el,* and the like; as, "Lamb, lambkin; goose, gosling; duck, duckling; hill, hillock; cock, cockerel," &c.

OF PREPOSITIONS USED AS PREFIXES.

I shall conclude this lecture by presenting and explaining a list of Latin and Greek prepositions which are extensively used in English as prefixes. By carefully studying their signification, you will be better qualified to understand the meaning of those words into the composition of which they enter, and of which they form a material part.

I. LATIN PREFIXES.

A, ab, abs—signify from or away; as, *a-vert*, to turn from; *ab-ject*, to throw away; *abs-tract*, to draw away.

Ad—to or at; as, *ad-here*, to stick to; *ad-mire*, to wonder at.

Ante—means before; as, *ante-cedent*, going before.

Circum—signifies round, about; as, *circum-navigate*, to sail round.

Con, com, co, col—together; as, *con-join*, to join together; *com-press*, to press together; *co-operate*, to work together; *col-lapse*, to fall together.

Contra—against; as, *contra-dict*, to speak against.

De—from, down; as, *de-duct*, to take from; *de-scend*, to go down

Di, dis—asunder, away; as, *di-lacerate*, to tear asunder; *dis-miss*, to send away.

E, ef, ex—out; as, *e-ject*, to throw out; *ef-flux*, to flow out; *ex-clude*, to shut out.

Extra—beyond; as, *extra-ordinary*, beyond what is ordinary.

In, im, il, ir—(*in*, Gothic, *inna*, a cave or cell;) as, *in-fuse*, to pour in. These prefixes, when incorporated with adjectives or nouns, commonly re-erse their meaning; as, *in-sufficient, im-polite, il-legitimate, ir-reverence, ir-esolute.*

Inter—between; as, *inter-pose*, to put between.

Intro—within, into; as, *intro-vert*, to turn within; *intro-duce*, to lead into.

Ob, op—denote opposition; as, *ob-ject*, to bring against; *op-pugn*, to oppose.

Per—through, by; as, *per-ambulate*, to walk through; *per-haps*, by haps.

Post—after; as, *post-script*, written after; *post-fix*, placed after.

Præ, pre—before; as, *pre-fix*, to fix before.

Pro—for, forth, forward; as, *pro-noun*, for a noun; *pro-tend*, to stretch forth; *pro-ject*, to shoot forward.

Præter—past, beyond; as, *preter-perfect*, pastperfect; *preter-natural*, be-yond the course of nature.

Re—again or back; as, *re-peruse*, to peruse again; *re-trace*, to trace back.

Retro—backwards; as, *retro-spective*, looking backwards.

Se—aside, apart; as, *se-duce*, to draw aside.

Sub—under; as, *sub-scribe*, to write under, or *sub-sign*.

Subter—under; as, *subter-fluous*, flowing under.

Super—above or over; as, *super-scribe*, to write above; *super-vise*, to overlook.

Trans—over, beyond, from one place to another; as, *trans-port*, to carry over; *trans-gress*, to pass beyond.

II. GREEK PREFIXES.

A—signifies privation; as, *anonymous*, without name.

Amphi—both or two; as, *amphi-bious*, partaking of both or two natures.

Anti—against; as, *anti-masonry*, against masonry.

Dia—through; as, *dia-meter*, line passing through a circle.

Hyper—over; as, *hyper-critical*, over or too critical.

Hypo—under, implying concealment or disguise; as, *hypo-crite*, one dis-sembling his real character.

Meta—denotes change or transmutation; as, *meta-morphose*, to change the shape.

Para—contrary or against; as, *para-dox*, a thing contrary to received opinion.

Peri—round about; as, *peri-phrasis*, circumlocution.

Syn, syl, sym—together; as, *syn-tax*, a placing together; *syn-od*, a meet-ing or coming together; *syl-lable*, that portion of a word which is taken to-gether; *sym-pathy*, fellow-feeling, or feeling together.

RULES OF SYNTAX,

WITH ADDITIONAL EXERCISES IN FALSE SYNTAX.

The third part of Grammar is SYNTAX, which treats of the agreement and government of words and of their proper arrangement in a sentence.

SYNTAX consists of two parts, *Concord* and *Gov ernment*.

CONCORD is the agreement which one word has with another, in gender, person, number, or case.

For the illustration of agreement and government, see pages 52, and 53.

For the definition of a sentence, and the transposition of its words and members, see pages 119, 124, 128, and 167.

The principal parts of a simple sentence are the *nominative* or subject, the *verb* or attribute, or word that makes the affirmation, and the *object*, or thing affected by the action of the verb; as, "A wise *man governs* his *passions*." In this sentence, *man* is the subject; *governs*, the attribute; and *passions* the object.

A PHRASE is two or more words rightly put together, making sometimes a part of a sentence, and sometimes a whole sentence.

ELLIPSIS is the omission of some word or words, in order to avoid disagreeable and unnecessary repetitions, and to express our ideas concisely, and with strength and elegance.

In this recapitulation of the rules, Syntax is presented in a condensed form, many of the essential NOTES being omitted. This is a necessary consequence of my general plan, in which Etymology and Syntax, you know are blended. Hence, to ac-quire a complete knowledge of Syntax from this work, you must look over the whole.

You may now proceed and parse the following additional exercises in false Syntax; and, as you analyze, endeavor to correct all the errors without looking at the Key. If, in correcting these examples, you should be at a loss in assigning the reasons why the constructions are erroneous, you can refer to the manner adopted in the foregoing pages.

RULE I.

The article *a* or *an* agrees with nouns in the *singular* number only, individually or collectively; as, " *A* star, *an* eagle, *a* score, *a* thousand."

RULE II.

The definite article *the* belongs to nouns in the singular or *plural* number; as, " *The* star, *the* stars; *the* hat, *the* hats."

Note 1. A nice distinction in the meaning is sometimes effected by the use or omission of the article *a*. If I say, " He behaved with *a* little reverence," my meaning is positive. But if I say, " He behaved with little reverence," my meaning is negative. By the former, I rather praise a person; by the latter, I dispraise him. When I say, " There were few men with him," I speak diminutively, and mean to represent them as inconsiderable; whereas, when I say, " There were *a* few men with him," I evidently intend to make the most of them.

2. The indefinite article sometimes has the meaning of *every* or *each*; as, " They cost five shillings *a* dozen;" that is, ' *every* dozen.'
  " A man he was to all the country dear,
  " And passing rich with forty pounds *a* year !"
that is, ' *every* year.'

3. When several adjectives are connected, and express the various qualities of things individually different, though alike in name, the article should be repeated; but when the qualities all belong to the same thing or things, the article should not be repeated. " *A* black and *a* white calf," signifies, A black *calf*, and a white *calf*; but " *A* black and white calf," describes the two colors of *one* calf.

RULE III.

The nominative case governs the verb; as, " *I* learn, *thou* learnest, *he* learns, *they* learn."

RULE IV.

The verb must agree with its nominative in number and person; as, " The bird *sings*, the birds *sing*, thou *singest*."

Note 1. Every verb, when it is not in the infinitive mood, must have a nominative, expressed or implied; as, " Awake, arise;" that is, Awake *ye*; arise *ye*

2. When a verb comes between two nouns, either of which may be considered as the subject of the affirmation, it must agree with that which is more naturally its subject; as, " The wages of sin *is* death; His meat *was* locusts and wild honey;" " His pavilion *were* dark *waters* and thick *clouds*."

EXAMPLES OF FALSE SYNTAX.

Frequent commission of sin harden men in it.

Great pains has been taken to reconcile the parties.

So much both of ability and merit, are seldom found.

The sincere is always esteemed.

Not one of them are happy.

What avails the best sentiments, if people do not live suitably o them ?

Disappointments sinks the heart of man ; but the renewal of hope give consolation.

The variety of the productions of genius, like that of the operations of nature, are without limit.

A variety of blessings have been conferred upon us.

Thou cannot heal him, it is true, but thou may do something to relieve him.

In piety and virtue consist the happiness of man.

O thou, my voice inspire,
Who touched Isaiah's hallowed lips with fire.

Note 1. Will martial flames for ever fire thy mind,
And never, never be to Heaven resigned ?

He was a man whose inclinations led him to be corrupt, and had great abilities to manage the business.

Note 2. The crown of virtue is peace and honor.

IIis chief occupation and enjoyment were controversy.

RULE V.

When an address is made, the noun or pronoun addressed, is put in the nominative case *independent ;* as, " *Plato,* thou reasonest well ; " " Do, *Trim,* said my uncle Toby."

Note 1. A noun is independent, when it has no verb to agree with it.

2. Interjections require the objective case of a pronoun of the *first* person after them, but the nominative of a noun or pronoun of the *second* or *third* person ; as, " Ah ! *me;* Oh ! *thou;* O ! *virtue.*"

RULE VI.

A noun or pronoun placed before a participle, and being independent of the rest of the sentence, is in the nominative case *absolute ;* as, " *Shame being lost,* all virtue is lost ; " " The *sun being risen,* we travelled on."

Note. Every nominative case, except the case absolute and independent, should belong to some verb expressed or understood ; as, " To whom thus, *Adam ;* " that is, *spoke.*

FALSE SYNTAX.

Him Destroyed,
Or won to what may work his utter loss,
All this will follow soon.

Note.—Two substantives, when they come together, and do not signify the same thing, the former must be in the genitive case.

Virtue, however it may be neglected for a time, men are so constituted as ultimately to acknowledge and respect genuine merit.

RULE VII.

Two or more nouns, or nouns and pronouns, signifying the same thing, are put, by apposition, in the same case; as, "*Paul,* the *apostle;*" "*Joram,* the *king;*" "*Solomon,* the *son* of David, *king* of Israel, wrote many proverbs."

NOTE. A noun is sometimes put in apposition with a sentence; as, "The sheriff has just seized and sold his valuable library—(*which was*) *a misfortune* that greatly depressed him."

FALSE SYNTAX.

We ought to love God, he who created and sustains all things.

The pronoun *he* in this sentence, is improperly used in the nominative case. It is the object of the action of the transitive verb "love," and put by apposition with "God;" therefore it should be the objective case, *him,* according to Rule 7. (Repeat the Rule, and correct the following.)

I saw Juliet and her brother, they that you visited.
They slew Varus, he that was mentioned before.
It was John, him who preached repentance.
Adams and Jefferson, them who died on the fourth of July 1826, were both signers and the firm supporters of the Declaration of Independence.
Augustus the Roman emperor, him who succeeded Julius Cesar, is variously described by historians.

RULE VIII.

Two or more nouns, or nouns and pronouns, in the *singular* number, connected by copulative conjunctions, must have verbs, nouns, and pronouns, agreeing with them in the *plural;* as, "Socrates *and* Plato *were* wise; *they* were eminent *philosophers.*"

NOTE 1. When *each* or *every* relates to two or more nominatives in the singular, although connected by a copulative, the verb must agree with each of them in the singular; as, "*Every* leaf, *and every* twig, *and every* drop of water, *teems* with life."

2. When the singular nominative of a complex sentence, has another noun joined to it with a preposition, it is customary to put the verb and pronoun agreeing with it, in the singular; as, " Prosperity with humility, *renders its* possessor truly amiable ;" " The General, also, in conjunction with the officers, *has* applied for redress."

FALSE SYNTAX.

Coffee and sugar grows in the West Indies : it is exported ir large quantities.

Two singular nouns coupled together, form a plural idea. The verb *grows* is improper, because it expresses the action of both its nominatives, " coffee and sugar," which two nominatives are connected by the copulative conjunction, *and ;* therefore the verb should be plural, *grow ;* and then it would agree with coffee *and* sugar, according to Rule 8. (Repeat the Rule.) The pronoun *it*, as it represents both the nouns, " coffee and sugar," ought also to be plural, *they*, agreeably to Rule 8. The sentence should be written thus, " Coffee and sugar *grow* in the West Indies : *they are* exported in large quantities."

Time and tide waits for no man.

Patience and diligence, like faith, removes mountains.

Life and health is both uncertain.

Wisdom, virtue, happiness, dwells with the golden mediocrity.

The planetary system, boundless space, and the immense ocean, affects the mind with sensations of astonishment.

What signifies the counsel and care of preceptors, when you think you have no need of assistance ?

Their love, and their hatred, and their envy, is now perished.

Why is whiteness and coldness in snow ?

Obey the commandment of thy father, and the law of thy mother ; bind it continually upon thy heart.

Pride and vanity always render its possessor despicable in the eyes of the judicious.

There is error and discrepance in the schemes of the orthoepists, which shows the impossibility of carrying them into effect.

EXAMPLES FOR THE NOTE.

Every man, woman, and child, were numbered.

Not proper ; for, although *and* couples things together so as to present the whole at one view, yet *every* has a contrary effect : it distributes them, and brings each separately and singly under consideration. *Were* numbered is therefore improper. It should be, " *was* numbered," in the singular, according to the Note. (Repeat it.)

When benignity and gentleness reign in our breasts, every person and every occurrence are beheld in the most favorable light.

RULE IX.

Two or more nouns, or nouns and pronouns, in the *singular* number, connected by disjunctive conjunctions, must have verbs, nouns, and pronouns, agreeing with them in the *singular;* as, " Neither John *nor* James *has* learned *his* lesson."

NOTE 1.. When singular pronouns, or a noun and pronoun, of different persons, are disjunctively connected, the verb must agree, in person, with that which is placed nearest to it; as, " Thou *or* I *am* in fault; I *or* thou *art* to blame; I, *or* thou, *or* he, *is* the author of it." But it would be better to say " Either I am to blame or thou art," &c.

2. When a disjunctive occurs between a singular noun or pronoun and a plural one, the verb must agree with the plural noun or pronoun, which should generally be placed next to the verb ; as, " Neither poverty *nor riches* were injurious to him;" " I *or* they were offended by it."

Constructions like these ought generally to be avoided.

FALSE SYNTAX.

Ignorance or negligence have caused this mistake.

The verb, *have* caused, in this sentence, is improperly used in the plural, because it expresses the action, not of *both*, but of either the one or the other of its nominatives; therefore it should be in the singular, *has* caused ; and then it would agree with " ignorance *or* negligence," agreeably to Rule 9 (Repeat the Rule.)

A circle or a square are the same in idea.

Neither whiteness nor redness are in the porphyry.

Neither of them are remarkable for precision.

Man is not such a machine as a clock or a watch, which move merely as they are moved.

When sickness, infirmity, or reverse of fortune, affect us, the sincerity of friendship is proved.

Man's happiness or misery are, in a great measure, put into his own hands.

Despise no infirmity of mind or body, nor any condition of life, for they may be thy own lot.

The prince, as well as the people, were blameworthy.

RULE X.

A collective noun or noun of multitude, conveying *unity* of idea, generally has a verb or pronoun agreeing with it in the *singular;* as, "The *meeting was* large, and *it* held three hours."

NOTE. Rules 10, and 11, are limited in their application. See page 59.

FALSE SYNTAX.

The nation are powerful.

The fleet were seen sailing up the channel.

The church have no power to inflict corporal punishment.

The flock, and not the fleece, are, or ought to be, the objects of the shepherd's care.

That nation was once powerful; but now they are feeble.

RULE XI.

A noun of multitude, conveying *plurality* of idea, must have a verb or pronoun agreeing with it in the *plural;* as, " The *council were* divided in *their* sentiments."

FALSE SYNTAX.

My people doth not consider.

The multitude eagerly pursues pleasure as its chief good.

The committee was divided in its sentiments, and it has referred the business to the general meeting.

The people rejoices in that which should give it sorrow.

RULE XII.

A noun or pronoun in the possessive case, is governed by the noun it possesses; as, " *Man's* happiness;" " *Its* value is great."

NOTE 1. When the possessor is described by a circumlocution, the possessive sign should generally be applied to the last term only; as, " The *duke of Bridgewater's* canal; The *bishop of Landaff's* excellent book; The *captain of the guard's* house." This usage, however, ought generally to be avoided. The words do not literally convey the ideas intended. What nonsense to say, " This is *the governor of Ohio's* house !"

2. When nouns in the possessive case are in apposition, and follow each other in quick succession, the possessive sign is generally annexed to the last only; as, " For *David* my *servant's* sake; *John* the *Baptist's* head; The canal was built in consequence of *De Witt Clinton* the *governor's* advice."

But when a pause is proper, and the governing noun not expressed, the sign should be applied to the first possessive only, and understood to the rest; as, " I reside at Lord *Stormont's,* my old *patron* and *benefactor.*"

3. *Its,* the possessive case of *it,* is often improperly used for *'tis,* or, *it is;* as, " *Its* my book: *Its* his," &c.; instead of, " *It is* my book; or, *'Tis* my book; *It is* his; or, *'Tis* his."

4. Participles frequently govern nouns and pronouns in the possessive case, as, " In case of his *majesty's dying* without issue, &c.; Upon *God's having ended* all his works, &c.; I remember *its being reckoned* a great exploit; At *my coming* in he said," &c. But in such instances, the participle with its adjuncts may be considered a substantive phrase, according to Note 2, Rule 28.

5. Phrases like these, " A work of *Washington Irving's;* A brother of *Joseph's;* A friend of *mine;* A neighbor of *yours,*" do not, as some have supposed, each contain a double possessive, or two possessive cases, but they may be thus construed; " A work of (*out of,* or, *among the number of*) *Washington Irving's works;* that is, One of the works of *Washington Irving,* One of the brothers of *Joseph;* One friend of *my friends;* One neighbor of *your neighbors.*"

FALSE SYNTAX.

Homers works are much admired.

Nevertheless, Asa his heart was not perfect with the Lord.

James Hart, his book, bought August the 19, 1829.

Note 1. It was the men's, women's, and children's lot to suffer great calamities.

This is Peter's, John's, and Andrew's occupation.

Note 2. This is Campbell's the poet's production.

The silk was purchased at Brown's, the mercer's and haberdasher's.

Note 4. Much will depend on the pupil composing frequently.

Much depends on this rule being observed.

The measure failed in consequence of the president neglecting to lay it before the council.

RULE XIII.

Personal pronouns must agree with the nouns for which they stand, in *gender* and *number;* as, "*John* writes, and *he* will soon write well."

NOTE. You, though frequently employed to represent a singular noun, is always *plural in form;* therefore the verb connected with it should be plural; as, "My friend, you *were* mistaken." See pages 99 and 100

FALSE SYNTAX

Every man will be rewarded according to their works.

Incorrect, because the pronoun *their* does not agree in gender or number with the noun "man," for which it stands; consequently Rule 13, is violated. *Their* should be *his;* and then the pronoun would be of the masculine gender, singular number, agreeing with *man*, according to Rule 13. (Repeat the Rule.)

An orator's tongue should be agreeable to the ear of their audience.

Rebecca took goodly raiment, and put them on Jacob.

Take handfuls of ashes, and let Moses sprinkle it towards heaven, in the sight of Pharaoh, and it shall become small dust.

No one should incur censure for being tender of their reputation.

Note. Horace, you was blamed ; and I think you was worthy of censure.

Witness, where was you standing during the transaction ? How far was you from the defendant ?

RULE XIV.

Relative pronouns agree with their antecedents, in *gender, person,* and *number ;* as, "Thou *who lovest* wisdom ;" "I *who speak* from experience."

NOTE. When a relative pronoun is preceded by two antecedents of different persons, the relative and the verb may agree in person with either, but not without regard to the sense ; as, "I am the man *who command* you ;" or,

" I am the man *who commands* you." The meaning of the first of these examples will more obviously appear, if we render it thus: " I who command you, am the *man*."

When the agreement of the relative has been fixed with either of the preceding antecedents, it must be preserved throughout the sentence; as, " I am the *Lord, that maketh* all things; *that stretcheth* forth the heavens alone; *that spreadeth* abroad the earth by myself," &c.

FALSE SYNTAX.

Thou who has been a witness of the fact, canst state it.

The wheel killed another man, which make the sixth which have lost their lives by this means.

Thou great First Cause, least understood!

Who all my sense confined.

Note, 2d part. Thou art the Lord, who didst choose Abraham, and brought him forth out of Ur of the Chaldees.

RULE XV.

The relative is the nominative case to the verb, when no nominative comes between it and the verb; as, "The master *who* taught us, was eminent."

FALSE SYNTAX.

If he will not hear his best friend, whom shall be sent to admonish him.

This is the man whom, he informed me, was my benefactor.

RULE XVI.

When a nominative comes between the relative and the verb, the relative is governed by the following verb, or by some other word in its own member of the sentence; as, "He *whom* I *serve,* is eternal."

NOTE 1. *Who, which, what,* the relative *that,* and their compounds, *whomever, whomsoever,* &c., though in the objective case, are always placed before the verb; as, " He *whom* ye *seek,* has gone hence."

2. Every relative must have an antecedent to which it relates, either expressed or implied; as, " *Who* steals my purse, steals trash;" that is, *he* who.

3. The pronouns *whichsoever, whatsoever,* and the like, are sometimes elegantly divided by the interposition of the corresponding nouns; as, " On *which* side *soever* the king cast his eyes," &c.

4. The pronoun *what* is sometimes improperly used instead of the conjunction *that;* as, " He would not believe but *what* I was in fault." It should be, " but *that,*" &c.

FALSE SYNTAX.

That is the friend who I sincerely esteem.

Not proper, because *who,* which is the object of the action expressed by the transitive verb " esteem," is in the nominative case. It ought to be *whom,* in the objective; and then it would be governed by esteem, according to Rule 16. (Repeat the Rule:)—and, also, according to Rule 20. "That is the friend *whom* I sincerely esteem."

They who much is given to, will have much to answer for.

From the character of those who you associate with, your own will be estimated.

He is a man who I greatly respect.

Our benefactors and tutors are the persons who we ought to ove, and who we ought to be grateful to.

They who conscience and virtue support, may smile at the caprices of fortune.

Who did you walk with?

Who did you see there?

Who did you give the book to?

RULE XVII.

When a relative pronoun is of the interrogative kind, it refers to the word or phrase containing the answer to the question for its *subsequent*, which subsequent must agree in *case* with the interrogative; as, " *Whose* book is that? *Joseph's;*" " *Who* gave you this? *John.*"

NOTE. Whether the interrogative *really refers* to a subsequent or not, is doubtful; but it is certain that the subsequent should agree in case with the interrogative.

FALSE SYNTAX.

Who gave John those books? Us. Of whom did you buy them? Of a bookseller, he who lives in Pearl-street.

Who walked with you? My brother and him.

Who will accompany me to the country? Her and me.

RULE XVIII.

Adjectives belong to, and qualify nouns, expressed or understood; as, "He is a *good*, as well as a *wise* man."

NOTE 1. Adjectives frequently belong to pronouns; as, " *I* am *miserable; He* is *industrious.*"

2. Numeral adjectives belong to nouns, which nouns must agree in number with their adjectives, when of the *cardinal* kind; as, " Ten *feet;* Eighty *fathoms.*" But some anomalous and figurative expressions form an exception to this rule; as, " A fleet of *forty sail;*" " *Two hundred head of cattle.*"

3. Adjectives sometimes belong to verbs in the infinitive mood, or to a part of a sentence; as, " *To see* is *pleasant;* To be blind is *unfortunate;* To die for our country is *glorious.*"

4. Adjectives are often used to modify the sense of other adjectives, or the action of verbs, and to express the quality of things in connexion with the

action by which that quality is produced; as, " *Red hot* iron; *Pale blue* lining; *Deep sea-green* sash; The apples boil *soft;* Open your hand *wide;* The clay burns *white;* The fire burns *blue;* The eggs boil *hard.*"

5. When an adjective is preceded by a preposition, and the noun is understood, the two words may be considered an adverbial phrase; as, " In general, in particular;" that is, generally, particularly.

6. Adjectives should be placed next to the nouns which they qualify; as, " A tract of *good* land."

7. We should generally avoid comparing such adjectives as do not literally admit of comparison; such as, *more impossible, most impossible; more unconquerable, more perfect, &c.* See REMARKS on adjectives, page 76.

8. When an adjective or an adverb is used in comparing two objects, it should be in the comparative degree; but when more than two are compared, the superlative ought to be employed; as, " Julia is the *taller* of the two; Her specimen is the *best* of the three."

FALSE SYNTAX.

Note 2. The boat carries thirty tun.

The chasm was twenty foot broad, and one hundred fathom in depth.

Note 6. He bought a new pair of shoes, and an elegant piece of furniture.

My cousin gave his fine pair of horses for a poor tract of land.

Note 7. The contradictions of impiety are still more incomprehensible.

It is the most uncertain way that can be devised.

This is a more perfect model than I ever saw before.

Note 8. Which of those two cords is the strongest?

I was at a loss to determine which was the wiser of the three.

RULE XIX.

Adjective pronouns belong to nouns, expressed or understood; as, " *Any* man, *all* men."

NOTE 1. The demonstrative adjective pronouns must agree in number with their nouns; as, " *This* book, *these* books; *that* sort, *those* sorts."

2. The pronominal adjectives, *each, every, either, neither, another,* and *one,* agree with nouns in the singular number only; as, " *Each* man, *every* person, *another* lesson;" unless the plural nouns convey a collective idea: as, " *Every* six months."

3. *Either* is often improperly employed instead of *each;* as, " The king of Israel, and Jehoshaphat the king of Judah, sat *either* of them on his throne." *Each* signifies *both* taken separately; *either* implies only *the one* or *the other* taken disjunctively:—" sat *each* on *his* throne."

FALSE SYNTAX.

Note 1. Those sort of favors do real injury.

They have been playing this two hours.

These kind of indulgences soften and injure the **mind.**

He saw one or more persons enter the garden.

Note 2. Let each esteem others better than themselves.

There are bodies, each of which are so small as to be invisible.

Every person, whatever their station may be, are bound by the laws of morality and religion.

Note 3. On either side of the river was the tree of life.

Nadab and Abihu took either of them his censer.

RULE XX.

Active-transitive verbs govern the objective case; as, " Cesar conquered *Pompey;*" " Columbus discovered *America;*" " Truth ennobles *her.*"

FALSE SYNTAX.

Ye who were dead, hath he quickened.

Ye, in the nominative case, is erroneous, because it is the object of the action expressed by the transitive verb " hath quickened ;" and therefore it should be *you*, in the objective case. *You* would then be governed by " hath quickened," agreeably to Rule 20. *Active-transitive verbs govern the objective case.*

Who did they entertain so freely ?

They who opulence has made proud, and who luxury has corrupted, cannot relish the simple pleasures of nature.

He and they we know, but who are ye ?

She that is negligent, reprove sharply.

He invited my brother and I to pay him a visit.

Who did they send on that mission ?

They who he has most injured, he had the greatest reason to love.

RULE XXI.

The verb *to be* may have the same case after it as before it; as, " *I* am the *man;*" " I believe *it* to have been *them;*" " *He* is the *thief.*"

NOTE 1. When nouns or pronouns next preceding and following the verb *to be*, signify the *same thing*, they are *in apposition*, and, therefore, in the *same case*. Rule 21 is predicated on the principle contained in Rule 7.

2. The verb *to be* is often understood : as, " The Lord made *me man ;* He made *him what* he was ;" that is, " The Lord made me *to be* man ; He made him *to be that which* he was." " They desired me to call *them brethren ;*" i. e. *by the name of* brethren. " They named *him John ;*" i. e. *by the name of* John ; or, by the *name* John ; putting these two nouns in *apposition*.

FALSE SYNTAX.

I know it to be they.

Improper, because *it* is in the objective case before the verb " to be," and *they* is in the nominative after ; consequently, Rule 21 is violated. *They* is in apposition with *it*, therefore *they* should be *them*, in the objective after to be, according to Rule 21. (Repeat the Rule.)

Be composed, it is me.

I would not act thus, if I were him.

Well may you be afraid; it is him, indeed.

Who do you fancy him to to be?

Whom do men say that I am? Whom say ye that I am?

If it was not him, who do you imagine it to have been?

He supposed it was me; but you knew that it was him.

RULE XXII.

Active-intransitive and passive verbs, the verb *to become*, and other neuter verbs, have the same case after them as before them, when both words refer to, and signify, the same thing; as, " *Tom* struts a *soldier;*" " *Will* sneaks a *scrivener;*" " *He* was called *Cesar;*" " The *general* was saluted *emperor;*" " *They* have become *fools.*"

NOTE 1. Active-intransitive verbs sometimes assume a transitive form, and govern the objective case; as, " *To dream* a *dream; To run* a *race; To walk* the *horse; To dance* the *child; To fly* the *kite.*"

2. According to a usage too common in colloquial style, an agent not literally the correct one, is employed as the nominative to a passive verb, which causes the verb to be followed by an *objective* case without the possibility of supplying before it a preposition: thus, " *Pitticus* was offered a large *sum* by the king;" " *She* was promised *them* (the *jewels*) by her mother;" " *I* was asked a *question.*" It would be better sense, and more agreeable to the idiom of our language, to say, " A large *sum* was offered *to Pitticus;*" "*They* were promised *(to) her;*" " A *question* was put *to me.*"

3. Some passive verbs are formed by using the participles of compound active verbs. To *smile*, to *wonder*, to *dream*, are intransitive verbs, for which reason they have no passive voice; but, to *smile on*, to *wonder at*, to *dream of*, are compound active-transitive verbs, and, therefore, admit of a passive voice; as, " He *was smiled on* by fortune; The accident is not *to be wondered at;*"

" There are more things in heaven and earth, Horatio,

" Than *are dreamed of* in your philosophy."

RULE XXIII.

A verb in the infinitive mood may be governed by a verb, noun, adjective, participle, or pronoun; as, " *Cease* to do evil;" " We all have our *talent* to be improved;" " She is *eager* to learn;" " They are *preparing* to go;" " Let *him* do it."

ILLUSTRATION. The supposed principle of *government* referred to in this rule, may be thus illustrated. In the sentence, " Cease to do evil," the peculiar manner in which *cease* is introduced, *requires* or *compels* us to put the verb *do* in the infinitive mood; and, according to the genius of our language, we cannot express this act of doing, when thus connected with *cease*, in any other mood, unless we change the construction of the sentence. Hence we say, that *cease* governs the mood of the verb *do*. Similar remarks may be applied to the words *talent, eager, preparing,* and *him,* in the respective examples under the rule.

Many respectable grammarians refer the government of this mood invariably to the preposition *to* prefixed, which word they do not, of course, consider a part of the verb. Others contend, and with some plausibility, that this mood is not governed by any particular word. If we reject the idea of government, as applied to the verb in this mood, the following rule, if substituted for the foregoing, might, perhaps, answer all practical purposes.

RULE.

A verb in the infinitive mood, refers to some noun or pronoun, as its subject or actor.

ILLUSTRATION of the examples under Rule XXIII. " To do" refers to *thou* understood for its agent ; " to be improved" refers to *talent ;* "to learn,' to *she ;* " to go," to *they ;* and " to do," refers to *him.*"

NOTE 1.   The infinitive mood absolute stands independent of the rest of the sentence ; as, " *To confess* the truth, I was in fault."

2. The infinitive mood is sometimes governed by conjunctions or adverbs; as, " An object so high *as to be* invisible ;" " He is wise *enough to deceive ;*" " The army is *about to march.*"

RULE XXIV.

The infinitive mood, or part of a sentence, is frequently put as the nominative case to a verb, or the object of an active-transitive verb ; as, " *To play* is pleasant ;" " Boys love *to play ;*" " *That warm climates shorten life,* is reasonable to suppose ;" " He does not consider *how near he approaches to his end.*"

NOTE.   *To,* the sign of the infinitive mood, is sometimes properly omitted ; as, " I heard him *say* it ;" instead of, " to *say* it."

RULE XXV.

The verbs which follow *bid, dare, need, make, see, hear, feel, help, let,* and their participles, are in the infinitive mood without the sign *to* prefixed ; as, "He bids me *come ;*" "I dare *engage ;*" " Let me *go ;*" "Help me *do it ;*" i. e. *to come, to go, to do* it, &c. " He is *hearing* me *recite.*"

FALSE SYNTAX.

Bid him to come.

He durst not to do it without permission.

Hear him to read his lesson.

It is the difference in their conduct, which makes us to approve the one, and to reject the other.

It is better live on a little, than outlive a great deal.

I wish him not wrestle with his happiness.

RULE XXVI.

Participles have the same government as the verbs have from which they are derived; as, "I saw the tutor *instructing* his *pupils.*"

Note. The present participle with the definite article *the* before it, becomes a noun, and must have the preposition *of* after it. *The* and *of* must both be used, or both be omitted; as, " By *the* observing *of* truth, you will command respect;" or, " By observing truth," &c.

FALSE SYNTAX.

Note. We cannot be wise and good without the taking pains for it.

The changing times and seasons, the removing and setting up kings, belong to Providence alone.

These are the rules of grammar, by observing of which you may avoid mistakes.

RULE XXVII.

The present participle refers to some noun or pronoun denoting the subject or actor; as, " I see a *boy running.*"

RULE XXVIII.

The perfect participle belongs, like an adjective, to some noun or pronoun, expressed or understood; as, " I saw the *boy abused.*"

Note 1. Participles of neuter verbs have the same case after them as before them; as, " *Pontius Pilate* being *Governor* of Judea, and *Herod* being *Tetrarch,*" &c.

2. A participle with its adjuncts, may sometimes be considered as a substantive or participial phrase, which phrase may be the subject of a verb, or the object of a verb or preposition; as, " *Taking from another without his knowledge or assent,* is called stealing; He studied to avoid *expressing himself too severely;* I cannot fail of *having money,* &c.; By *promising much and performing but little,* we become despicable."

3. As the perfect participle and the imperfect tense of irregular verbs, are sometimes different in their form, care must be taken that they be not indiscriminately used. It is frequently said, ' He begun,' for ' he began;' ' He run,' for ' he ran;' ' He come,' for ' he came;' the participles being here used instead of the imperfect tense; and much more frequently is the imperfect tense employed instead of the participle; as, ' I had wrote,' for ' I had written;' ' I was chose,' for ' I was chosen;' ' I have eat,' for ' I have eaten.' ' He would have spoke;'—*spoken.* ' He overrun his guide ;'—*overran.* ' The sun had rose;'—*risen.*

FALSE SYNTAX.

I seen him. I have saw many a one.

Seen is improper, the perfect participle being used instead of the imperfect tense of the verb. It ought to be, " I *saw* him," according to Note 3. *Have saw* is also erroneous, the imperfect tense being employed instead of the perfect participle. The perfect tense of a verb is formed by combining the auxiliary *have* with its perfect participle : therefore the sentence should be written thus, " I have *seen* many a one :" Note 3.

Note 3. He done me no harm, for I had wrote my letter before he come home.

Had not that misfortune befel my cousin, he would have went to Europe long ago.

The sun had already arose, when I began my journey.

Since the work is began, it must be prosecuted.

The French language is spoke in every state in Europe.

He writes as the best authors would have wrote, had they writ on the same subject.

RULE XXIX.

Adverbs qualify verbs, participles, adjectives, and other adverbs; as, " A *very good* pen *writes extremely well;*" " By *living temperately,*" &c.

NOTE 1. Adverbs are generally set before adjectives or adverbs, after verbs, or between the auxiliary and the verb ; as, " He made a *very sensible* discourse, and was *attentively* heard."

2. When the qualifying word which follows a verb, expresses *quality*, it must be an adjective, but when it expresses *manner*, an adverb should be used ; as, " She looks *cold;* She looks *coldly* on him ; He feels *warm;* He feels *warmly* the insult offered to him." If the verb *to be* can be substituted for the one employed, an adjective should follow, and not an adverb ; as, " She looks [*is*] *cold;* The hay smells [*is*] *sweet;* The fields look [*are*] *green;* The apples taste [*are*] *sour;* The wind blows [*is*] *fresh.*"

3. It is not strictly proper to apply the adverbs *here, there,* and *where,* to verbs signifying motion, instead of the adverbs *hither, thither, whither :* thus, " He came *here* [*hither*] hastily;" " They rode *there* [*thither*] in two hours;" " *Where* [*whither*] will he go ?" But in familiar style, these constructions are so far sanctioned as sometimes to be admissible.

4. The use of *where,* instead of *in which,* in constructions like the following, is hardly admissible : " The immortal sages of '76, formed a charter, *where* [*in which*] their rights are boldly asserted."

5. As the adverbs *hence, thence,* and *whence,* literally supply the place of a noun and preposition, there appears to be a solecism in employing a preposition in conjunction with them : " *From whence* it follows;" " He came *from thence* since morning." Better, " *whence* it follows;" " He came *thence.*" The following phrases are also exceptionable : " The *then* ministry;" " The *above* argument;" " Ask me *never* so much dowry;" " Charm he *never* so wisely." Better, " The ministry *of that time* or *period;*" " The *preceding* argument;" " *Ever* so much dowry;" " *Ever* so wisely."

FALSE SYNTAX.

Note 1. It cannot be impertinent or ridiculous therefore to remonstrate.

He was pleasing not often, because he was vain.

These things should be never separated.

We may happily live, though our possessions are small.

RULE XXX.

Two negatives destroy one another, and are generally equivalent to an affirmative; as, "Such things are *not un*common;" i. e. they are common.

NOTE. When one of the two negatives employed is joined to another word, it forms a pleasing and delicate variety of expression; as, "His language, though inelegant, is *not un*grammatical;" that is, it is grammatical.

But, as two negatives, by destroying each other, are equivalent to an affirmative, they should not be used when we wish to convey a *negative* meaning. The following sentence is therefore inaccurate: "I can*not* by *no* means allow him what his argument must prove." It should be, "I cannot by *any* means," &c., or, "I *can* by *no* means."

FALSE SYNTAX.

Note, 2d part. I don't know nothing about it.
I did not see nobody there. Nothing never affects her.
Be honest, nor take no shape nor semblance of disguise.
There cannot be nothing more insignificant than vanity.
Precept nor discipline is not so forcible as example.

RULE XXXI.

Prepositions govern the objective case; as, "He went *from* Utica *to* Rome, and then passed *through* Redfield."

FALSE SYNTAX.

Each is accountable for hisself.
They settled it among theirselves.
It is not I who he is displeased with.
Who did you go with?
Who did you receive instruction from?

RULE XXXII.

Home, and nouns signifying *distance*, time *when, how long*, &c. are generally governed by a preposition *understood*; as, "The horse ran a mile;" "He came *home* last June;" "My friend lived four *years* at college;" that is, ran *through the space of* a mile; or, ran *over a space called* a mile; *to* his home *in* last June; *during* four years, &c.

NOTE 1. The prepositions *to* and *for* are often understood, chiefly before the pronouns; as, "Give [to] *me* a book; Get [for] *him* some paper."

2. *To* or *unto*, is, by some, supposed to be understood after *like* and *unlike;* as, "He is *like* [unto] his brother; She is *unlike* [to] him." Others consider this mode of expression an idiom of the language, and maintain that *like* governs the objective following it.

3. Nouns signifying extension, duration, quantity, quality, or value, are used without a governing word; as, "The Ohio is one thousand *miles* long; She is ten *years* old; My hat is worth ten *dollars*" These are sometimes considered anomalies. See page 163.

RULE XXXIII.

Conjunctions connect nouns and pronouns in the same case; as, "The master taught *her* and *me* to write;" "*He* and *she* are associates."

FALSE SYNTAX.

My brother and him are grammarians.

You and me enjoy great privileges.

Him and I went to the city in company; but John and him returned without me.

Between you and I there is a great disparity of years.

RULE XXXIV.

Conjunctions generally connect verbs of like moods and tenses; as, "If thou sincerely *desire, and* earnestly *pursue* virtue, she *will* assuredly *be found* by thee, *and prove* a rich reward."

NOTE 1. When different moods and tenses are connected by conjunctions, the nominative must be repeated; as, "He *may return*, but *he will* not *tarry*."

2. Conjunctions implying contingency or doubt, require the subjunctive mood after them; as, "*If* he *study*, he will improve." See pages 135, 145, and 155.

3. The conjunctions *if, though, unless, except, whether*, and *lest*, generally require the subjunctive mood after them.

4. Conjunctions of a positive and absolute nature, implying no doubt, require the indicative mood; as, "*As* virtue *advances, so* vice *recedes*."

FALSE SYNTAX.

Did he not tell me his fault, and entreated me to forgive him?

Professing regard, and to act differently, discovers a base mind.

Note 1. He has gone home, but may return.

The attorney executed the deed, but will write no more.

Note 2. I shall walk to-day, unless it rains.

If he acquires riches, they will corrupt his mind.

RULE XXXV.

A noun or pronoun following the conjunction *than, as,* or *but*, is nominative to a verb, or governed by a verb or preposition, expressed or understood; as, "Thou art wiser *than* I [*am*.*]* "I saw nobody *but* [*I saw*] him."

NOTE 1. The conjunction *as*, when it is connected with *such, many,* or *same*, is sometimes, though erroneously, called a *relative pronoun*; as, "Let *such* as presume to advise others," &c.; that is, Let *them who*, &c. See page 116.

2. An ellipsis, or omission of some words, is frequently admitted, which must be supplied in the mind in order to parse grammatically; as, "Wo is me;" that is, *to* me; "To sleep all night;" i. e. *through* all *the* night; "He has gone a journey;" i. e. *on* a journey; "They walked a league;" i. e. *over a space called* a league.

3. When the omission of words would obscure the sense, or weaken its force, they must be expressed.

4. In the use of prepositions, and words that relate to each other, we should pay particular regard to the meaning of the words or sentences which they connect: all the parts of a sentence should correspond to each other, and a regular and clear construction throughout should be carefully preserved.

FALSE SYNTAX.

They are much greater gainers than me.

They know how to write as well as him; but **he is a better** grammarian than them.

They were all well but him.

None were rewarded but him and me.

Jesus sought none but they who had gone astray.

REMARKS ON THE TENSES.

1. In the use of verbs, and other words and phrases which, *in point of time*, relate to each other, a due regard to that relation should be observed.

Instead of saying, "The Lord *hath given*, and the Lord *hath taken* away;" we should say, "The Lord *gave*, and the Lord *hath taken* away." Instead of, "I *remember* the family more than twenty years;" it should be, "I *have remembered* the family more than twenty years."

2. The best rule that can be given for the management of the tenses, and of words and phrases which, in point of time, relate to each other, is this very general one; *Observe what the sense necessarily requires.*

To say, "I *have* visited Washington last summer; I *have seen* the work more than a month ago," is not good *sense*. The constructions should be, "I *visited* Washington, &c.; I *saw* the work, &c." "This mode of expression *has been* formerly much admired:"—"*was* formerly much admired." "If I *had have* been there;" "If I *had have* seen him;" "*Had* you *have* known him," are solecisms too gross to need correction. We can say, I *have* been, I *had* been; but what sort of a tense is, *had have been*? To place *had* before the *defective* verb ought, is an error equally gross and illiterate:—"*had* ought, *hadn't* ought." This is as low a vulgarism as the use of *theirn, hern,* and *hizzen, tother, furder, baynt, this ere,* I *seed* it, I *tell'd* him.

3. When we refer to a past action or event, and no part of that time in which it took place; remains, the *imperfect* tense should be used; but if there is still remaining some portion of the time in which we declare that the thing has been done, the *perfect* tense should be employed.

Thus, we say, "Philosophers *made* great discoveries in the last century;"

" He *was* mucn afflicted last year ;" but when we refer to the present cen tury, year, week day, &c. we ought to use the *perfect* tense ; as, " Philoso phers *have made* great discoveries in the present century ;" " He *has been* much afflicted this year ;" " I *have read* the president's message this week ;" " We *have heard* important news this morning ;" because these events occur red in this century, this year, this week, and to-day, and still there remains a part of this century, year, week, and day, of which I speak.

In general, the perfect tense may be applied wherever the action is con nected with the present time, by the actual existence either of the autho. of the work, though it may have been performed many centuries ago ; but if neither the author nor the work now remains, the perfect tense ought not to be employed. Speaking of priests in general, we may say, " They *have*, in all ages, *claimed* great powers ;" because the general order of the priest hood still exists ; but we cannot properly say, " The Druid priests *have claimed* great powers ;" because that order is now extinct. We ought, there fore, to say, " The Druid priests *claimed* great powers."

The following examples may serve still farther to illustrate the proper use and application of the tenses. " My brother has recently been to Philadel phia." It should be, " *was* recently at Philadelphia ;" because the adverb *recently* refers to a time completely past, without any allusion to the present time. " Charles is grown considerably since I have seen him the last time." Corrected, " Charles *has* grown, since I *saw* him," &c. " Payment was at length made, but no reason assigned for its being so long postponed." Cor rected, " for its *having been* so long postponed." " They were arrived an hour before we reached the city :"—" They *had* arrived."

" The workmen will complete the building at the time I take possession of it." It should be, " will *have completed* the building," &c. " This curious piece of workmanship was preserved, and shown to strangers for more than fifty years past :"—" *has been* preserved, and *been* shown to strangers," &c. " I had rather write than beg :"—" I *would* rather write than beg."

" On the morrow, because he would have known the certainty whereof Paul was accused of the Jews, he loosed him from his bands." It ought to be, " because he *would know ; or, being willing to know*," &c. " The blind man said, ' Lord, that I might receive my sight ;' " " If by any means I might attain unto the resurrection of the dead." In both these examples, *may* would be preferable to *might*. " I feared that I should have lost the parcel, before I arrived :"—" that I should *lose*." " It would have afforded me no satisfaction, if I could perform it." It ought to be, " if I could *have perform ed* it ;" or, " It *would afford* me no satisfaction, if I *could perform* it." " This dedication may serve for almost any book that has, is, or shall be published :" —" that *has been*, or *will be published*."

4. In order to employ the two tenses of the infinitive mood with propriety, particular attention should be paid to the meaning of what we express.

Verbs expressive of *hope, desire, intention*, or *command*, ought to be followed by the PRESENT tense of the *Infinitive mood.*

" Last week I intended to *have written*," is improper. The intention of writing was then *present* with me ; and, therefore, the construction should be, " I intended *to write*." The following examples are also inaccurate ; " I found him better than I expected *to have found* him ;" " My purpose was, after spending ten months more in commerce, *to have withdrawn* my wealth to another country." They should be, " expected *to find* him ;" " *to withdraw* my wealth."

" This is a book which proves itself to be written by the person whose name it bears." It ought to be "which proves itself *to have been written,*" &c. "To see him would have afforded me pleasure all my life." Corrected, "*To have seen* him;" or, "*To see* him *would afford* me pleasure," &c. "The arguments were sufficient to have satisfied all who heard them:"—"were sufficient *to satisfy.*" "History painters would have found it difficult to have invented such a species of beings:"—"*to invent* such a species."

5. General and immutable truths ought to be expressed in the *present* tense.

Instead of saying, "He did not know that eight and twenty *were* equal twenty and eight;" "The preacher said very audibly, that whatever *wa* useful, *was* good;" "My opponent would not believe, that virtue *was* always advantageous.;" The constructions should be, "*are* equal to twenty;" "whatever *is* useful, *is* good;"."virtue *is* always advantageous."

EXAMPLES IN FALSE SYNTAX PROMISCUOUSLY ARRANGED.

We adore the Divine Being, he who is from eternity to eternity.

On these causes depend all the happiness or misery which exist among men.

The enemies who we have most to fear, are those of our own hearts.

Is it me or him who you requested to go?

Though great has been his disobedience and his folly, yet if he sincerely acknowledges his misconduct, he shall be forgiven.

There were, in the metropolis, much to amuse them.

By exercising of our memories, they are improved.

The property of my friend, I mean his books and furniture, were wholly consumed.

Affluence might give us respect in the eyes of the vulgar, but will not recommend us to the wise and good.

The cares of this world, they often choke the growth of virtue.

They that honor me, I will honor; and them that despise me, shall be lightly esteemed.

I intended to have called last week, but could not.

The fields look freshly and gayly since the rain.

The book is printed very neat, and on fine wove paper.

I have recently been in Washington, where I have seen Gen. Andrew Jackson, he who is now president.

Take the two first, and, if you please, the three last.

The Chinese wall is thirty foot high.

It is an union supported by an hypothesis, merely.

I have saw him who you wrote to; and he would have came back with me, if he could.

Not one in fifty of those who call themselves deists, understand the nature of the religion which they reject.

If thou studiest diligently, thou will become learned.

Education is not attended to properly in Spain.

He know'd it was his duty ; and he ought, therefore, to do it.

He has little more of the great man besides the title.

Richard acted very independent on the occasion.

We have done no more than it was our duty to have done.

The time of my friend entering on business, soon arrived.

His speech is the most perfect specimen I ever saw.

Calumny and detraction are sparks which, if you do not blow,
hey will go out of themselves.

Those two authors have each of them their merit.

  Reasons whole pleasure, all the joys of sense,
  Lies in three words, health, peace, and competence.

A great mass of rocks thrown together by the hand of nature
with wildness and confusion, strike the mind with more grandeur,
than if they were adjusted to one another with the accuratest
symmetry.

A lampoon or a satire do not carry in them robbery or murder.

The side A, with the sides B and C, compose the triangle.

If some persons opportunities were never so favorable, they
would be too indolent to improve.

It is reported that the governor will come here to-morrow.

Beauty and innocence should be never separated.

Extravagance and folly may reduce you to a situation where
you will have much to fear and little to hope.

Not one in fifty of our modern infidels are thoroughly versed
in their knowledge of the Scriptures.

Virtue and mutual confidence is the soul of friendship. Where
these are wanting, disgust or hatred often follow little differences.

An army present a painful sight to a feeling mind.

To do good to them that hate us, and, on no occasion, to seek
revenge, is the duty of a christian.

The polite, accomplished libertine, is but miserable amidst all
his pleasures : the rude inhabitant of Lapland is happier than him.

There are principles in man, which ever have, and ever will,
incline him to offend.

This is one of the duties which requires great circumspection.

They that honor me, them will I honor.

Every church and sect have opinions peculiar to themselves.

Pericles gained such an ascendant over the minds of the Athe-
nians, that he might be said to attain a monarchical power in
Athens.

Thou, Lord, who hath permitted affliction to come upon us, shall
deliver us from it in due time.

That writer has given us an account of the manner in which
christianity has formerly been propagated among the heathens.

Though the measure be mysterious, it is not unworthy of your attention.

In his conduct was treachery, and in his words, faithless professions.

After I visited Europe, I returned to America.

I have not, nor shall not, consent to a proposal so unjust.

I had intended yesterday to have walked out, but I have been again disappointed.

Five and eight makes thirteen ; five from eight leaves three.

If he goes to Saratoga next week, it will make eight times that he has visited that renowned watering place.

I could not convince him, that a forgiving disposition was nobler than a revengeful one. I consider the first, one of the brightest virtues that ever was or can be possessed by man.

The college consists of one great, and several smaller edifices.

He would not believe, that honesty was the best policy.

The edifice was erected sooner than I expected it to have been.

Surely, goodness and mercy shall follow me all the days of my life ; and I will dwell in the house of the Lord for ever.

If a man have a hundred sheep, and one of them be gone astray, doth he not leave the ninety and nine, &c. ?

He might have completed his task sooner, but he could not do it better.

The most ignorant and the most savage tribes of men, when they have looked round on the earth, and on the heavens, could not avoid ascribing their origin to some invisible, designing cause, and felt a propensity to adore their Creator.

CRITICAL NOTES AND OBSERVATIONS.

OBSERVATION 1. The following absurd phrases so common in the sacred desk and elsewhere, should be carefully avoided by all who regard common sense :—" Sing the *two first* and *three last* verses." Just as if there could be more than *one* first and *one* last. There may be a *first two*, a *second two*, &c. ; a *first three*, a *second three*, a *last three*. " Within the *two last* centuries ;" " The second syllable of the *three first* words ;" " The *three first* of these orthoepists have no rule by which their pronunciation is regulated :"—" the *last two* centuries ;" " the *first three* words ;" " the *first three* of these or thoepists."

2. Adjectives should not be used to express the manner of action. " The higher the river, the *swifter* it flows ;" " James learns *easier* than Juliet ; he sees *deeper* into the millstone than she :"—" the *more swiftly* it flows ;" " learns *more easily* ; *farther* into the millstone." " He conducted the *boldest* of any :"—" the *most boldly*."

3. *More* requires *than* after it. The following sentences are therefore improper : " He was more beloved, but not so much admired, *as* Cinthio ; '

"Richard is more active, but not so studious, *as* his companion." The legitimate mode of supplying the ellipses in these constructions, will show their gross impropriety: thus, "He was more beloved *as* Cinthio;" "Richard is more active *as* his companion," &c.

4. Adverbs, as illustrated on page 85, are generally *substitutes* for two or more words belonging to other parts of speech. "Will you accompany me to Europe next summer?" "*Yes.*" "Do you believe that the voyage will restore your health?" "*No.*" In these examples, the adverbs *yes* and *no*, are substitutes for whole sentences, and, therefore, do not qualify any words understood. *Yes*, in this instance, literally means, "*I will accompany you to Europe next summer;*" and *no*, "*I do not believe that the voyage will restore my health.*" Many other adverbs are often employed in a similar manner.

"*Firstly*," is often improperly used instead of the adverb *first;* "a *good deal*," instead of, *much*, or, a *great deal.*

5. A nice distinction should be observed in the use of *such* and *so.* The former may be employed in expressing *quality;* the latter, in expressing a *degree* of the quality; as, "*Such* a temper is seldom found;" "*So* bad a temper is seldom found." In the following examples, *so* should be used instead of *such:* "He is *such* an extravagant young man, that I cannot associate with him;" "I never before saw *such* large trees."

The affected use of cardinal, instead of ordinal numbers, ought not to be imitated. "On page *forty-five;*" "Look at page *nineteen;*"—*forty-fifth, nineteenth.*

6. In the choice and application of prepositions, particular regard should be paid to their meaning as established by the idiom of our language and the best usage. "In my proceedings, I have been actuated from the conviction, that I was supporting a righteous cause;" "He should have profited from those golden precepts;" "It is connected to John with the conjunction *and;*" "Aware that there is, in the minds of many, a strong predilection in favor of established usages;" "He was made much on at Argos;" "They are resolved of going;" "The rain has been falling of a long time;" "It is a work deserving of encouragement." These examples may be corrected thus, "actuated *by* the conviction;" "*by* those golden precepts;" "*by* the conjunction and;" "a predilection *for;*" "much *of* at Argos;" "*on* going;" "falling a long time;" "deserving encouragement."

7. The preposition *to* is used before nouns of place, where they follow verbs or participles of motion; as, "I went *to* Washington." But *at* is employed after the verb *to be;* as, "I have been *at* Washington;" "He has been *to* New York, *to* home," &c. are improper. The preposition *in* is set before countries, cities, and large towns; "He lives *in* France, *in* London, *in* Philadelphia, *in* Rochester." But before single houses, and cities and villages which are in distant countries, *at* is commonly used; as, "He lives *at* Park-place;" "She resides *at* Vincennes." People in the northern states may say, "They live *in* New Orleans, or, *at* New Orleans."

8. Passive agents to verbs in the infinitive mood, should not be employed as active agents. The following are solecisms: "This house to let;" "Horses and carriages to let;" "Congress has much business to perform this session;" because the agents, *house, horses* and *carriages*, and *business*, which are really *passive*, are, according to these constructions, rendered as active. The expressions should be, "This house to *be* let;" "Horses and carriages to *be* let;" "much business to *be performed.*"

9. AMBIGUITY.—"Nothing is more to be desired than wisdom." Not *literally* correct, for *wisdom* is certainly more to be desired than *nothing;* but, as a figurative expression, it is well established and unexceptionable.

"A crow is a large black bird:"—a large, *black—bird.*

"I saw a horse—fly through the window:"—I saw a *horsefly.*

"I saw a ship gliding under full sail through a spy glass." I saw, through a spy glass, a ship gliding under full sail.

"One may see how the world goes with half an eye." One may see with half an eye, how the world goes.

"A great stone, that I happened to find, after a long search, by the sea shore, served me for an anchor." This arrangement of the members and circumstances of this sentence, confines the speaker's *search to the sea shore;* whereas, he meant, "A *large stone, which,* after a long search, I happened *to find by the sea shore,* served me for an anchor."

"I shall only notice those called personal pronouns." I shall notice *only* those called personal pronouns.

10. TAUTOLOGY.—Avoid words which add nothing to the sense; such as, "*Now* extant, *free* gratis, *slow* mope, *cold* snow, a *hot* sun, a *flowing* stream, a *dull* blockhead, *wise* sages." "I am just going to go there;" I am *about* to go.

11. ABSURDITIES AND IMPROPRIETIES.—"I can learn him many things." It ought to be, "I can *teach* him." To *learn,* is to *acquire* or *receive* information; to *teach,* means to *communicate* it.

"I don't think it is so." You *do think,* that it is *not* so.

Ever, always. "I have ever been of this mind." I have *always* been. *Ever* and *always* are not synonymous. *Ever* refers to *one* indefinite period of time; as, "If he *ever* become rich:" *always* means *at all times.*

Excuse, pardon. The former signifies to release from an obligation which refers to the future; the latter, to forgive a neglect or crime that is past. "Excuse me for neglecting to call yesterday:" *pardon* me.

Remember, recollect. We *remember* a thing which we retain in our mind; we *recollect* it, when, though having gone from the mind, we have power to call it back.

Defect, deficiency. A thing which is incomplete in any of its parts, is *defective;* a total absence of the thing, is a *deficiency.*

This subject will be resumed in the appendix to this work.

CORRECTIONS IN ORTHOGRAPHY.

From among those words which are often erroneously spelled, the following are selected and corrected according to Johnson, and to Cobb's Dictionary.

INCORRECT.	CORRECT.	INCORRECT.	CORRECT.
Abridgement	Abridgment	camblet	camlet
abscision	abscission	camphire	camphor
achievment	achievement	canvas	canvass
adze	addice	carcase	carcass
agriculturalist	agriculturist	centinel	sentinel
ancle	ankle	chace	chase
attornies	attorneys	chalibeate	chalybeate
baise	baize	chamelion	chameleon
bason	basin	chimist	chemist
bass	base	chimistry	chemistry
bombazin	bombasin	cholic	colic
boose	bouse	chuse	choose
boult	bolt	cimetar	cimeter
buccaneer	bucanier	clench	clinch
burthen	burden	cloke	cloak
bye	by	cobler	cobbler
calimanco	calamanco	chimnies	chimneys

Incorrect.	Correct.	Incorrect.	Correct.
chesnut	chestnut	maneuver	manoeuvre
clue	clew	merchandize	merchandise
connection	connexion	misprison	misprision
corset	corslet	monies	moneys
cypher	cipher	monied	moneyed
cyphering	ciphering	negociate	negotiate
dactyl	dactyle	negociation	negotiation
develope	develop	noviciate	novitiate
dipthong	diphthong	ouse	ooze
dispatch	despatch	opake	opaque
doat	dote	paroxism	paroxysm
drouth	drought	partizan	partisan
embitter	imbitter	patronize	patronise
embody	imbody	phrenzy	phrensy
enquire	inquire	pinchers	pincers
enquirer	inquirer	plow	plough
enquiry	inquiry	poney	pony
ensnare	insnare	potatoe	potato
enterprize	enterprise	quere	query
enthral	inthrall	recognize	recognise
entrench	intrench	reindeer	raindeer
entrenchment	intrenchment	reinforce	re-enforce
entrust	intrust	restive	restiff
enwrap	inwrap	ribbon	riband
epaulette	epaulet	rince	rinse
etherial	ethereal	sadler	saddler
faggot	fagot	sallad	salad
fasset	faucet	sceptic	skeptic
fellon	felon	sceptical	skeptical
fie	fy	scepticism	skepticism
germ	germe	segar	cigar
goslin	gosling	seignor	seignior
gimblet	gimlet	serjeant	sergeant
grey	gray	shoar	shore
halloe	halloo	soothe	sooth
highth	height	staunch	stanch
hindrance	hinderance	streight	straight
honied	honeyed	suitor	suiter
impale	empale	sythe	scythe
inclose	enclose	tatler	tattler
inclosure	enclosure	thresh	thrash
indict	endict	thwak	thwack
indictment	endictment	tipler	tippler
indorse	endorse	tranquility	tranquillity
indorsement	endorsement	tripthong	triphthong
instructor	instructer	trissyllable	trisyllable
insure	ensure	valice	valise
insurance	ensurance	vallies	valleys
judgement	judgment	vise	vice
laquey	lackey	vollies	volleys
laste	last	waggon	wagon
licence	license	warrantee	warranty
loth	loath	whoopingcough	hoopingcough
lothsome	loathsome	woe	wo
malcontent	malecontent	yeast	yest

CORRECTIONS IN ORTHOEPY.

The following words being often erroneously pronounced by polite people, as well as by the vulgar, their correction, in this place, agreeably to *Cobb's Dictionary*, it is presumed, will be useful to many. Some of the mispronunciations given are *provincial*.

Fåte, får, fåll, fåt—mĕ, mĕt—pĭne, pĭn—nŏ, nŏr, nŏt, mŏve—tŭbe, tŭb, bŭll —ŏĭl—fŏŭnd—*thin*—THIS.

ORTHOGRA-PHY.	IMPROPER.	PRONOUNCED.	ORTHOGRA-PHY.	IMPROPER.	PRONOUNCED.
Again	å-gåne'	å-gĕn'	Edge	åje	ĕdje
Against	å-gånste'	å-gĕnst	Either	ī'THŭr	ē'THŭr
Ally	ål'lĕ	ål-lī'	English	ĕng'lĭsh	ĭng'glĭsh
Are	åre	år	Era	ĕ'rĕ	ē'rå
Azure	åzh'ŭr	å'zhŭre	Ere	ĕre	åre
Bade	både	båd	Fasten	fås'tn	fås'sn
Beard	bård	bēĕrd	Fearful	fĕr'fŭl	fēĕr'fŭl
Been	bĕn *or* bēĕn	bĭn	Figure	fĭg'gŭr	fĭg'ŭre
Bleat	blååt	blēĕt	Fiend	fĕnd	fēĕnd
Boil	bīle	bŏĭl	First	fŭst	fŭrst
Bonnet	bŭn'nĕt	bŏn'nĭt	Foliage	fŏĭl'åje	fŏ'lĕ-åje
Brooch	brŏtsh	brŏŏtsh	Fortune	fŏr'tshŭn	fŏr'tshŭne
Canal	kå-nåwl'	kå-nål'	Fortnight	fŏrt'nĭt	fŏrt'nĭte
Catch	kĕtsh	kåtsh	Fountain	fŏŭn'tn	fŏŭn'tĭn
Causeway	krŏs'wå	kåwz'wå	Fracture	fråk'tshŭr	fråk'tshŭre
Chalice	kål'ĭs	tshål'ĭs	Fragrance	fråg'rånse	frå'grånse
Chasten	tshås'tn	tshåse'sn	Futile	fŭ'tĭle	fŭ'tĭl
Chimney	tshĭm'blĕ	tshĭm'nĕ	Gather	gĕTH'ŭr	gåTH'ŭr
Chine	tshĭme	tshĭne	Get	gĭt	gĕt
Choir	kŏĭr	kwĭre	Girth	gŭrt	gĕrth
Clevy	klĕv'ĭs	klĕv'vĕ	Goal	gŏŏl	gŏle
Clinch	klĕnsh	klĭnsh	Going	gŏne *or* gŏ'ĭn	gŏ'ĭng
Column	kŏl'yŭm	kŏl'lŭm	Gold	gŏŏld	gŏld
Combat	kŏm'båt	kŭm'båt	Gum	gŏŏm	gŭm
Comma	kŏm'mĕ	kŏm'må	Grudge	be-grĕtsh'	grŭdje
Coquet	kŏ-kwĕt'	kŏ-kĕt'	Gypsum	gĭp'sŭm	jĭp'sŭm
Corps	kŏrps	kŏre	Has	hĕz	håz
Cover	kĭv'ŭr	kŭv'ŭr	Have	håve	håv
Deaf	dĕĕf	dĕf	Heard	hēĕrd	hĕrd
Decisive	dĕ-sĭs'ĭv	dĕ-sĭ'sĭv	Hearth	hŭrth *or* håth	hårth
Depot	dĕ'pŏt	dĕ-pŏ'	Hiss	sĭss	hĭss
Depute	dĕp'ŭ-tĭze	dĕ-pŭte'	Hoist	hĭste'	hŏĭst
Deputed	dĕp'ŭ-tĭzd	dĕ-pŭ'tĕd	Homely	hŭm'blĕ	hŏme'lĕ
Design	dĕ-zĭne'	dĕ-sĭne'	Hoof	hŭf	hŏŏf
Dint	dĕnt	dĭnt	Hostler	håws'lŭr	ŏs'lŭr
Docile	dŏ'sĭle	dŏs'sĭl	Humble	hŭm'bl	ŭm'bl
Disgust	dĭs-gŭst'	dĭz-gŭst'	Jesting	jĕĕst'ĭn	jĕst'ĭng
Dismay	dĭs-må'	dĭz-må'	Kettle	kĭt'tl	kĕt'tl
Disown	dĭs-ŏne'	dĭz-ŏne'	Lecture	lĕk'tshŭr	lĕk'tshŭre
Dost	dŏst	dŭst	Leisure	lĕzh'ŭr	lē'zhŭre
Doth	dŏth	dŭth	Lever	lĕv'ŭr	lē'vŭr
Does	dŏŏz	dŭz	Lid	lĕd	lĭd
Drain	drĕĕn	dråne	Lilach	lå'lŏk	lī'låk
Drought	drŏŭth	drŏŭt	Loam	lŏŏm	lŏme
Drowned	drŏŭnd'ĕd	drŏŭnd	Loo	lŭ	lŏŏ
Ductile	dŭk'tĭle	dŭk'tĭl	Maintain	måne-tåne'	mĕn-tåne'

ORTHOGRAPHY	IMPROPER.	PRONOUNCED.	ORTHOGRAPHY.	IMPROPER.	PRONOUNCED.
Matron	măt′rŭn	mā′trŭn	Roof	rŭff	rōōf
Mermaid	măre′măde	mĕr′măde	Sacred	săk′rĕd	sā′krĕd
Mountain	mŏŭn′tn	mŏŭn′tĭn	Said	săde	sĕd
Nature	nā′tshŭr	nā′tshŭre	Sat	sĕt	săt
Neither	nī′ᴛʜŭr	nĕ′ᴛʜŭr	Says	săze	sĕz
Oblige	ŏ-blĕĕje′	ŏ-blīje′	Scarce	skărse	skārse
Oblique	ŏ-blĕĕk′	ŏb-līke′	Schedule	skĕd′ŭle	sĕd′jŭle
Of	ŏf	ŏv	Shut	shĕt	shŭt
Oil	īle	ŏīl	Since	sĕnse	sĭnse
Only	ŏn′le or ŭn′lĕ	ōne′lĕ	Sleek	slĭk	slĕĕk
Panther	păne′tŭr	păn′thŭr	Sliver	slīv′vŭr	slĭ′vŭr
Parent	păr′ĕnt	pā′rĕnt	Slothful	slăwth′fŭl	slŏth′fŭl
Partner	părd′nŭr	părt′nŭr	Soot	sŭt	sŏŏt
Pasture	păs′tshŭr	păs′tshŭre	Spikenard	spĭg′nŭt	spīke′nărd
Patron	păt′rŭn	pā′trŭn	Spoil	splle	spŏīl
Pincers	pĭnsh′ŭrz	pĭn′sŭrz	Steelyard	stĭl′yŭrdz	stĕĕl′yărd
Pith	pĕth	pĭth	Stamp	stŏmp	stămp
Plait	plĕĕt	plăte	Stint	stĕnt	stĭnt
Poem	pŏme	pō′ĕm	Sword	swŏrd	sōrd
Point	pĭnte	pŏīnt	Synod	sī′nŏd	sĭn′ŭd
Pother	pŏᴛʜ′ŭr	pŭᴛʜ′ŭr	Therefore	ᴛʜăre′fōre	ᴛʜĕr′fōre
Precept	prĕs′sĕpt	prē′sĕpt	Thill	fĭl	thĭl
Preface	prē′făse	prĕf′făs	To	tŏ	tōō
Prelude	prē′lŭde	prĕl′ŭde	Tour	tŏŭr	tōōr
Process	prŏ′sĕs	prŏs′sĕs	Treble	trĭb′bl	trĕb′bl
Product	prŏ′dŭkt	prŏd′ŭkt	Towards	tŏ-wărdz′	tŏ′ŭrdz
Progress	prŏ′grĕs	prŏg′rĕs	Trophy	trŏf′fĕ	trō′fĕ
Profile	prŏ′fīle	prŏ-fĕĕl′	Tuesday	tshŭz′dĕ	tūze′dĕ
Pumpion	pŭngk′ĭn	pŭmp′yŭn	Verdure	vŭr′jŭr	vĕr′jŭre
Put	pŭt (verb)	pŭt	Vizier	vĭ′zhŭr	vĭz′yĕĕr
Quoit	kwăte	kwŏīt	Volume	vŏl′lŭm	vŏl′yŭme
Rapine	ră′pīne	răp′ĭn	Were	wăre	wĕr
Rear	răre	rĕĕr	Yea	yă	yĕ
Reptile	rĕp′tīle	rĕp′tĭl	Yes	yĕs	yĭs
Rid	rĕd	rĭd	Yest	yĕĕst or ĕĕst	yĕst
Rind	rīne	rĭnd	Yet	yĭt	yĕt
Rinse	rĕnse	rĭnse	You	yŭ	yŏŏ
Rosin	rŏz′ŭm	rŏz′ĭn	Your	yŭre	yŏŏr
Routine	rŏŭ tène	rŏŏ-tĕĕn′	Youth	yŭth	yŏŏth

ORTHOGRAPHY.	IMPROPER.	PRONOUNCED.
Ague and fever	fĕ′vŭrn-ă′gŭr	ā′gŭ-and fĕ′vŭr
Alternate	âwl-tĕr′năte	ăl-tĕr′năte
Annunciate	ăn-nŭn′shăte	ăn-nŭn′shĕ-ăte
Andiron	hănd′ī-ŭrn	ănd′ī-ŭrn
Antipodes	ăn′tĕ-pŏdz	ăn-tĭp′ŏ-dĕĕz
Apparent	ăp-păr′ĕnt	ăp-pā′rĕnt
Architecture	ărtsh′ĕ-tĕk-tshŭr	ăr′-kĕ-tĕk-tshŭre
Assumption	ăs-sŭmp′shŭn	ăs-sŭm′shŭn
Auxiliary	ăwks-ĭl′ă-rĕ	ăwg-zĭl′yă-rĕ
Certiorari	săsh-ŭr-ăr′ŭr	sĕr-shĕ-ŏ-rā′rĭ
Christianity	krĭs-tshăn′ĕ-tĕ	krĭs-tshĕ-ăn′ĕ-tĕ
Clandestine	klăn-dĕs′tīne	klăn-dĕs′tĭn
Coadjutor	-kŏ-ăd′jŭ-tŭr	kŏ-ăd-jŭ′tŭr
Compendium	kŏm-pĕn′dĕ-ŭm	kŏm-pĕn′jĕ-ŭm

ORTHOGRAPHY.	INCORRECT.	PRONOUNCED.
Connoisseur	kŏn-nĭs-sùre′	kŏ-nês-sàre′
Courteous	kŏre′tè-ûs	kûr′tshè-ûs
Coverlet	kŭv′ûr-lĭd	kŭv′ûr-lêt
Cowardice	kŏŭ′ûrd-ĭse	kŏŭ′ûrd-ĭs
Decrepit	dè-krĭp′ĭd	dè-krêp′ĭt
Demonstrate	dêm′ŏn-stràte	dè-mŏn′stràte
Desideratum	dè-sĭd-êr-àt′ûm	dè-sĭd-è-rà′tûm
Diamond	dĭ′mûnd	dĭ′à-mûnd
Discrepance	dĭs-krêp′ǎn-sè	dĭs′krè-pánse
Disfranchise	dĭs-frǎn′tshĭze	dĭs-frǎn′tshĭz
Dishonest	dĭs-ŏn′êst	dĭz-ŏn′êst
Disorder	dĭs-ŏr′dûr	dĭz-ŏr′dûr
Electrify	è-lêk′tûr-ĭze	è-lêk′trè-fĭ
Emaciate	è-mà′shàte	è-mà′shè-àte
Expatiate	êks-pà′shàte	êks-pà′shè-àte
Expiatory	êks-pĭ′à-tŏ-rè	êks′pè-à-tûr-rè
Extempore	êks-têm′pŏre	êks-têm′pŏ-rè
Feminine	fêm′è-nĭne	fêm′è-nĭn
Frequently	frêk′wênt-lè	frè′kwênt-lè
Genuine	jên′ù-ĭne	jên′ù-ĭn
Guardian	gàr-dèèn′	gyàr′dè-ân
Gymnastic	gĭm-nàs′tĭk	jĭm-nàs′tĭk
Hallelujah	hàl-lè-lù′jà	hàl-lè-lŏŏ′yà
Hospital	hŏs′pĭt-àl	ŏs′pè-tàl
Humorous	hù′mûr-ûs	yù′mûr-ûs
Idea	ĭ-dè′	ĭ-dè′à
Ignoramus	ĭg-nŏ-rǎm′ûs	ĭg-nŏ-rà′mûs
Indecorous	ĭn-dêk′ŏ-rûs	ĭn-dè-kŏ′rûs
Irradiate	ĭr-rǎd′è-àte	ĭr-rà′dè-àte
Literati	lĭt-êr-àt′ĭ	lĭt-êr-à′tĭ
Maintenance	màne-tàne′ànse	mên′tè-nànse
Masculine	màs′kù-lĭne	màs′kù-lĭn
Mercantile	mûr′kǎn-tĭle mûr-kǎn-tèèl′ mûr-kǎn′tĭl	mêr′kǎn-tĭl
Meliorate	mè-lĭ′ŏ-ràte	mè′lè-ŏ-ràte
Molestation	mŏ-lès-tà′shûn-	mŏl-ês-tà′shûn
Museum	mù′zè-ûm	mù-zè′ûm
National	nà′shûn-àl	nàsh′ûn-àl
Nomenclature	nŏ-mên′klà-tùre	nŏm-ên-klà′tshùre
Nominative	nŏm′è-tĭv	nŏm′è-nà-tĭv
Obstreperous	ŏb-strŏp′pù-lûs	ŏb-strêp′êr-ûs
Octavo	ŏk-tà′vŏ	ŏk-tà′vŏ
Oratory	ŏr′à-tŏ-rè	ŏr′à-tûr-rè
Parentage	pà′rênt-àje	pàr′ênt-àje
Partiality	pàr-shàl′lè-tè	pàr-shè-àl′lè-tè
Patronage	pà′trûn-àje	pàt′rûn-ĭje
Patriarch	pàt′rè-àrk	pà′trè-àrk
Patriot	pàt′rè-ût	pà′trè-ût
Patriotism	pàt′rè-ût-ĭzm	pà′trè-ût-ĭzm
Philologist	fĭ-lŏl′lŏ-jĭst	fè-lŏl′lŏ-jĭst
Philosophy	fĭ-lŏs′ŏ-fè	fè-lŏs′ŏ-fè
Philosophical	fĭ-lŏ-sŏf′ĭk-àl	fĭl-ŏ-zŏf′è-kàl
Plagiarism	plǎ′gà-rĭzm	plà′jà-rĭzm
Possess	pŏs-sès′	pŏz-zès′

ORTHOGRAPHY.	INCORRECT.	PRONOUNCED.
Possessive	pŏs-sĕs'sĭv	pŏz-zĕs'sĭv
Possession	pŏs-sĕsh'ŭn	pŏz-zĕsh'ŭn
Preventive	prė-vėnt'å-tĭv	prė-vėnt'ĭv
Pronunciation	prŏ-nŭn-sė-à'shŭn	prŏ-nŭn-shė-à'shŭn
Propitiation	prŏ-pĭs-ė-à'shŭn	prŏ-pĭsh-ė-à'shŭn
Prophecy	prŏv'ė-sĭ (noun)	prŏf'ė-sė (noun)
Prophesy	prŏv'ė-sĭ (verb)	prŏf'ė-sĭ (verb)
Ratio	rà'shŏ	rà'shė-ŏ
Rational	rà'shŭn-ål	råsh'ŭn-ål
Sacrament	så'krå-mėnt	såk'rå-mėnt
Sacrifice	så'krė-fĭze *or* (fĭs)	såk'rė-fĭze
Stereotype	stėr'ŏ-tĭpe	stė'rė-ŏ-tĭpe
Stupendous	stŭ-pĕn'dŭ-ŭs } stŭ-pĕn'jŭs }	stŭ-pĕn'dŭs
Synonyme	sė-nŏn'ė-mė	sĭn'ŏ-nĭm
Transparent	trăns-pår'ėnt	trăns-på'rėnt
Transparency	trăns-pår'ėn-sė	trăns-på'rėn-sė
Tremendous	trė-mėn'dŭ-ŭs } trė-mėn'jŭs }	trė-mėn'dŭs
Verbatim	vėr-båt'ĭm	vėr-bà'tĭm
Volcano	vŏl-kà'nŏ	vŏl-kà'nŏ
Whiffletree	hwĭp'pl-trė	hwĭf'fl-trėė

NOTE 1.—When the words *learned, blessed, loved, &c.* are used as participial adjectives, the termination *ed* should generally be pronounced as a separate syllable; as, " A *learn-ed* man; The *bless-ed* Redeemer;" but when they are employed as verbs, the *ed* is contracted in pronunciation; as, " He *learn'd* his lesson; They are *lov'd;* I have *walk'd*."

2. The accent of the following words falls on those syllables expressed in the *italic* characters: Eu ro *pe* an, hy me *ne* al, Ce sa *re* a, co ad *ju* tor, ep i cu *re* an, *in* ter est ed, *in* ter est ing, *rep* a ra ble, *rec* og nise, *leg* is la ture, *ob* li ga to ry, in *com* pa ra ble, ir *rep* a ra ble, in *ex* o ra ble. In a large class of words, the vowels *a, e,* and *ai,* should be pronounced like long *a* in *late;* such as, *fare, rare, there, their, where, air, chair, compare, declare,* &c. In the words *person, perfect, mercy, interpret, determine,* and the like, the vowel *e* before *r,* is often *erroneously* sounded like short *u.* Its proper sound is that of *e* in *met, pet, imperative.*

3. With respect to the pronunciation of the words *sky, kind, guide,* &c. it appears that a mistake extensively prevails. It is believed that their common pronunciation by the vulgar, is the *correct* one, and agreeable to the pronunciation intended by Mr. John Walker. The proper diphthongal sounds in skėl, kyĭnd, gyĭde, are adopted by the common mass, and *perverted* by those who, in their unnatural and affected pronunciation of these words, say, skė-l, kė-ĭnde, gė-ĭde. This latter mode of pronouncing them in two syllables, is as incorrect and ridiculous as to pronounce the words *boil, toil,* in two syllables; thus, bŏ-ĭl, tŏ-ĭl.

4. *My, wind.* When *my* is contrasted with *thy, his, her, your,* &c. it is pronounced, mĭ : in all other situations, it is pronounced, mė; as, " *My me*] son, give ear to *my* [*me*] counsel." When *wind* ends a line in poetry, and is made to rhyme with *mind, bind, kind,* &c. it is pronounced, wĭnd; but, in other situations, it is pronounced, wĭnd.

" Lo, the poor Indian! whose untutored mind
" Sees God in clouds, or hears him in the *wind*."

PROVINCIALISMS.

CONTRACTIONS, VULGARISMS, AND OTHER IMPROPRIETIES.

As each of the following provincialisms and vulgarisms, has its locality in some one section or other of our country, it is hoped that these corrections will be found useful in the districts to which the various phrases respectively belong.

IMPROPER.	CORRECT.	IMPROPER.	CORRECT.
Aint	Are not	åk'tèw-èl	åk'tshŭ-ål
haint	have not	èd'èw-kåte	èd'jŭ-kåte
taint	'tis not	fåtʜ'ŭr	få'ʜŭr
baint	are not	heft	weight
maint	may not	stoop	porch
wont	will not	stent	task
wer'nt	were not	helve	handle
waunt	was not	muss	disorder
woodent	would not	dump	unload
mussent	must not	scup	swing
izzent	is not	shay	gig or chaise
wazzent	was not	cutter	one-horse sleigh
hezzent	has not	staddle	sapling
doozzent	does not	foxy	reddish
tizzent	'tis not	suple	spry or supple
whool	who will		

COMMON IN NEW ENGLAND OR NEW YORK.

don't
can't
i'll
'tis

IN PENNSYLVANIA.

IMPROPER.	CORRECT.	IMPROPER.	CORRECT.
Akst	áskt	Strenth	strength
bèn	bĭn	lenth	length
hŭl	hŏle	brenth	breadth
hŭm	hŏme	ort	ought
stŭn	stŏne	nan	what
dŏŏz	dŭz	wisht	wish
glåss	glåss	wunst	once
måss	måss	ouch	oh
bråss	bråss	cheer	chair
påss	påss	spook	ghost
flåwnt	flånt	furnentz	opposite
hĭz'zn	hĭz	wanity	vanity
hŏŭ'zn	hŏŭz'ĭz	in wain	in vain
ån'shènt	åne'tshènt	ornary	ordinary
ån'jèl	åne'jèl	for by	to spare
dån'jŭr	dåne'jŭr	we bit	small piece
utrån'jŭr	stråne'jŭr	disremember	do not remember
tshåm'bŭr	tshåme'bŭr		

IRISH.

IMPROPER.	CORRECT.
nå'tŭr	nå'tshŭre
nåt'ŭr-èl	nåtsh'ŏ-rål
fŏr'tĭn	fŏr'tshŭne
fŏr'tèw-nåte	fŏr'tshŭ-nåte
vŭr'tèw	vèr'tshŭ
vŭr'tèw-ŭs	vèr'tshŭ-ŭs
Dŏŏr	dŏre
flŏŏr	flŏre
ŏnd	ånd
lŏss	lŏŏz
kŏŏrse	kŏrse
sŏŏrse	sŏrse
tĭll	tŏŏ
pŭt	pŭt
fŭt	fŭt
å-kŏŏnt'	åk-kŏŭnt'
pŭl'pĭt	pŭl'pĭt
påre'sŭn	pår'sn

IMPROPER.	CORRECT.	IMPROPER.	CORRECT.
Md. Va. Ky. Miss. &c.		shĕt *or* shŭt	rĭd
тнȧr	тнȧre	tŏtĕ *or* fŏtch	kȧr′rĕ, fĕtsh, *or*
whȧr	hwȧre		brĭng
bȧr [bear]	bȧre	hŏp′d	hĕlpt
wȧr	wĕr	cȧ-hŏŏt′	pȧrt′nŭr-shĭp
mŏŭt	mĭte [might]	mȧr′bl	mŏŏv ŏff
gwĭne	gŏ′ĭng		

NOTE. *Clever, pretty, ugly, curious, expect, guess,* and *reckon,* though correct English words, have, among the common people of New England and New York, a provincial application and meaning. With them, a *clever* man, is one of a gentle and obliging disposition; instead of, a man of distinguished talents and profound acquirements. *Pretty* and *ugly,* they apply to the *disposition* of a person, instead of, to his *external appearance.* In these states, one will often hear, " I *guess* it rains," when the speaker *knows* this to be a fact, and, therefore, *guessing* is uncalled for. " I *expect* I can go ;" or, " I *reckon* I can ;" instead of, " I *suppose* or *presume.*" In New England, a clergyman is often called a *minister,* in New York, a *priest,* and south of N. Y. a *parson.* The last is preferable.

NEW ENGLAND OR NEW YORK.	CORRECTED.
I be goin. He lives to hum.	I *am* going. He lives *at* home.
Hese ben to hum this two weeks.	*He has been at home these* 2 weeks.
You haddent ought to do it. Yes had ought.	You ought *not* to do it. *Certainly* I ought.
Taint no better than hizzen.	*'Tis* no better than *his.*
Izzent that are line writ well ?	*Is not* that line well *written ?*
Tizzent no better than this ere.	*It is* no better, or, it is *not any* better than this.
The keows be gone to hum, neow, and I'mer goin arter um.	The *cows are* gone *home,* and *I am going after them.*
He'll be here, derights, and bring yourn and thairn.	He *will* be here, directly, and bring yours and theirs.
He touch'd the stun which I shew him, an di guess it made him sithe, for twas cissing hot.	He touched the *stone* which I *showed* him, and it made him *sigh,* for *it was hissing* hot.
Run, Thanel, and cut a staddle, for to make a lever on. Ize jest agoneter go, daddy.	Go, Nathaniel, and cut a *sapling,* to make a *lever of.* I *was about* to go, or, *intending* to go *immediately,* father.
Where shell I dump my cart, square? Dump it yender. Whats the heft of your load ?	Where *shall* I *unload* my cart ? *Yonder. What is* the *weight* of your load ?
When ju git hum from Hafford ? A fortnit ago. You diddent, did ye? Ju see my Danel, whose sot up a tarvern there ? No. Hede gone afore I got there. O, the pesky criter! Hele soon be up a stump.	When *did you return from Hartford?* A *fortnight* ago. *Is it possible! Did* you see my *son Daniel, who has opened a public house* there ? No. *He had left before* I *arrived* there. O, the *paltry fellow! He will* soon *come to naught.*
My frinds supurb mansion is delightfully sitewated on a nate-eral mound of considerable hithe. It hez a long stoop in front; but it is furder from the city than I'de like my hum.	My *friend's* superb mansion is de lightfully *situated* on a *natural* mound of considerable *height.* It *has* a long *porch* in front; but it is *farther* from the city than I *would* like to *reside.*
I know'd the gal was drownded, and I tell'd the inquisitioners, that ize	I *knew* the *girl had been drowned,* and I *told* the *jury of inquest, that I was*

NEW ENGLAND.

nither geestin nor jokin about it; but if they'd permit me to give em my ideze, they'd obleege me. So I par-severed, and carried my pinte. You don't say so. Be you from Barkshire? I be. Neow I swan! if I aint clean beat. You baint from the Jarseys, be ye? Yes. Gosh! then I guess you kneow heow to tend tarvern.

CORRECTED.

not jesting about it; but, by permitting me to give them my view of the subject, they would oblige me. So, I persever-ed, and gained my point. Indeed! Are you from Berkshire? I am. Really I am surprised.

Are you from New Jersey? Yes. Then I presume you know how to ten a tavern

IN PENNSYLVANIA.

I seen him. Have you saw him? Yes, I have saw him wunst; and that was before you seed him.

I done my task. Have you did yours? No, but I be to do it.

I be to be there. He know'd me.

Leave me be, for Ime afear'd.

I never took notice to it.

I wish I haddent did it; howsum-ever, I dont keer: they cant skeer me.

Give me them there books.

He ort to go; so he ort.

No he orten.

Dont scrouge me.

I diddent go to do it.

Aint that a good hand write?

Nan? I know'd what he meant, but I never let on.

It is a long mile to town. Ah! I thought 'twas unle a short mile.

CORRECTED.

I saw him. Have you seen him? Yes, once; and that was before you saw him.

I have done my task. Have you done yours? No, but I must.

I shall be there; or, I must be there. He knew me.

Let me be, for I am afraid.

I never took notice of it: or, better thus, I never noticed it.

I wish I had not done it: however, I disregard them. They cannot scare me.

Give me those books.

He ought to go, really.

He ought not.

Don't crowd me.

I did not intend to do it.

Is not that beautiful writing?

What? I knew what he meant, but I kept that to myself.

It is a little over a mile to town. Ah! I supposed it to be less than a mile.

IRISH.

Not here the day; he went till Pittsburg.

Let us be after pairsing a wee bit.

Where did you loss it?

CORRECTED.

He is not here to-day. He went to Pittsburg.

Let us parse a little.

Where did you lose it?

MD. VA. KY. OR MISS.

Carry the horse to water.

Tote the wood to the river.

Have you focht the water?

I've made 200 bushels of corn this year.

He has run against a snag.

Is that your plunder, stranger?

He will soon come of that habit.

I war thar, and I seen his boat was loadend too heavy.

Whar you gwine

Hese in cohoot with me.

Did you get shet of your tobacca?

Who hoped you to sell it?

CORRECTED.

Lead the horse to water; or, water the horse.

Carry the wood to the river.

Have you fetched, or brought, the water?

I have raised 200 bushels of corn this year.

He has got into difficulty.

Is that your baggage, sir?

He will soon overcome, or get rid of, that habit.

I was there, and I saw that his boat was too heavily laden, or loaded.

Where are you going?

He is in partnership with me.

Did you get rid, or dispose of, your tobacco?

Who helped you to sell it?

PROSODY.

PROSODY treats of the modulations of the voice according to the usages of the language we speak, and the sentiments we wish to express: hence, in its most extensive sense, it comprises all the laws of elocution.

Prosody is commonly divided into two parts: the first teaches the true pronunciation of words, comprising *accent*, *quantity*, *emphasis*, *pause*, and *tone ;* and the second, the laws of *versification.*

Accent. Accent is the laying of a peculiar stress of the voice on a particular letter or syllable in a word, that it may be better heard than the rest, or distinguished from them ; as, in the word *presúme*, the stress of the voice must be on the letter *u*, and the second syllable, *sume*, which syllable takes the accent.

Every word of more syllables than one, has one accented syllable. For the sake of euphony or distinctness in a long word, we frequently give a secondary accent to another syllable besides the one which takes the principal accent; as, `tes ti mo' ni `al, a ban' don `ing.

Quantity. The quantity of a syllable is that time which is occupied in pronouncing it. It is considered as long or short.

A vowel or syllable is long, when the accent is on the vowel ; which causes it to be slowly joined in pronunciation with the following letters ; as, " Fāll, bāle, mōōd, hōūse, fēaturé."

A syllable is short, when the accent is on the consonant ; which causes the vowel to be quickly joined to the succeeding letter ; " as, ănt, bŏnnĕt, hŭngĕr."

A long syllable generally requires double the time of a short one in pronouncing it ; thus, " māte" and " nōte" should be pronounced as slowly again as " măt" and " nŏt."

Emphasis. By emphasis is meant a stronger and fuller sound of the voice, by which we distinguish some word or words on which we design to lay particular stress, and to show how they affect the rest of the sentence. Sometimes the emphatic words must be distinguished by a particular tone of voice, as well as by a greater tress.

Emphasis will be more fully explained under the head of Elocution.

Pauses. Pauses or rests, in speaking and reading, are a total cessation of the voice during a perceptible, and, in many cases, a measurable space of time.

Tones. Tones are different both from emphasis and pauses; consisting in the modulation of the voice, or the notes or variations of sound which we employ in the expression of our sentiments.

Emphasis affects particular words and phrases ; but tones affect sentences, paragraphs, and sometimes a whole discourse.

PUNCTUATION.

PUNCTUATION is the art of dividing written composition into sentences or parts of sentences, by points or stops, in order to mark the different pauses which the sense and an accurate pronunciation require.

The *Comma* represents the shortest pause ; the *Semicolon,* a pause double that of the comma ; the *Colon,* double·that of the semicolon ; and the *Period,* double that of the colon.

Punctuation is a modern art. The ancients were entirely unacquainted with the use of points ; and wrote, not only without any distinction of members and periods, but also without any distinction of words. This custom continued till the year 360 before Christ. How the ancients read their works, written in this manner, it is not easy to conceive. After the practice of joining words together had ceased, notes of distinction were placed at the end of every word. This practice continued a considerable time.

As it appears that the present usage of points did not take place while manuscripts and monumental inscriptions were the only known methods of conveying knowledge, we must conclude, that it was introduced with the art of printing. The introduction was, however, gradual : all the points did not appear at once. The colon, semicolon, and note of admiration, were produced some time after the others. The whole set, as they are now used, became established, when learning and refinement had made considerable progress.

As the rules of punctuation are founded altogether on the grammatical construction of sentences, their application pre-supposes, on the part of the student, a knowledge of Syntax. Although they admit of exceptions, and require a continual exercise of judgment and literary taste in applying them properly, they are of great utility, and justly merit our particular attention.

The great importance of acquiring a thorough knowledge of punctuation, and of attending strictly to the application of its rules, is established by the single fact, that *the meaning of a sentence is often totally perverted by the omission or misapplication of points* To illustrate the correctness of this remark, numerous example might be selected. The following border on the ridiculous: "Mr. Jared Hurton having gone to sea his wife, desires the prayers of this church ;" "Tryon, who escaped from the jail on Friday last, is 22 years of age, has sandy hair, light eyes, thin visage, with a short nose turned up about six feet high, &c." Corrected ; " Mr. Jared Hurton having gone to sea, his wife desires the prayers of this church ;" " thin visage, with a short nose turned up, about six feet high, &c."

Before one enters upon the study of punctuation, it is necessary for him to understand what is meant by an *adjunct, a simple senence*, and a *compound sentence*.

An *adjunct* or *imperfect phrase* contains no assertion, or does not amount to a proposition or sentence ; as, " Therefore ;" " studious of praise ;" " in the pursuit of commerce."—For the definition of a sentence, and a compound sentence, turn to page 119.

When two or more adjuncts are connected with the verb in the same manner, and by the same preposition or conjunction, the sentence is compound, and may be resolved into as many simple ones as there are adjuncts ; as, " They have sacrificed their *health* and *fortune*, at the *shrine* of vanity, *pride*, and *extravagance*." But when the adjuncts are connected with the verb in a different manner, the sentence is simple ; as, " Grass of an excellent *quality*, is produced in great *abundance* in the northern regions of our country."

COMMA.

RULE 1. The members of a simple sentence should not, in general, be separated by a comma ; as, " Every part of matter swarms with living creatures."

Exercises in Punctuation.—Idleness is the great fomenter of all corruptions in the human heart. The friend of order has made half his way to virtue. All finery is a sign of littleness.

RULE 2. When a simple sentence is long, and the nominative is accompanied with an inseparable adjunct of importance, it may admit a comma immediately before the verb ; as, " The good taste *of the present age*, has not allowed us to neglect the cultivation of the English language ;" " Too many *of the pretended friendships of youth*, are mere combinations in pleasure."

Exercises.—The indulgence of a harsh disposition is the introduction to future misery. To be totally indifferent to praise or censure is a real defect in character. The intermixture of evil in human society serves to exercise the suffering graces and virtues of the good.

RULE 3. When the connexion of the different parts of a simple sentence, is interrupted by an adjunct of importance, the adjunct must be distinguished by a comma before and after it ; as, " His work is, *in many respects*, very imperfect. It is, *therefore*, not much approved." But when these interruptions are slight and unimportant, it is better to omit the comma; as, "Flattery is *certainly* pernicious;" "There is *surely* a pleasure in beneficence."

Exercises.—Charity like the sun brightens all its objects. Gentleness is in truth the great avenue to mutual enjoyment. You too have your failings. Humility and knowledge with poor apparel excel pride and ignorance under costly attire. The best men often experience disappointments. Advice should be seasonably administered. No assumed behavior can always hide the real character.

RULE 4. The nominative case independent, and nouns in apposition when accompanied with adjuncts, must be distinguished by commas; as, "My *son*, give me thy heart;" "Dear *Sir*, I write to express my gratitude for your many kindnesses;" "I am obliged to you, my *friends*, for your many favors;" "*Paul*, the *apostle*, of the Gentiles, was eminent for his zeal and knowledge;" "The *butterfly*, *child* of the summer, flutters in the sun."

But if *two* nouns in apposition are unattended with adjuncts, or if they form only a proper name, they should not be separated; as, "*Paul* the *apostle*, suffered martyrdom;" "The *statesman Jefferson*, wrote the declaration of Independence."

Exercises.—Lord thou hast been our dwelling place in all generations. Continue my dear child to make virtue thy chief study. Canst thou expect thou betrayer of innocence to escape the hand of vengeance? Death the king of terrors chose a prime minister. Hope the balm of life sooths us under every misfortune. Confucius the great Chinese philosopher was eminently good as well as wise. The patriarch Joseph is an illustrious example of true piety.

RULE 5. The nominative case absolute and the infinitive mood absolute with their adjuncts, a participle with words depending on it, and, generally, any imperfect phrase which may be resolved into a simple sentence, must be separated from the rest of the sentence by commas; as, "*His father dying*, he succeeded to the estate;" "*To confess the truth*, I was in fault;" "The king, *approving the plan*, put it in execution;" "He, *having finished his academical course*, has returned home, *to prosecute his professional studies*."

Exercises.—Peace of mind being secured we may smile at misfortune. To enjoy present pleasure he sacrificed his future ease and reputation. His talents formed for great enterprises could not fail of rendering him conspicuous. The path of piety and virtue pursued with a firm and constant spirit will assuredly lead to happiness. All mankind compose one family assembled under the eye of one common Father.

RULE 6. A compound sentence must be resolved into simple ones by placing commas between its members; as, "The decay, the waste, and the dissolution of a plant, may affect our spirits, and suggest a train of serious reflections."

Three or more nouns, verbs, adjectives, participles, or adverbs, connected by conjunctions, expressed or understood, must be separated by commas; as, " The husband, wife,* and children,† suffered extremely ;" " In a letter, we may advise, exhort, comfort, request, and discuss ;" " David was a brave, wise, and pious man ;" " A man, fearing, serving, and loving his Creator, lives for a noble purpose ;" " Success generally depends on acting prudently, steadily, and vigorously, in what we undertake."

Two or more nouns, verbs, adjectives, participles, or adverbs, occurring in the same construction, with their conjunctions understood, must be separated by commas; as, " Reason, virtue, answer one great aim ;" " Virtue supports in adversity, moderates in prosperity ;" " Plain, honest truth, needs no artificial covering ;" " We are fearfully, wonderfully framed."

Exercises.—We have no reason to complain of the lot of man nor of the mutability of the world. Sensuality contaminates the body depresses the understanding deadens the moral feelings of the heart and degrades man from his rank in creation.

Self-conceit presumption and obstinacy blast the prospects of many a youth. He is alternately supported by his father his uncle and his elder brother. The man of virtue and honor will be trusted relied upon and esteemed. Conscious guilt renders one mean-spirited timorous and base. An upright mind will never be at a loss to discern what is just and true lovely honest and of good report. Habits of reading writing and thinking are the indispensable qualifications of a good student. The great business of life is to be employed in doing justly loving mercy and walking humbly with our Creator. To live soberly righteously and piously comprehends the whole of our duty. In our health life possessions connexions pleasures there are causes of

---

* The correctness and importance of this rule appear to be so obvious, as to render it not a little surprising, that any *writer*, possessing the least degree of rhetorical taste, should reject it. I am bold to affirm, that it is observed by every correct reader and speaker ; and yet, strange as it may seem, it is generally violated by those printers who punctuate by the ear, and all others who are influenced by their pernicious example ; thus, " The head, the heart and the hands, should be constantly and actively employed in doing good." Why do they not omit the comma where the conjunction is understood ? It would be doing no greater violence to the principles of elocution ; thus, " The head the heart and the hands, should be, &c." or thus, " The head the heart, and the hands, should be employed," &c. Who does not perceive that the latter pause, where the conjunction is expressed, is as necessary as the former, where the conjunction is understood ? And, since this is the case, what fair objection can be made to the following method of punctuation ? " The head, the heart, and the hands, should be constantly and actively employed in doing good ;" " She is a woman, gentle, sensible, well-educated, and religious."

† As a considerable pause in pronunciation is necessary between the las noun and the verb, a comma should be inserted to denote it ; but as no pause is allowable between the last adjective and the noun, or between the last adverb and the verb, the comma, in such instances, is properly omitted ; thus, " David was a brave, wise, and *pious* man."

decay imperceptibly working. Deliberate slowly execute promptly. An idle trifling society is near akin to such as is corrupting. This unhappy person had been seriously affectionately admonished but in vain.

RULE 7. Comparative sentences whose members are short, and sentences connected with relative pronouns the meaning of whose antecedents is restricted or limited to a particular sense, should not be separated by a comma; as, "Wisdom is better than riches;" "No preacher is so successful as time;" "He accepted *what* I had rejected;" "Self-denial is the *sacrifice which* virtue must make;" "Subtract from many modern poets *all that* may be found in Shakspeare, and trash will remain;" "Give it to the *man whom* you most esteem." In this last example, the assertion is not of "man in general," but of "the man whom you most esteem."

But when the antecedent is used in a general sense, a comma is properly inserted before the relative; as, "*Man, who* is born of a woman, is of few days and full of trouble;" "There is no *charm* in the female sex, *which* can supply the place of virtue."

This rule is equally applicable to constructions in which the relative is understood; as, "Value duly the privileges you enjoy;" that is, "privileges *which* you enjoy."

Exercises.—How much better it is to get wisdom than gold! The friendships of the world can exist no longer than interest cements them. Eat what is set before you. They who excite envy will easily incur censure. A man who is of a detracting spirit will misconstrue the most innocent words that can be put together. Many of the evils which occasion our complaints of the world are wholly imaginary.

The gentle mind is like the smooth stream which reflects every object in its just proportion and in its fairest colors. In that unaffected civility which springs from a gentle mind there is an incomparable charm. The Lord whom I serve is eternal. This is the man we saw yesterday.

RULE 8. When two words of the same sort, are connected by a conjunction expressed, they must not be separated; as, "Libertines call religion, bigotry *or* superstition;" "True worth is modest *and* retired;" "The study of natural history, expands *and* elevates the mind;" "Some men sin deliberately *and* presumptuously." When words are connected in pairs, the pairs only should be separated; as, "There is a natural difference between merit *and* demerit, virtue *and* vice, wisdom *and* folly;" "Whether we eat *or* drink, labor *or* sleep, we should be temperate."

But if the parts connected by a conjunction are not short, they may be separated by a comma; as, "Romances may be said to be miserable rhapsodies, *or* dangerous incentives to evil."

Exercises.—Idleness brings forward and nourishes many bad passions. True friendship will at all times avoid a rough or careless behavior. Health and peace a moderate fortune and a few friends sum up all the undoubted

articles of temporal felicity. Truth is fair and artless simple and sincere
uniform and consistent. Intemperance destroys the strength of our bodies
and the vigor of our minds.

RULE 9. Where the verb of a simple member is understood,
a comma may, in some instances, be inserted; as, "From law
arises security; from security, curiosity; from curiosity, knowledge." But in others, it is better to omit the comma; "No station is so high, no power so great, no character so unblemished, as
to exempt men from the attacks of rashness, malice, and envy."

Exercises.—As a companion he was severe and satirical; as a friend captious and dangerous. If the spring put forth no blossoms in summer there
will be no beauty and in autumn no fruit. So if youth be trifled away without improvement manhood will be contemptible and old age miserable.

RULE 10. When a simple member stands as the object of a
preceding verb, and its verb may be changed into the infinitive
mood, the comma is generally omitted; as, "I suppose *he is at
rest;*" changed, "I suppose *him to be at rest.*"

But when the verb *to be* is followed by a verb in the infinitive
mood, which, by transposition, may be made the nominative case
to it, the verb *to be* is generally separated from the infinitive by
a comma; as, "The most obvious remedy is, *to withdraw from all
associations with bad men;*" "The first and most obvious remedy
against the infection, is, to withdraw from all associations with bad
men."

Exercises.—They believed he was dead. He did not know that I was the
man. I knew she was still alive. The greatest misery is to be condemned
by our own hearts. The greatest misery that we can endure is to be condemned by our own hearts.

NOTES.

1. When a conjunction is separated by a phrase or member from the member to which it belongs, such intervening phrase appears to require a comma
at each extremity; as, "They set out early, *and,* before the close of the day,
arrived at the destined place." This rule, however, is not generally followed
by our best writers; as, "If thou seek the Lord, he will be found of thee;
but if thou forsake him, he will cast thee off for ever;" "*But* if the parts
connected are not short, a comma may be inserted."

2. Several verbs succeeding each other in the infinitive mood, and having
a common dependance, may be divided by commas; as, "To relieve the
indigent, to comfort the afflicted, to protect the innocent, to reward the deserving, are humane and noble employments."

3. A remarkable expression, or a short observation, somewhat in the form
of a quotation, may be properly marked with a comma; as, "It hurts a
man's pride to say, *I do not know;*" "Plutarch calls lying, *the vice of slaves.*"

4. When words are placed in opposition to each other, or with some
marked variety, they must be distinguished by a comma; as,

"Tho' *deep,* yet *clear;* tho' *gentle,* yet not *dull;*
"*Strong,* without *rage;* without *o'erflowing, full.*"

"Good men, in this frail, imperfect state, are often found, not only in union
with, but in opposition *to,* the views and conduct of each other."

Sometimes when the word with which the last preposition agrees, is single, the comma may be omitted ; as, " Many states were in alliance *with*, and under the protection *of* Rome."

The same rule and restrictions apply, when two or more nouns refer to the same preposition ; as, " He was composed both under the *threatening*, and at the *approach*, *of* a cruel and lingering death;" " He was not only the *king*, but the *father of* his people."

5. The words, " as, thus, nay, so, hence, again, first, secondly, formerly, now, lastly, once more, above all, on the contrary, in the next place, in short," and all other words and phrases of a similar kind, must generally be separated from the context by a comma; *as*, " Remember thy best friend ; *former-ly*, the supporter of thy infancy ; *now*, the guardian of thy youth ;" " He feared want; *hence*, he overvalued riches ;" " *So*, if youth be trifled away," &c. " *Again*, we must, have food and clothing ;" " *Finally*, let us conclude."

The foregoing rules and examples are sufficient, it is presumed, to suggest to the learner, in all ordinary instances, the proper place for inserting the comma ; but in applying these rules, great regard must be paid to the length and meaning of the clauses, and the proportion which they bear to one another.

SEMICOLON.

The semicolon is used for dividing a compound sentence into two or more parts, not so closely connected as those which are separated by a comma, nor yet so little dependant on each other, as those which are distinguished by a colon.

RULE 1. When the preceding member of the sentence does not of itself give complete sense, but depends on the following clause, and sometimes when the sense of that member would be complete without the concluding one, the semicolon is used ; as in the following examples : " As the desire of approbation, when it works according to reason, improves the amiable part of our species ; so, nothing is more destructive to them, when it is governed by vanity and folly ;" " The wise man is happy, when he gains his own approbation ; the fool, when he gains the applause of those around him ;" " Straws swim upon the surface ; but pearls lie at the bottom."

Exercises.—The path of truth is a plain and safe path that of falsehood a perplexing maze. Heaven is the region of gentleness and friendship hell of fierceness and animosity. As there is a worldly happiness which God perceives to be no other than disguised misery as there are worldly honors which in his estimation are reproach so there is a worldly wisdom which in his sight is foolishness.

But all subsists by elemental strife
And passions are the elements of life.

RULE 2. When an example is introduced to illustrate a rule or proposition, the semicolon may be used before the conjunction *as ;* as in the following instance : Prepositions govern the objective case ; *as*, " She gave the book *to* him."

NOTE. In instances like the foregoing, many respectable punctuists employ the colon, instead of the semicolon.

COLON.

The Colon is used to divide a sentence into two or more parts less connected than those which are separated by a semicolon; but not so independent as separate, distinct sentences.

RULE 1. When a member of a sentence is complete in itself, but followed by some supplemental remark, or farther illustration of the subject, the colon may be properly employed; as, "Nature felt her inability to extricate herself from the consequences of guilt: the gospel revealed the plan of divine interposition and aid." "Great works are performed, not by strength, but by perseverance: yonder palace was raised by single stones; yet you see its height and spaciousness."

Exercises.—The three great enemies to tranquillity are vice superstition and idleness vice which poisons and disturbs the mind with bad passions superstition which fills it with imaginary terrors idleness which loads it with tediousness and disgust.

When we look forward into the year which is beginning what do we behold there? All my brethren is a blank to our view a dark unknown presents itself.

RULE 2. When a semicolon has preceded, or more than one, and a still greater pause is necessary, in order to mark the connecting or concluding sentiment, the colon should be applied; as, "A divine legislator, uttering his voice from heaven; an almighty governor, stretching forth his arm to punish or reward; informing us of perpetual rest prepared for the righteous hereafter, and of indignation and wrath awaiting the wicked: these are the considerations which overawe the world, which support integrity, and check guilt."

PERIOD.

When a sentence is complete, and so independent as not to be connected with the one which follows it, a period should be inserted at its close; as, "Fear God." "Honor the patriot." "Respect virtue."

In the use of many of the pauses, there is a diversity of practice among our best writers and grammarians. Compound sentences connected by conjunctions, are sometimes divided by the period; as, "Recreations, though they may be of an innocent kind, require steady government to keep them within a due and limited province. *But* such as are of an irregular and vicious nature, are not to be governed, but to be banished from every well-regulated mind."

The period should follow every abbreviated word; as, "A. D. N. B. U. S. Va. Md. Viz. Col. Mr."

DASH.

The Dash, though often used improperly by hasty and incoherent writers, may be introduced with propriety, where the sentence breaks off abruptly ; where a significant pause is required ; or where there is an unexpected turn in the sentiment ; as, " If thou art he, so much respected once—but, oh ! how fallen ! how degraded !" " If acting conformably to the will of our Creator ;—if promoting the welfare of mankind around us ;—if securing ou own happiness ;—are objects of the highest moment : then we are loudly called upon to cultivate and extend the great interests of religion and virtue."

A dash following a stop, denotes that the pause is to be greater than if the stop were alone ; and when used by itself, requires a pause of such length as the sense only can determine.

" Here lies the great—False marble, where ?
" Nothing but sordid dust lies here."

INTERROGATORY POINT.

The note of interrogation is used at the end of an interrogative sentence ; as, " Who adorned the heavens with such exquisite beauty ?"

Note. The interrogative point should not be employed in cases where it is only said, that a question has been asked ; as, " The Cyprians asked me, why I wept."

EXCLAMATORY POINT.

The note of exclamation is applied to expressions of sudden emotion, surprise, joy, grief, &c. and sometimes to invocations and addresses ; as, " How much vanity in the pursuits of men !" " What is more amiable than virtue !" " My friend ! this conduct amazes me !" "Hear me, O Lord ! for thy loving kindness is great !"

PARENTHESIS.

A parenthesis is a clause containing some useful remark, which may be omitted without injuring the grammatical construction ; as, " To gain a posthumous reputation, is to save a few letters (for what is a name besides ?) from oblivion."

" Know then this truth, (enough for man to know,)
" Virtue alone is happiness below."

Note. The parenthesis generally denotes a moderate depression of the voice ; and, as the parenthetical marks do not supply the place of a point, the clause should be accompanied with every stop which the sense woul require, if the parenthetical characters were not used. It ought to termi nate with the same kind of point which the member has that precedes it ; as " He loves nobly, (I speak of friendship,) who is not jealous when he has partners of love."

" Or why so long (in life if long can be)
" Lent Heav'n a parent to the poor and me ?" .

Parentheses, however, containing interrogations or exclamations, form an exception to this rule; as, "If I grant his request, (and who could refuse it?) I shall secure his esteem and attachment."

APOSTROPHE AND QUOTATION.

The Apostrophe is used to abbreviate a word, and also to mark the possessive case of a noun; as, " 'tis, for *it is; tho*,' for *though; o'er,* for *over;*" " A *man's* poverty."

A Quotation marks a sentence taken in the author's own language; as, " The proper study of mankind is man."

When an author represents a person as speaking, the language of that person should be designated by a quotation; as, At my coming in, he said, " You and the physician are come too late.'

A quotation contained within another, should be distinguished by two *single* commas; as, " Always remember this ancient maxim 'Know thyself.'"

DIRECTIONS FOR USING CAPITAL LETTERS.

It is proper to begin with a capital,

1. The first word of every sentence.

2. Proper names, the appellations of the Deity, &c.; as, " James Cincinnati, the Andes, Huron;" " God, Jehovah, the Almighty the Supreme Being, Providence, the Holy Spirit."

3. Adjectives derived from proper names, the titles of books, nouns which are used as the subject of discourse, the pronoun *I* and the interjection *O*, and every line in poetry; as, " American, Grecian, English, French; Irving's Sketch Book, Percival's Poems; I write; Hear, O earth!"

APPENDIX.

VERSIFICATION.

POETRY is the language of passion, or of enlivened imagination.

VERSIFICATION, in English, is the harmonious arrangement of a particular number and variety of accented and unaccented syllables, according to particular laws.

RHYME is the correspondence of the sound of the last syllable in one line, to the sound of the last syllable in another; as,

" O'er the glad waters of the dark-blue *sea*,
" Our thoughts as boundless and our souls as *free*."

BLANK VERSE consists in poetical thoughts expressed in regular numbers, but without the correspondence of sound at the end of the lines which constitutes rhyme.

POETICAL FEET consist in a particular arrangement and connexion of a number of accented and unaccented syllables.

They are called *feet*, because it is by their aid that the voice, as it were, *steps* along through the verse in a measured pace.

All poetical feet consist either of two, or of three syllables; and are reducible to eight kinds; four of two syllables, and four of three, as follows:

DISSYLLABLE.	TRISYLLABLE.
A Trochee – ᴜ	A Dactyle – ᴜ ᴜ
An Iambus ᴜ –	An Amphibrach ᴜ – ●
A Spondee – –	An Anapaest ᴜ ᴜ –
A Pyrrhic ᴜ ᴜ	A Tribrach ᴜ ᴜ ᴜ

A Trochee has the first syllable accented, and the last unaccented; as, Hātefŭl, péttish:

> Rĕstlĕss mōrtăls tōil fŏr nāught.

An Iambus has the first syllable unaccented, and the last accented; as, Bĕtrăy, consíst:

> Thĕ sĕas shăll wăste, thĕ skĭes ĭn smōke dĕcāy.

A Dactyle has the first syllable accented, and the two latter unaccented; as, Lābŏrĕr, póssible:

> Frōm thĕ lŏw plĕasūres ŏf this făllĕn nātŭre.

An Anapaest has the first two syllables unaccented, and the last accented; as, Cŏntrăvēne, acquiésce:

> At thĕ clōse ŏf thĕ dāy whĕn thĕ hămlĕt ĭs stĭll.

A Spondee; as, The păle mōōn: a Pyrrhic; as, ŏn thĕ tall tree: an Amphibrach; as, Dĕlightfŭl: a Tribrach; as, Numĕrăblĕ.

RHETORIC.

GRAMMAR instructs us how to express our thoughts correctly. RHETORIC teaches us to express them with force and elegance.

The former is generally confined to the correct application of words in constructing single sentences. The latter treats of the proper choice of words, of the happiest method of constructing sentences, of their most advantageous arrangement in forming a discourse, and of the various kinds and qualities of composition. The principles of rhetoric are principally based on those unfolded and illustrated in the science of grammar. Hence, an acquaintance with the latter, and, indeed, with the liberal arts, is a prerequisite to the study of rhetoric and belles-lettres.

COMPOSITION.

It may be laid down as a maxim of eternal truth, that *good sense* is the foundation of all good writing. One who understands a subject well, will scarcely write ill upon it.

Rhetoric, or the art of persuasion, requires in a writer, the union of good sense, and a lively and chaste imagination. It is, then, her province to teach him to embellish his thoughts with elegant and appropriate language, vivid imagery, and an agreeable variety of expression. It ought to be his aim,

> "To mark the point where sense and dulness meet."

STYLE.—PERSPICUITY AND PRECISION.

STYLE is the peculiar manner in which we express our concep-
tions by means of language. It is a picture of the ideas which
rise in our minds, and of the order in which they are produced.

The qualities of a good style, may be ranked under two heads.
perspicuity and *ornament*.

PERSPICUITY, which is considered the fundamental quality of a
good style, claims attention, first, to single words and phrases;
and, secondly, to the construction of sentences. When consid
ered with respect to words and phrases, it requires these three
qualities, *purity, propriety,* and *precision*.

Purity of language consists in the use of such words and such
constructions as belong to the language which we speak, in opposition to words and phrases belonging to other languages, or which
are obsolete or new-coined, or employed without proper authority.

Propriety is the choice of those words which the best usage
has appropriated to the ideas which we intend to express by them.
It implies their correct and judicious application, in opposition to
low expressions, and to words and phrases which would be less
significant of the ideas which we wish to convey. It is the
union of purity and propriety, which renders style graceful and
perspicuous.

Precision, from *præcidere*, to cut off, signifies retrenching all
superfluities, and pruning the expression in such a manner as to
exhibit neither more nor less than an exact copy of the ideas
intended to be conveyed.

STRUCTURE OF SENTENCES.

A proper construction of sentences is of so great importance
in every species of composition, that we cannot be too strict or
minute in our attention to it.

Elegance of style requires us generally to *avoid* many short or long sentences in succession; a monotonous correspondence of one member to another; and the commencing of a piece, section, or paragraph, with a long
sentence.

The qualities most essential to a perfect sentence, are *Unity,
Clearness, Strength,* and *Harmony*.

UNITY is an indispensable property of a correct sentence. A
sentence implies an arrangement of words in which only *one* pro
position is expressed. It may, indeed, consist of parts; but
these parts ought to be so closely bound together, as to make on
the mind the impression, not of many objects, but of only one.
In order to preserve this unity, the following rules may be useful.

1. *In the course of the sentence, the scene should be changed as little as
possible.* In every sentence there is some leading or governing word, which,
if possible, ought to be continued so from the beginning to the end of it.

The following sentence is not constructed according to this rule : " After we came to anchor, they put me on shore, where I was saluted by all my friends, who received me with the greatest kindness." In this sentence, though the objects are sufficiently connected, yet, by shifting so frequently the place and the person, the *vessel*, the *shore*, *we*, *they*, *I*. and *who*, they appear in so disunited a view, that the mind is led to wander for the sense. The sentence is restored to its proper unity by constructing it thus : " Having come to anchor, I was put on shore, where I was saluted by all my friends, who re ceived me with the greatest kindness."

2. *Never crowd into one sentence things which have so little connexion, tha they would bear to be divided into two or more sentences.* The violation of this rule produces so unfavorable an effect, that it is safer to err rather by too many short sentences, than by one that is overloaded and confused.

3. *Avoid all unnecessary parentheses.*

CLEARNESS. *Ambiguity*, which is opposed to clearness, may arise from a bad choice, or a bad arrangement of words.

A leading rule in the arrangement of sentences, is, that *those words or members most nearly related, should be placed in the sentence as near to each other as possible, so as thereby to make their mutual relation clearly appear.* This rule ought to be observed,

1. *In the position of adverbs.* " By greatness," says Mr. Addison, " I do not only mean the bulk of any single object, but the largeness of a whole view." The improper situation of the adverb *only*, in this sentence, renders it a limitation of the verb *mean*, whereas the author intended to have it qualify the phrase, *a single object;* thus, " By greatness, I do not mean the bulk of any single object *only*, but the largeness of a whole view."

2. *In the position of phrases and members.* " Are these designs which any man who is born a Briton, in any circumstances, in any situation, ought to be ashamed or afraid to avow ?" Corrected : " Are these designs which any man who is born a Briton, ought to be ashamed or afraid, *in any circumstances, in any situation*, to avow ?"

3. *In the position of pronouns.* The reference of a pronoun to its noun, should always be *so clear that we cannot possibly mistake it :* otherwise the noun ought to be repeated. " It is folly to pretend to arm ourselves against the accidents of life, by heaping up treasures, which nothing can protect us against but the good providence of our Heavenly Father." *Which*, in this sentence, grammatically refers to *treasures;* and this would convert the whole period into nonsense. The sentence should have been thus constructed, " It is folly to pretend, by heaping up treasures, to arm ourselves against the *accidents* of life, against *which* nothing can protect us but the good providence of our Heavenly Father."

STRENGTH. By the *strength* of a sentence is meant such an arrangement of its several words and members, as exhibits the sense to the best advantage, and gives every word and member its due weight and force.

1 The first rule for promoting the strength of a sentence, is, to *take from t all redundant words and members.* Whatever can be easily supplied in th mind, should generally be omitted ; thus, " Content with deserving a triumph he refused the honor of it," is better than to say, " *Being* content with de serving a triumph." &c. " They returned back again to the same city from whence they came forth." If we expunge from this short sentence *five* words which are were expletives, it will be much more neat and forcible

thus, "They returned to the city whence they came." But we should be cautious of pruning so closely as to give a hardness and dryness to the style. Some leaves must be left to shelter and adorn the fruit.

2. *Particular attention to the use of copulatives, relatives, and all the particles employed for transition and connexion, is required.* In compositions of an elevated character, the *relative* should generally be inserted. An injudicious repetition of *and* enfeebles style; but when enumerating objects which we wish to have appear as distinct from each other as possible, it may be repeated with peculiar advantage; thus, "Such a man may fall a victim to ower; but truth, *and* reason, *and* liberty, would fall with him."

3. *Dispose of the capital word or words in that part of the sentence in which they will make the most striking impression.*

4. *Cause the members of a sentence to go on rising in their importance one above another.* In a sentence of two members, the longer should generally be the concluding one.

5. *Avoid concluding a sentence with an adverb, a preposition, or any inconsiderable word, unless it be emphatical.*

6. *Where two things are compared or contrasted with each other, a resemblance in the language and construction should be observed.*

FIGURES OF SPEECH.

Figures of Speech may be described as that language which is prompted either by the imagination, or by the passions. They generally imply some departure from simplicity of expression; and exhibit ideas in a manner more vivid and impressive, than could be done by plain language. Figures have been commonly divided into two great classes; Figures of *Words*, and Figures of *Thought*.

Figures of Words are called *Tropes*, and consist in a word's being employed to signify something that is different from its original meaning; so that by altering the word, we destroy the figure.

When we say of a person, that he has a fine *taste* in wines, the word taste is used in its common, literal sense; but when we say, he has a fine *taste* for painting, poetry, or music, we use the word figuratively. "A good man enjoys comfort in the midst of adversity," is simple language; but when it is said, "To the upright there ariseth *light* in *darkness*," the same sentiment is expressed in a figurative style, *light* is put in the place of *comfort*, and *darkness* is used to suggest the idea of *adversity*.

The following are the most important figures:

1. A METAPHOR is founded on the resemblance which one object bears to another; or, it is a comparison in an abridged form.

When I say of some great minister, "That he upholds the state like a *pillar* which supports the weight of a whole edifice," I fairly make a comparison; but when I say of such a minister, "That he is the *pillar* of state," the word pillar becomes a metaphor. In the latter construction, the comparison between the minister and a pillar, is made in the mind; but it is expressed without any of the words that denote comparison.

Metaphors abound in all writings. In the scriptures they may be found in vast variety. Thus, our blessed Lord is called a vine, a lamb, a lion, &c.;

. and men, according to their different dispositions, are styled wolves, sheep, dogs, serpents, vipers, &c.

Washington Irving, in speaking of the degraded state of the American Aborigines who linger on the borders of the " white settlements," employs the following beautiful metaphor: " The proud *pillar* of their independence has been shaken down, and the whole moral *fabric* lies in ruins."

2. AN ALLEGORY may be regarded as a metaphor continued; o it is several metaphors so connected together in sense, as fre- q ntly to form a kind of parable or fable. It differs from a sin- gle metaphor, in the same manner that a cluster on the vine differs from a single grape.

The following is a fine example of an allegory, taken from the 60th psalm; wherein the people of Israel are represented under the image of a vine. " Thou hast brought a vine out of Egypt: thou hast cast out the heathen and planted it. Thou preparedst room before it; and didst cause it to take deep root, and it filled the land. The hills were covered with the shadow of it, and the boughs thereof were like the goodly cedars. She sent out her boughs into the sea, and her branches into the river."

3. A SIMILE or COMPARISON is when the resemblance between two objects, whether real or imaginary, is expressed in form.

Thus, we use a simile, when we say, " The actions of princes are like those great rivers, the course of which every one beholds, but their springs have been seen by few." " As the mountains are round about Jerusalem, so the Lord is round about his people." " The music of Caryl was like the memory of joys that are past, pleasant and mournful to the soul." " Our Indians are like those wild plants which thrive best in the shade, but which wither when exposed to the influence of the sun."

> " The Assyrian came down, like the wolf on the fold,
> And his cohorts were gleaming with purple and gold;
> And the sheen of their spears was like stars on the sea,
> When the blue wave rolls nightly on deep Galilee."

4. A METONYMY is where the cause is put for the effect, or the effect for the cause; the container for the thing contained; or the sign for the thing signified.

When we say, " They read *Milton*," the cause is put for the effect, mean- ing " Milton's *works*." " Gray hairs should be respected;" here the effect is put for the cause; meaning by " gray hairs," *old age*, which produces gray hairs. In the phrase, " The kettle boils," the container is substituted for the thing contained. " He addressed the *chair*;" that is, the person in the chair.

5. A SYNECDOCHE OR COMPREHENSION. When the whole is put for a part, or a part for the whole; a genus for a species, or a species for a genus; in general, when any thing less, or any thing more, is put for the precise object meant, the figure is called a Synecdoche.

Thus, " A fleet of twenty *sail*, instead of, *ships*." " The *horse* is a noble animal;" " The *dog* is a faithful creature:" here an individual is put for the species. We sometimes use the " head" for the *person*, and the " waves" for the *sea*. In like manner, an attribute may be put for a subject; as, " Youth" for the *young*, the " deep" for the *sea*.

6. PERSONIFICATION or PROSOPOPŒIA is that figure by which we attribute life and action to inanimate objects. When we say, "The ground *thirsts* for rain," or, "the earth *smiles* with plenty;" when we speak of "ambition's being *restless*," or, "a disease's being *deceitful;*" such expressions show the facility, with which the mind can accommodate the properties of living creatures to things that are inanimate.

The following are fine examples of this figure:
"Cheer'd with the grateful smell, old *Ocean smiles;*"
"The wilderness and the solitary place shall be glad for them; and the desert shall rejoice and blossom as the rose."

7. AN APOSTROPHE is an address to some person, either absent or dead, as if he were present and listening to us. The address is frequently made to a personified object; as, "Death is swallowed up in victory. O *death!* where is thy sting? O *grave!* where is thy victory?"

"Weep on the rocks of roaring winds, O *maid* of Inistore; bend thy fair head over the waves, thou fairer than the ghost of the hills, when it moves in a sun-beam at noon over the silence of Morven."

8. ANTITHESIS. Comparison is founded on the resemblance, antithesis, on the contrast or opposition, of two objects.

Example. "If you wish to enrich a person, study not to *increase* his *stores,* but to *diminish* his *desires.*"

9. HYPERBOLE or EXAGGERATION consists in magnifying an object beyond its natural bounds. "As swift as the wind; as white as the snow; as slow as a snail;" and the like, are extravagant hyperboles.

"I saw their chief, tall as a rock of ice; his spear, the blasted fir; his shield, the rising moon; he sat on the shore, like a cloud of mist on the hills."

10. VISION is produced, when, in relating something that is past, we use the present tense, and describe it as actually passing before our eyes.

11. INTERROGATION. The literal use of an interrogation, is to ask a question; but when men are strongly moved, whatever they would affirm or deny with great earnestness, they naturally put in the form of a question.

Thus Balaam expressed himself to Balak: "The Lord is not man, that he should lie, nor the son of man, that he should repent. Hath he said it? and shall he not do it? Hath he spoken it? and shall he not make it good?"
"Hast thou an arm like God? or canst thou thunder with a voice like him?"

12. EXCLAMATIONS are the effect of strong emotions, such a surprise, admiration, joy, grief, and the like.

"O that I had in the wilderness a lodging place of way-faring men!" "O that I had wings like a dove! for then would I fly away, and be at rest!"

13. IRONY is expressing ourselves in a manner contrary to our thoughts; not with a view to deceive, but to add force to our

remarks. We can reprove one for his negligence, by saying, "You have taken great care, indeed."

The prophet Elijah adopted this figure, when he challenged the priests of Baal to prove the truth of their deity. "He mocked them, and said, Cry aloud for he is a god : either he is talking, or he is pursuing, or he is on a journey, or, peradventure, he sleepeth, and must be waked."

14. AMPLIFICATION or CLIMAX consists in heightening all the ircumstances of an object or action, which we desire to place n a strong light.

Cicero gives a lively instance of this figure, when he says, "It is a crime to put a Roman citizen in bonds : it is the height of guilt to scourge him ; little less than parricide to put him to death : what name, then, shall I give to the act of crucifying him ?"

KEY.

Corrections of the False Syntax arranged under the Rules and Notes.

RULE 4. Frequent commission of sin *hardens* men in it. Great pains *have* been taken, &c.—*is* seldom found. The sincere *are*, &c.—*is* happy. What *avail*, &c.—Disappointments *sink*—the renewal of hope *gives*, &c.—*is* without limit. *has* been conferred upon us.—Thou *canst* not heal—but thou *mayst* do, &c.—*consists* the happiness, &c.—Who *touchedst*, or *didst touch* Isaiah's hallowed lips with fire.

Note 1. And *wilt thou* never be to Heaven resigned ?—And *who* had great abilities, &c.

Note 2. *Are* peace and honor.—*was* controversy.

RULE 7. *Them* that you visited.—*him* that was mentioned.—*he* who preached repentance, &c.—*they* who died.—*he* who succeeded.

RULE 8. Time and tide *wait*, &c.—*remove* mountains.—*are* both uncertain.—*dwell* with, &c.—*affect* the mind, &c.—What *signify* the counsel and care, &c.—*are* now perished.—Why *are* whiteness and coldness, &c.—bind *them* continually, &c.—render *their* possessor, &c.—There *are* error and discrepance—which *show*, &c.

RULE 9. *Is* the same in idea.—*is* in the porphyry.—*is* remarkable, &c.— which *moves* merely as *it is* moved.—*affects* us, &c.—Man's happiness or misery *is*, in a great measure, &c.—for *it* may be, &c.—*was* blameworthy.

RULE 10. The nation *is* powerful.—The fleet *was* seen, &c.—The church *has*, &c.—*is*, or ought to be, the *object*, &c.—*it* is feeble.

RULE 11. My people *do*, &c.—The multitude eagerly *pursue* pleasure as *their*, &c.—*were* divided in *their* sentiments, and *they have* referred, &c.— The people *rejoice*—give *them* sorrow.

RULE 12. *Homer's* works are, &c.—*Asa's* heart. *James Hart's* book.

Note 1. It was the *men, women*, and children's lot, &c. or, *It was the lot of* the men, women, and children.—*Peter, John*, and Andrew's, &c.

Note 2. This is *Campbell* the poet's production ; or, *The production of Campbell, &c.*—The silk was purchased at Brown's the *mercer* and *haberdasher.*

Note 4. The *pupil's* composing, &c.—*rule's* being observed.—of the *president's* neglecting to lay it before the council.

RULE 13. Of *his* audience.—put *it* on Jacob.—sprinkle *them*—and they shall, &c.—of *his* reputation.

Note. You *were* blamed ; you *were* worthy.—where *were* you ?—how far *were* you?

RULE 14. Who *hast* been, &c.—*who is* the sixth *that has* lost *his life* by this means.

Who all my sense *confinedst ;* or, *didst confine.*

Note. And *who broughtest* him forth out of Ur.

RULE 15. *Who* shall be sent, &c.—This is the man *who,* &c.

RULE 16. They *to whom* much is given, &c.—*with whom* you associate &c.—*whom* I greatly respect, &c.—*whom* we ought to love, and *to whom, &c* —They *whom* conscience, *&c.*—With *whom* did you walk ?—*Whom* did you see ?—To *whom* did you give the book ?

RULE 17. Who gave John those books ? *We.*—*him* who lives in Pearl street—My brother and *he.*—*She* and *I.*

RULE 18 : *Note* 2. Thirty *tuns.*—twenty *feet*—one hundred *fathoms.*

Note 6. He bought a pair of *new* shoes—piece of *elegant* furniture.—pair of *fine* horses—tract of *poor* land.

Note 7. Are still more *difficult to be comprehended.*—most *doubtful,* or *precarious* way, &c.—*This model comes nearer perfection than any I,* &c.

RULE 19 : *Note.* That sort.—*these* two hours.—*This* kind, &c.—He saw one *person,* or more *than one,* enter the garden.

Note 2. Better than *himself.*—*is* so small.—*his* station may be, *is* bound by the laws.

Note 3. On *each* side, &c.—took *each* his censer.

RULE 20. *Whom* did they, &c.—They *whom* opulence,—*whom* luxury, &c —*Him* and *them* we know, &c.—*Her* that is negligent, &c.—my brother and *me, &c.*—*Whom* did they send, &c.—*Them whom* he, &c.

RULE 21. It is *I.*—If I were *he.*—it is *he,* indeed.—*Whom* do you, &c.— *Who* do men say, &c.—and *who* say ye, &c.—*whom* do you imagine it to have been ?—it was *I;* but you knew that it was *he.*

RULE 25. Bid him *come* —durst not *do* it.—Hear him *read, &c.*—makes us *approve* and *reject, &c.*—better *to* live—than *to* outlive, &c.—*to* wrestle.

RULE 26 : *Note.* The taking *of* pains : or, without taking pains, &c.— The changing *of* times,—the removing and setting up *of* kings.

RULE 28 : *Note* 3. He *did* me—I had *written*—he *came* home.—*befallen* my cousin—he would have *gone.*—already *risen.*—is *begun.*—is *spoken.*— would have *written*—had they *written, &c.*

RULE 29 : *Note* 1. It cannot, *therefore,* be, &c.—he was *not often* pleasing.—should *never* be separated.—We may live *happily, &c.*

RULE 30 : *Note.* I don't know *any thing ;* or, I *know* nothing, &c.—I did not see *anybody ;* or, I saw *nobody, &c.*—Nothing ever *affects* her.—*and* take no shape *or* semblance, &c.—There *can* be nothing, &c.—*Neither* precept *nor* discipline is so forcible as example.

RULE 31. For *himself.*—among *themselves.*—*with whom* he is, &c.—*With whom* did, &c.—*From whom* did you receive instruction ?

RULE 33. My brother and *he,* &c.—You and *I, &c.* *He* and I—John and *he, &c.*—Between you and *me, &c.*

RULE 34. And *entreat* me, *&c.*—and *acting* differently, *&c.*

Note 1. But *he* may return—but *he* will write no more.

Note 2. Unless it *rain.*—If he *acquire* riches, *&c.*

RULE 35. Than *I.*—as well as *he,* than *they.*—but *he.*—but *he* and *I.*—but *them* who had gone astray.

Promiscuous Examples.—*Him* who is from eternity, *&c.*—*depends* all the happiness,—which *exists, &c.*—the enemies *whom, &c.*—Is it *I* or *he whom* you requested ?—Though great *have* been,—sincerely *acknowledge.*—There *was,* in the metropolis.—exercising our memories.—*was* consumed.—Affluence *may* give—but *it* will not.—of this world often choke.—*Them* that honor,—and *they* that despise.—I intended to *call* last week.—the fields look *fresh* and *gay.*—very *neatly, finely woven* paper.—where I *saw* Gen. Andrew Jackson, *him* who.—Take the *first two,—last three.*—thirty *feet* high.—*a* union,—*a* hypothesis.—I have *seen* him *to whom* you wrote, he would have *come* back, or *returned.*—*understands* the nature,—he *rejects.*—If thou *study,* —thou *wilt* become.—is not *properly* attended to.—He *knew.*—therefore, to *have* done it,—*than* the title.—very *independently.*—duty to *do.*—my *friend's* entering.—is the *best* specimen, or it *comes nearer* perfection *than any, &c.*— blow *them,* will go, &c.—*Each of those two authors has his* merit.—*Reason's* whole.—*lie* in.—*strikes* the mind,—than if *the parts had been adjusted,*—with *perfect* symmetry.

Satire *does* not carry in *it.*—*composes* the triangle.—*persons'* opportunities were *ever.*—It *has been* reported.—should *never* be.—situation *in which.*—is thoroughly versed in *his.*—*are* the soul,—*follows* little.—An army *presents.* —*are* the *duties* of a christian.—happier than *he.*—*always* have *inclined,* and *which always* will incline him to offend.—which *require* great.—*Them* that honor me, will I.—*has* opinions peculiar to *itself.*—that *it may* be said *he' attained* monarchical.—*hast* permitted,—*wilt* deliver.—*was* formerly propagated.—the measure *is,*—unworthy your.—*were* faithless.—After I *had* visited. —nor sha!l *I,* consent.—Yesterday I intended to *walk* out, but *was.*—*make* or *are* thirteen,—*leave* three.—If he *go,*—make *the eighth time* that he *will have* visited.—*is* nobler.—was possessed, or *that ever* can be.—one great *edifice,*—smaller *ones.*—honesty *is.*—it to *be.*—*will* follow me,—I *shall* dwell. —*is* gone astray.—he could not *have done.*—*feeling* a propensity.

PUNCTUATION.

COMMA.

Corrections of the Exercises in Punctuation.

RULE 1. Idleness is the great fomenter of all corruptions in the human heart. The friend of order has made half his way to virtue. All finery is a sign of littleness.

RULE 2. The indulgence of a harsh disposition, is the introduction to future misery. To be totally indifferent to praise or censure, is a real defect in character. The intermixture of evil in human society, serves to exercise the suffering graces and virtues of the good.

RULE 3. Charity, like the sun, brightens all its objects. Gentleness is, in truth, the great avenue to mutual enjoyment. You, too, have your failings. Humility and knowledge with poor apparel, excel pride and ignorance, under costly attire. The best men often experience disappointments. Advice should be seasonably administered. No assumed behavior can always hide the real character.

RULE 4. Lord, thou hast been our dwelling place in all generations. Continue, my dear child, to make virtue thy chief study. Canst thou expect, thou betrayer of innocence, to escape the hand of vengeance? Death, the king of terrors, chose a prime minister. Hope, the balm of life, sooths us under every misfortune. Confucius, the great Chinese philosopher, was eminently good, as well as wise. The patriarch Joseph is an illustrious example of true piety.

RULE 5. Peace of mind being secured, we may smile at misfortune. To enjoy present pleasure, he sacrificed his future ease and reputation. His talents, formed for great enterprises, could not fail of rendering him conspicuous. The path of piety and virtue, pursued with a firm and constant spirit, will assuredly lead to happiness. All mankind compose one family, assembled under the eye of one common Father.

RULE 6. We have no reason to complain of the lot of man, nor of the mutability of the world. Sensuality contaminates the body, depresses the understanding, deadens the moral feelings of the heart, and degrades man from his rank in creation.

Self-conceit, presumption, and obstinacy, blast the prospect of many a youth. He is alternately supported by his father, his uncle, and his elder brother. The man of virtue and honor, will be trusted, relied upon, and esteemed. Conscious guilt renders one mean-spirited, timorous, and base. An upright mind will never be at a loss to discern what is just and true, lovely, honest, and of good report. Habits of reading, writing, and thinking, are the indispensable qualifications of a good student. The great business of life is, to be employed in doing justly, loving mercy, and walking humbly with our God. To live soberly, righteously, and piously, comprehends the whole of our duty.

In our health, life, possessions, connexions, pleasures, there are causes of decay imperceptibly working. Deliberate slowly, execute promptly. An idle, trifling society, is near akin to such as is corrupting. This unhappy person had been seriously, affectionately admonished, but in vain.

RULE 7. How much better it is to get wisdom than gold. The friendships of the world can exist no longer than interest cements them. Eat what is set before you. They who excite envy, will easily incur censure. A man who is of a detracting spirit, will misconstrue the most innocent words that can be put together. Many of the evils which occasion our complaints of the world, are wholly imaginary.

The gentle mind is like the smooth stream, which reflects every object in its just proportion, and in its fairest colors. In that unaffected civility which springs from a gentle mind, there is an incomparable charm. The Lord, whom I serve, is eternal. This, is the man we saw yesterday.

RULE 8. Idleness brings forward and nourishes many bad passions. True friendship will, at all times, avoid a rough or careless behavior. Health and peace, a moderate fortune, and a few friends, sum up all the undoubted articles of temporal felicity. Truth is fair and artless, simple and sincere, uniform and consistent. Intemperance destroys the strength of our bodies and the vigor of our minds.

RULE 9. As a companion, he was severe and satirical; as a friend, captious and dangerous. If the spring put forth no blossoms, in summer there will be no beauty, and in autumn, no fruit. So, if youth be trifled away without improvement, manhood will be contemptible, and old age, miserable.

RULE 10. They believed he was dead. He did not know that I was the man. I knew she was still alive. The greatest misery is, to be condemned by our own hearts. The greatest misery that we can endure, is, to be condemned by our own hearts.

SEMICOLON.

RULE 1. The path of truth is a plain and safe path; that of falsehood is a perplexing maze. Heaven is the region of gentleness and friendship; hell, of fierceness and animosity. As there is a worldly happiness, which God perceives to be no other than disguised misery; as there are worldly honors, which, in his estimation, are a reproach; so, there is a worldly wisdom, which, in his sight, is foolishness.

But all subsists by elemental strife;
And passions are the elements of life.

COLON.

RULE 1. The three great enemies to tranquillity, are vice, superstition, and idleness : vice, which poisons and disturbs the mind with bad passions; superstition, which fills it with imaginary terrors; idleness, which loads it with tediousness and disgust.